The Heart of David

Building the Spiritual Temple

Dr. Jeffrey Hazim

You are all living stones.

"You also, as living stones, are being built up a Spiritual House,
a holy priesthood, to offer up spiritual sacrifices
acceptable to God through Jesus Christ."
1 Peter 2:5

xulon PRESS

The Heart of David
by Dr. Jeffrey Hazim
Sinai Calvary Ministries

Printed in the United States of America

ISBN 1-60034-249-3

Graphic Artists: Elimir Garcia, David Utrera, Silvia Eames
Artwork on Cover: Jutta Herold
Cover Design: David Utrera

www.theheartofdavid.com
www.xulonpress.com

A Message from Sinai Calvary Ministries

"All of the creation eagerly waits for the revealing of the sons of God."

Jesus preached about the Gospel of the Kingdom. He said: *"The harvest truly is plentiful, but the laborers are few. Therefore pray the Lord of the harvest to send out laborers into His harvest." "It has been given to you to know the mysteries of the Kingdom of Heaven." "And this Gospel of the Kingdom will be preached in all the world as a witness to all the nations, and then the end will come."* Our mission and devotion are to solve the mysteries of the Kingdom of Heaven, make the Gospel of the Kingdom clear to the world, and equip laborers for a harvest of righteousness. If you have questions or comments, please visit us online at **www.theheartofdavid.com.**

Disclaimer

This book is part of a package of prophetic ideas that we are in the process of formulating and documenting. It is an attempt at making the Gospel of the Kingdom clear to the world. It is by no means an exhaustive work, but a small part of a much larger work in progress. These ideas have slowly matured through study and debate, and have been presented for testing and critique to the best available minds within our limited community. However, none of these prophetic ideas are written in stone. It is our attempt to "put a stake in the ground," a common point of reference from which wider critique and participation can be received. We will continue to pursue "all truth" (John 16:13), not truth defined by the winds of opinion or sacred tradition, but truth derived through diligent, thoughtful, and prayerful Biblical scholarship and dialog, all under the guidance of the Holy Spirit. Truth must always be beautiful, systematic, and predictive. We reserve the right; in fact, we declare our responsibility, to change any and all ideas that ultimately do not conform to truth. This is our pledge. Due to the nature of "a work in progress," there may be ideas written here that have since matured. There may even be models that have already been removed because they were unable to stand up to the rigorous demands of "all truth." For updates and changes visit us online at **www.theheartofdavid.com.**

Stephen Duame & Dr. Jeffrey Hazim
Sinai Calvary Ministries

In The Beginning...

Dedication & Thanks

I dedicate this book to the ministry started by our Lord and Savior Jesus Christ, and to every servant of His who wishes to complete His work by believing that unity of the faith is possible. It is written to every bondservant of our Master who desires to press on toward the upward call in Christ Jesus, being conformed into His fullness and stature and image.

First and foremost, I want to thank my wife Andrea. Without her, I would not have the inspiration and challenge everyday of seeking to become more like Jesus. And because of her, I have three boys: Isaiah, Cyrus, and Shiloh. I believe they will someday be leaders in the Solomon Generation. She supported me to take the time to write 35-40 hours per week (for 18 months) in addition to the full time needed to run our practice. She sacrificed much for which I am eternally grateful.

I want to thank: Stephen, my close friend and teacher, who has helped God birth in me a desire to see with spiritual eyes and a heart for understanding the prophetic; Mike, who forever holds me to the highest standards and encourages me freely; Dennis, who constantly responds to truth and reminds me that there are still good men in the world; Jay, who has always been my most influential prayer partner; Gerry, who has never been afraid of truth; Chris, who has the boldness of a lion, and thankfully, is learning to become as gentle as a dove; Ron for his enthusiasm to grow in God's Word; Jason, who takes truth and runs with it; Ivan, for his positive attitude and encouraging words; and finally I give special thanks to Dolores, who has served as a tireless inspiration. I dedicate this book to you and thank all of you for your support and encouragement.

To all the men of my morning Bible studies, where many seeds have been planted and cultivated. I thank you for your ears to hear and your heart to obey, especially my brother-in-law Jerry who has always inspired me, by example, to be an excellent husband. To all the men of my evening studies who strive to "make the message of the Kingdom" clear to the world, I thank you.

To my second family: Silvia, Karen, Dr. Mike, Andrea, Marisol, Elimir, Christina, and Jean, who have tirelessly helped me turn my practice into a ministry. Thank you for your support, and also for putting up with me during the hard times. And to Jutta, who brought my vision for the cover of this book to life; I praise God for the gift He has given you. Also, a very special thanks to David, whose artwork inside the book is nothing short of inspired. You captured the heart of each section perfectly. I thank and bless you all for your help.

In addition, I want to thank all those who gave me input along the way, especially those who proofed the various versions of the manuscript and offered insight toward a clearer vision: Mike, Kathy, Renne, Dolores, Jason, Bonny, Larry, and Cristina. I would also like to thank Elimir for helping organize all the fine details "behind the scenes," and for her masterful job at formatting the entire book. Every detail that I could not handle was dumped in her lap (and then some). I could not have done it without you. I appreciate your vision, dedication, and talent.

Special thanks go out to Chaim Goldman, my close friend, who acted as chief editor. He offered invaluable input and feedback, always doing so with a unique sense of humor (a tenth fruit of the Spirit, if you will). The uncontrollable laughs helped me through tough times. Remember Chaim, I have it all in writing!

And finally I dedicate this work to my mom and dad. It was my dad who taught me to see outside the box, and it was my mom who taught me how to love. And it is with this love that I bring you *The Heart of David*.

Special Acknowledgment

I could not in good conscience take credit for authoring this book without special acknowledgement of my close friend and mentor, Stephen Duame. Many of the ideas and prophetic concepts contained in *The Heart of David* were born out of years of prayer and contemplation, as Stephen sought the LORD for His deepest truths. It was together with Stephen, over countless hours of meetings and Bible studies, that the Prophetic Framework of this book was constructed. It is truly on the shoulders of his brilliance that I bring you *The Heart of David*.

Thank you Stephen,
Jeff

Table of Contents

In the Beginning

Section 1- The Captive Heart

Section 2- A Voice in the Wilderness

Section 3- The Solomon Generation

Into Eternity

Prologue
(Do not skip!)

A call to radical, faith-based obedience to God is going forth into the Church. What will it take to come to the measure of the stature of the fullness of Christ? Through *The Heart of David*, I intend to inspire God's people to search for the deeper things of God and to help create unity of the faith among those who will one day establish God's Kingdom on earth. A wise old friend once said, "If you believe you have something to do with establishing God's Kingdom, you're right; and if you don't, you're also right. It's up to you."

Let's open the chambers and peer deeply into *The Heart of David*. David had a heart of praise, one that rejoiced in God's ways, sought after the LORD in all things, and delighted to do His will. He had a never-ending joy that sprung forth from knowing God. However, David did something that few other men in history would dare to do. He was able to anticipate God's desires, and was bold enough to declare them aloud before ever being told! What can a man accomplish for God, who loves Him so deeply, and wants to honor Him so completely that he can foresee the divine plan of his Creator? My prayer for you is that, like David, you too would develop such an uninhibited intimacy with God that your love for Him would inspire you to share David's vision and join me in his daring prayer.

However, this is not just another story about the renowned king of Israel. In *The Heart of David*, we explore the magnificence of using Biblical blueprints to uncover the "mysteries of the Kingdom of Heaven." On our voyage to the Promised Land, we will journey from Captivity, through the Wilderness, and ultimately find ourselves standing at the shore of the Jordan. Along the way we will discover our high calling. What will it take to cross over? Mix unshakable faith, a giant slayer with the heart of David, and the awesome power of the Holy Spirit, and what we have is the recipe to part the waters. Step into the river, and pass over on dry ground!

The high calling of the Church requires radical, faith-based obedience to God's commandments. However, THINK NOT that I have come to add anything to the blood of Christ. No doctrinal point presented in this book should be interpreted as adding to the requirement for eternal salvation. I confess only one way to everlasting life, faith in the shed blood of Jesus Christ, a free gift from God. Radical, faith-based obedience should be your gift in return. Obedience is not a duty, but it should be your desire.

All Scriptures used are quoted from the New King James Version (NKJV) of the Holy Bible, Copyright Nelson (1983), unless otherwise noted. I converted the actual Scriptural text into italics to make it stand out from other text in the book. In some cases, I used bold highlights or included a more detailed rendition from the Greek or Hebrew, from which the English is translated. I did this to emphasize the main points I was drawing from the text. Be aware that the bold, italic, and Greek/Hebrew do not appear in the Nelson NKJV. The emphasis is that of the author.

Appendix D contains a chart of major Prophetic Themes that you will find throughout this book. You can use it as a guide, if you wish, and refer back to it while reading *The Heart of David*. The far left column contains the prophetic themes or major concepts presented, while the far right column displays my desired outcome for you as the reader. In the center, I have indicated in which chapters you will find each particular premise elaborated. For a larger printable version of this chart, visit TheHeartofDavid.com.

Think about it!

"Think about it!" Icon: Alongside certain subsections, I included a special alert symbol. It is there to alert you about the nature of the material you are about to read. In every case where the symbol is present, the material is complex and requires your undivided attention. Do not attempt to read these sections while engaged in casual reading or when you are tired and not fully attentive. Instead, allow time for deep thought and meditation, even time to reread the section, if necessary, so you can contemplate these vital and complex issues. As the author, while editing this manuscript, I could not even fully comprehend these sections myself if working while tired. The alert remains "ON!" until you no longer see the line to the left of the text.

About the Cover: The cover of the book was inspired by a vision of the author after God birthed the idea for *The Heart of David*. God's prophetic plan for humanity is represented by the three dwelling places for God's Spirit. First, God descended on the Tabernacle in the Wilderness. He then occupied the Temple of Solomon, all the while making it well known that He could never be contained in a Temple made with hands. Finally, He will occupy the Spiritual Temple where His Name will dwell for all time.

Introduction

T here are many prayers in the Bible. Most of them call out to God to do something for us. The question remains: What can we do for Him? One prayer, above all others, is the answer to this question. Once saved, God gifts us with "free will," the opportunity to make choices. Are you willing to surrender your free will back to God? This new "freedom" makes us accountable to Him. In reality, true spiritual freedom is having no options; you simply decide that God's way is the only way! Are you willing to offer your life as a living sacrifice? If you are, read on and discover the prayer that God is waiting for you to pray. All of creation is groaning with expectation for the manifestation of the sons of God. Will you be bold enough to proclaim the prayer that will reveal the sons of God? If you are, carry on and make your intentions known. Oh, and by the way, prepare yourself for change!

Throughout this book we will rely on repetitive patterns demonstrated in Scripture to help us recognize and read "Scriptural Blueprints." These blueprints are the secret to a deep and significant understanding of Scripture. The first key to understanding the depths of Scripture is to understand that there are predictable patterns throughout. These follow a common prophetic technique of "overlay" where one picture or pattern is overlaid by another to add detail. Secondly, you must know how to spot these predictable patterns. And finally, you must become skilled at interpreting them.

In Matthew 16, Jesus uses the weather to demonstrate the predictable nature of things. "*In the evening when the sky is red you can predict fair weather, and in the morning when the sky is red and overcast you can say stormy weather. How then is it that you can discern the face of the weather but you cannot discern the signs of the times?"* Take notice of the many catastrophic events that have recently taken place around the world. You too must be able to discern the signs of the times. Therefore, you must be watchful for patterns. You must be able to read the blueprint.

There are many famous models of prayer, or blueprints of prayer, in the Scriptures. The Lord's Prayer, probably the most famous of all, is found in Luke 11:2-4: *"Our Father in heaven, Hallowed be Your name. Your Kingdom come. Your will be done on earth as it is in heaven. Give us day by day our daily bread. And forgive us our sins, for we also forgive everyone who is indebted to us. And do not lead us into temptation, but deliver us from the evil one."* This is the model prayer, or blueprint of prayer, instructed by Jesus.

Some prayers are blueprints for blessings, like the Aaronic or priestly blessing over Israel in Numbers 6:22-27, when the LORD spoke to Moses saying: *"Speak to Aaron and his sons, saying, 'This is the way you shall bless the children of Israel. Say to them: "The LORD bless you and keep you; The LORD make His face shine upon you, and be gracious to you; The LORD lift up His countenance upon you, And give you peace."' So they shall put My name on the children of Israel, and I will bless them."*

Some prayers model provision and protection like that of Jabez in 1 Chronicles 4:10. Jabez called on the God of Israel saying, *"Oh, that You would bless me indeed, and enlarge my territory, that Your hand would be with me, and that You would keep me from evil, that I may not cause pain!"* So God granted him what he requested. Still others are blueprints of prayers for forgiveness, thanksgiving, repentance, and battle.

One model prayer may be the one that has been echoed by more pastors and evangelists than any other throughout all of history, and is beyond a doubt the single most unifying prayer in all of Christianity. It's the defining prayer of the faith. It is called for more often and is without question the most important prayer any person will ever pray. It is the Sinner's Prayer or prayer of salvation in Roman 10:9-13: *...that if you confess with your mouth the Lord Jesus and believe in your heart that God has raised Him from the dead, you will be saved. For with the heart one believes unto righteousness, and with the mouth confession is made unto salvation. For the Scripture says, "Whoever believes on Him will not be put to shame."* For

18

there is no distinction between Jew and Greek, for the same LORD *over all is rich to all who call upon Him. For "whoever calls on the name of the* LORD *shall be saved."*

Although there is no need to recite any specific prayer to "get saved," without a true confession similar to Romans 10:9-13, one cannot even enter the family of God. This then, as a model prayer, stands above all others when teaching and preaching to a lost, unbelieving world. When evangelizing and preaching the Gospel of Salvation to the lost, it is, in a sense, the "high calling." When witnessing to the unsaved, leading them to a confession of faith is the goal. The "Sinner's Prayer" will forever remain the model prayer for shining light into darkness.

The prayer of Salvation deals with the issue of sin. The blood of Jesus is the atoning sacrifice and has paid the price for all of our sins, and therefore, after we repent and pray the prayer of salvation, sin should no longer be the focus in our lives. With this prayer we **move away** from sin.

As for your experience of being born again and having become a member of the family of God, does the prayer of salvation remain the most important prayer for you? As a Believer, is confessing your faith unto salvation the high calling? Is walking towards the altar to rededicate your life on any given Sunday the upward call in Christ Jesus? Is it the ultimate high calling on the Christian heart? I don't believe it is.

During the course of your life, all of the prayers mentioned earlier: repentance, blessings, provision, protection, thanksgiving, or forgiveness, are and will be of extreme value. But what if, for the moment, we set aside the focus on our **own individual needs and desires** in prayer and look at our function as members of the Body of Christ? We may begin to have "eyes to see" and "ears to hear" a new and higher calling.

If salvation is not the high calling, then what is? After salvation, I believe there is one blueprint prayer, which exceeds all others in importance, that will lead to this high calling. This act of faith, this one request, supersedes every other that a Believer might pray for during his life as a disciple of Jesus Christ. I believe the fulfillment of this prayer request will bring the Christian faith to maturity and face-to-face with our high calling.

I strongly believe that if, with a willing heart, you are called to pray this prayer along with me and countless other Believers; we will see the hand of God Almighty move in the earth like in no other generation. The second most important prayer overall and the most important prayer a Believer could ever pray is not one that moves us away from sin, but **towards God** the Father and towards being conformed into the image of our Lord and Savior Jesus Christ.

As the Apostle Paul wrote in Philippians 3:13-14, *Brethren, I do not count myself to have apprehended; but one thing I do, forgetting those things which are behind and reaching forward to those things which are ahead, I press toward the goal for the prize of the **upward call** of God in Christ Jesus.* And the upward call, as expressed so well in Ephesians 4:13, is: *Till we all come to the unity of the faith and of the knowledge of the Son of God, to a perfect man, **to the measure of the stature of the fullness of Christ.*** Simply stated, Paul was born again and at the same time did not consider himself to have already apprehended the prize of the upward call. In short, salvation cannot be the high calling However, obtaining the measure of the stature of the fullness of Christ is!

Considering this point of view, should you accept yourself as an imperfect, destined-to-sin victim of being human? Not if you forget what is behind and press on towards what rests ahead.

> ➤ *(Hebrews 12:1-2) Therefore we also, since we are surrounded by so great a cloud of witnesses, let us lay aside every weight, and the sin which so easily ensnares us, and let us run with endurance the race that is set before us, looking unto Jesus, the **author and finisher of our faith**, who for the joy that was set before Him endured the cross, despising the shame, and has sat down at the right hand of the throne of God.*

He is the author and **finisher** of our faith. Therefore, it is possible to obtain the measure of the stature of the fullness of Christ. Have you ever seriously considered reaching this high calling?

Can you be conformed into the image of Christ? Is it possible to attain the heart of Jesus? If you dedicate your life to completing the process that Jesus started on the cross; if you run the race with certainty; I believe it is possible to attain. Prayerfully you will agree by the time you complete this book.

➤ **(1 Corinthians 9:24-26)** *Do you not know that those who run in a race all run, but one receives the prize? Run in such a way that you may obtain it. And everyone who competes for the prize is temperate in all things. Now they do it to obtain a perishable crown, but we for an imperishable crown.* **Therefore I run thus: not with uncertainty.** *Thus I fight: not as one who beats the air.*

You must shed the attitude that you cannot do absolutely everything the Lord asks of you. You must discard the belief that you cannot become everything He died for you to become. You must run the race with certainty.

However, the road to being conformed into the image of Christ is a tough one and will take you on a path through the Wilderness. You must guard yourself from any doctrine that makes your walk as a Christian seem easy. Paul warned in his second letter to Timothy 4:3-4: *For the time will come when they will not endure sound doctrine, but according to their own desires, because* **they have itching ears,** *they will heap up for themselves teachers; and they will* **turn their ears away from the truth,** *and be turned aside to fables.* Itching ears only want to hear a feel good message. Those that want their ears tickled will not be lovers of truth. The truth is that you can do all things through Christ who strengthens you. You can be conformed into His image. You can be like Jesus. But it will take total sacrifice and the death of your will. Jesus tells us to "Be perfect, just as my Father in heaven is perfect." Does this thought bother you; or does the possibility of perfection truly excite you? Prayerfully, the Holy Spirit will guide you to the truth during our time together.

Do you remember when you prayed the prayer of salvation, when you confessed with your mouth and believed in your heart that Jesus is Lord and that God the Father raised Him from the dead? Do you recall your born again experience, when you first believed? Do you remember when you called on the name of the LORD for the first time, whether it was during a Church service, or an evangelical outreach, or with a friend who witnessed to you, watching a TV ministry, reading the Bible, or perhaps you were alone with the Lord when He called you? Do you remember the move of the Holy Spirit in your life after you got saved, after you prayed that prayer? Some changes were sudden and dramatic while others were slow and painful. Nevertheless, there were changes.

If your testimony does not resemble any of this, then this book is not really for you. You must stop here and pray for salvation and truly be repentant. You must make Jesus the Lord and Savior of your life. You first must be a child of God before you can be an heir to His inheritance. You need to be born again and grafted into the family of God first, before you can consider praying the most important and dramatic prayer that any member of God's family can pray.

If your witness is that you truly are born again, then you probably also have many other testimonies since the day you first believed. You probably can testify of numerous occasions when God moved in your life in a powerful way. You know the saying, "Be careful what you pray for; you just might get it!" The prayer that I propose is the most important prayer you will ever pray as a Believer is the Prayer of David.

As you may have guessed from the title of this book, *The Heart of David*, David is the key prophetic figure in this book, and his life is the blueprint that I am inviting you to emulate. Be careful if you pray this prayer; it will change your walk forever! Just like your prayer for Jesus to come into your heart and change you when you got saved, this prayer will invite the Holy Spirit into your life to do a radical work of transformation in you. This prayer is the Believer's equivalent of the Sinner's Prayer. What you ask for will change your faith forever. By proclaiming this prayer, you step out of the Wilderness into the Promised Land. Please be patient however. My advice to you is that you DO NOT skip ahead to discover this prayer without laying the groundwork first. If you do, it will have very little meaning and, most likely, only leave you disappointed and confused.

God said that David was "a man after His own heart." He is the only man in all of Scripture that God gives this title. We had better take notice of what a man after the heart of God is all about. Even though David made huge mistakes, he remained in the favor of God Almighty because of his repentant heart. He so understood the heart of God that he was able to step out and pray what I consider to be the boldest prayer in all of Scripture. It's with this heart and with this intention that I write this book.

Prayer is powerful. Pray with a heart like David's and you might change the world. God is looking for His children to first become sensitive enough to recognize what may be the most powerful prayer in all of Scripture. Secondly, He is looking for volunteers to step forward in unity, enthusiastic to humbly proclaim this prayer for all the Church and the entire world to hear. If willing, we might participate in the most exciting events the world has ever known. In the words of Jesus Himself, "*And this Gospel of the Kingdom will be preached in all the world as a witness to all the nations, and then the end will come.*"

Join me now as we hear his prayer and seek *The Heart of David*.

Section One:
The Captive Heart

Chapter One

Fertile Soil

Let us not frivolously spread our seed on rocks and pathways.
Let us soak the seed and cultivate the land and plant our seed in fertile soil.
Dr. Jeff Hazim

Let's open the chambers and peer deeply into *The Heart of David*. David had a heart of praise; one that rejoiced in God's ways, sought after the LORD in all things, and delighted to do His will. He had a never-ending joy that sprung forth from knowing God. David did something that few other men in history would dare to do. He anticipated God's plan before ever being told and was bold enough to declare it aloud! My prayer for you is that, like David, you too would develop such an uninhibited intimacy with God that your love for Him would inspire you to share David's vision and join me in his daring prayer.

However, this is not just a story about the renowned king of Israel. In *The Heart of David*, we explore the magnificence of using Biblical blueprints to decipher the "mysteries of the Kingdom of Heaven." On our voyage to the Promised Land, we will journey from Captivity, through the Wilderness, and ultimately find ourselves standing at the shore of the Jordan. Along the way we will discover our high calling. What will it take to cross over? Mix unshakable faith, a giant slayer with the heart of David, and the awesome power of the Holy Spirit, and what we have is the recipe to part the waters. Step into the river, and pass over on dry ground.

Before we move on to the details of David's prayer, we must first do some groundwork. Any farmer hoping for a good yield will cultivate his soil before he plants his seed. The soil is your heart and, more important-ly, the corporate heart of the Church. Ezekiel said it best when he prophesied that God would soften our hard hearts. In Ezekiel 36:26 the Lord says, *I will give you a new heart and put a new spirit within you; I will take the heart of stone out of your flesh and give you a heart of flesh.* It is my deepest desire that *The Heart of David* will prepare you for this heart transplant.

The first step in preparing for this surgery is coming up with the correct diagnosis. You won't seek a remedy if you don't know you have a disease. Diagnosing the condition of your heart can be done by using an excellent Biblical tool. The tool is learning to recognize and understand prophetic overlays. It is like learning to read a "Biblical Blueprint." I would like to introduce the first of the Biblical Blueprints that we will explore during the course of this book. It is that of the **Journey and Destination**. These two key elements will explain why it is a foregone conclusion that we all eventually need a heart transplant and that we must enter the Wilderness to get one. My prayer for you is that as you weave through the first section of the book called "The Captive Heart," you will come to the same conclusion.

The Journey & Destination

As a Believer, it is easiest for you to understand the *Journey and Destination* in its broadest sense. Let us use the concept of salvation, for example. Before Jesus, you were in the world. He redeemed you out of the world and set you apart to be saved for eternity. The blueprint looks something like this: You start in Captivity, take a journey through the Wilderness, and end at your destination— the Promised Land. You go from the world (captivity, bondage, sin, heart of stone) to the Wilderness where you face trials that test your faith, and which turn your heart of stone into a heart of flesh. James 1:2-4 says it like this: *My brethren, count it all joy when you fall into various trials, knowing that the testing of your faith produces patience. But let patience have its perfect work, that you may be perfect and complete, lacking nothing.* Becoming perfect and complete, lacking nothing, is the next stop after the Wilderness. It is called the Promised Land.

To summarize, it's Captivity—Wilderness—Promised Land. Just like Israel: Egypt—Desert—Canaan. In regard to salvation, as Believers, in a certain sense, you are already in the Promised Land. Your future is secure, albeit, you still face trials that test your faith and help you grow. These trials take place in the Wilderness. Patterns obviously repeat themselves over and over again in our lives and it is not unlikely that you will be at different locations on the journey in different areas of your life. Mini-cycles of these patterns may have you in the Promised Land at your job and in the Wilderness with your spouse. You may even be in the Captivity with your sports addiction and in the Wilderness with your children. Anyhow, you can see how it works. We have all experienced these patterns working in our lives and we all notice that we are at different stages in different areas of growth.

Corporately however, the Church is moving along on this **Journey** to a **Destination** as well. Now please don't get offended, but **concerning the heart,** technically, the Body of Christ is still on the Egyptian side of the Red Sea. We still need to be called into the Wilderness. Essentially, the Church is still part of the political, economic and religious systems of the world. God is saying to the world: "Let My People Go!" I understand if you have difficulty agreeing with this statement at this time. I only ask that you give it some time and let the Spirit minister to you. God is always faithful in revealing His truths in perfect timing. The Body of Christ, just like individuals, may be at different stages in different areas of growth. The Church may already be in the Wilderness in some aspects of its growth and may even be in the Promised Land in other respects. However, when considering its place on the world stage, the heart of the Church remains in Egypt; still part of the system, the institutions of the world remain deeply rooted within its fabric.

This can be a confusing concept because there are many smaller journeys within the single main journey, from Egypt through the Wilderness and into the Promised Land, which runs throughout history. For the Church, the smaller journeys repeat over and over again the same way they repeat for you as an individual. But the main journey runs its course one time through God's entire plan for mankind. Considering the Church's position in history, with regards to its heart, it is still in Egypt and needs to be called into the Wilderness. Let me make it perfectly clear. I am not attempting to criticize the Church, its accomplishments, or its place in history. Passing into the Wilderness is not a bad thing; it's not an inferior place or a punishment. For instance, our father Abraham was the first "Hebrew," the first "to cross over." He crossed over into the

Wilderness which was symbolic of progress in his faith, an advance. The Wilderness is a supernatural place of growth and transformation. It is the place where we become pure.

So, concerning the corporate heart of the Church, with respect to the last days before the Lord's return, it still does not occupy its rightful place of authority over the things of this world, and will need to enter trials in the Wilderness to be equipped with the promise of James 1:4: *"That you may be perfect and complete, lacking nothing."* Before you dismiss this possibility, give me a few more chapters. By the time you are half way through this book, you will probably agree. Again, this is in no way a criticism or condemnation of the Church as that would be denying the Spirit. I'm simply emphasizing that we MUST follow the blueprint of God's plan.

The Restoration

The spirit that calls the Church into the Wilderness must come first before the Lord's return. As you will soon learn, there must be a "restoration of all things" before Christ's second coming. This restoration takes place in the Wilderness and prepares God's people to pray the Prayer of David which will eventually lead us out of the Wilderness into the Promised Land.

The Forerunner

God always has forerunners who prepare the way for His people to follow. The forerunner must enter the Wilderness first, be tested and purified, become ready, and then declare a prayer like David's with complete conviction and faith. Each forerunner's duty is accomplished when he makes that prophetic journey across the Jordan and into the Promised Land, never doubting for a moment that the giants before him are no match for his faith. These brave predecessors complete their mission by going back to get the people. Just as Moses was exiled to the desert at 40 years of age and returned to Egypt at 80 to proclaim *"Let My people go!"* my prayer is that during the course of this book, the spirit of the **Wilderness Prophet** will get hold of your heart and inspire you to do the same. My hope is that you will be encouraged to leave your comfortable place in the world and head off into the Wilderness. It is in this desolate place that you will receive a new heart of flesh that will empower you to pray the Prayer of David with boldness, conviction, and faith. The power unleashed with this level of faith will part the Jordan and you will cross over on dry ground. But as you will learn in Chapter 9, Elisha goes with Elijah **back** from the "Promised Land" into the Wilderness, as a prototype of the mission of the forerunner. The forerunner, or the "firstfruits," of His harvest must complete the journey from Captivity to the Wilderness and into the Promised Land first. In doing so, they will serve as an example to the main body of His harvest who will later come out of Captivity in the greater Exodus. As a forerunner, you must follow the same pattern. You will pray the Prayer of David, and with a new heart go back and call the people out of Captivity. The main body will complete the journey for which you have paved the way. You will guide them through the Wilderness, lead them in the Prayer of David, and into the Promised Land.

The Heart

If your heart is too hard, burdened by the cares of the world, and you cannot receive this message, then you need to pray for the Lord to soften your heart. Pray with boldness and faith that He will begin to prepare the soil of your heart. If seed is sown on good soil, then *The Heart of David* will yield a bountiful harvest similar in magnitude to the harvest you reaped when you prayed for salvation with a genuine heart of faith.

If the spirit of the forerunner dwells in you and your heart is quickened by this possibility, you will at once be stirred by the words of the prophet Jeremiah. They should ring in your ears as a sweet sound, while they help you recall the powerful lesson taught by our Lord and Savior 600 years later.

Jeremiah 4:1-4

"If you will return, O Israel," says the LORD,
"Return to Me; And if you will put away your abominations
out of My sight, Then you shall not be moved.
And you shall swear, 'The LORD *lives,'*

In truth, in judgment, and in righteousness;
The nations shall bless themselves in Him,
And in Him they shall glory."
For thus says the LORD *to the men of Judah and Jerusalem:*

"Break up your fallow ground,
And do not sow among thorns.
Circumcise yourselves to the LORD,
And take away the foreskins of your hearts,
You men of Judah and inhabitants of Jerusalem,
Lest My fury come forth like fire,
And burn so that no one can quench it,
Because of the evil of your doings."

"Break up your fallow ground and do not sow among thorns." In these words, God uses soil as a metaphor for the heart. Jeremiah continues, *"Circumcise yourselves to the* LORD *and take away the foreskins of your hearts."* Jesus taught about the soil of the heart many years later as He recalled the words of the prophet and relayed the lesson to those who had ears to hear and eyes to see. Masterfully, in Matthew 13:3-9, He gave us the parable of the seed and the soil as a lesson about the condition of the heart.

Then He spoke many things to them in parables, saying: "Behold, a sower went out to sow. And as he sowed, some seed fell by the wayside; and the birds came and devoured them. Some fell on stony places, where they did not have much earth; and they immediately sprang up because they had no depth of earth. But when the sun was up they were scorched, and because they had no root they withered away. **And some fell among thorns,** *and the thorns sprang up and choked them. But others fell on* **good ground** *(fertile soil, a soft heart) and yielded a crop: some a hundredfold, some sixty, some thirty. He who has ears to hear, let him hear!"*

What then is the fruit of having a fertile heart? As we will see in a moment, according to Jesus the fruit is, *"Knowing the mysteries of the Kingdom of Heaven."* I don't know about you, but to me this is an incredible offer. Can you imagine understanding the Kingdom of Heaven? Many Believers today cannot even define what the "Kingdom of Heaven" is, let alone decipher its mysteries. Later in this book we will explore and define the Kingdom of Heaven. However, at this time it is sufficient that we merely understand, and I'm sure that Jesus would agree, that with a dull, unfertile heart, you will NEVER understand the deep mysteries of God. Jesus continues in Matthew 13:10-17:

*And the disciples came and said to Him, "Why do You speak to them in parables?" He answered and said to them, **"Because it has been given to you to know the mysteries of the Kingdom of Heaven**, but to them it has not been given. For whoever has, to him more will be given, and he will have abundance; but whoever does not have, even what he has will be taken away from him. Therefore I speak to them in parables, because seeing they do not see, and hearing they do not hear, nor do they understand. And in them the prophecy of Isaiah is fulfilled, which says: 'Hearing you will hear and shall not understand, And seeing you will see and not perceive; **For the hearts of this people have grown <u>dull</u>.** Their ears are hard of hearing And their eyes they have closed, Lest they should see with their eyes and hear with their ears, **Lest they should understand with their hearts and turn,** So that I should heal them.' But blessed are your eyes for they see, and your ears for they hear; for assuredly, **I say to you that many prophets and righteous men desired to see what you see, and did not see it, and to hear what you hear, and did not hear it.***

Again I ask, what is the fruit of having a fertile heart? Jesus puts it so well. *He answered and said to them,* **"Because it has been given to you to know the mysteries of the Kingdom of Heaven."** Isn't it exciting to know that we have the opportunity to see things that not even the great prophets of old could see? Jesus goes on to explain the parable in Matthew 13:18-23, which of course indicates that the condition of the heart is the most important factor in rightly dividing the word of the Kingdom. Simply stated, understanding the Kingdom of Heaven is a heart issue.

*"Therefore hear the parable of the sower: When anyone hears the **word of the Kingdom,** and does not understand it, then the wicked one comes and snatches away what was sown in his heart. This is he who received seed by*

the wayside. But he who received the seed on stony places, this is he who hears the word and immediately receives it with joy; yet he has no root in himself, but endures only for a while. For when tribulation or persecution arises because of the word, immediately he stumbles. Now he who received seed among the thorns is he who hears the word, and the cares of this world and the deceitfulness of riches choke the word, and he becomes unfruitful. But he who received seed on the good ground is he who hears the word and understands it, who indeed bears fruit and produces: some a hundredfold, some sixty, some thirty."

Thirty, sixty, a hundredfold what? What fruit is being multiplied? Answer: The mysteries to the Kingdom of Heaven. He plants a small seed in the soil of your heart and out of your heart should flow knowledge of the mysteries of the Kingdom of Heaven. The mysteries are to be solved and you have the key. Don't be like the disobedient servant Jesus teaches about in yet another parable. In the "Parable of the Talents" a servant hides his talent under a rock and when his master returns, he has only what his master left him and no more. The master dealt harshly with this servant for not "multiplying his talents." He called him a wicked servant and took the talent and gave it to the one who doubled his master's investment. This is a consistent theme throughout Jesus' teaching ministry. He confirms this way of the "Kingdom economy" in the parable of the soil above. *"For whoever has, to him more will be given, and he will have abundance; but whoever does not have, even what he has will be taken away from him."*

Our Master has left us with gifts and talents. He went away and sent a helper to assist us in multiplying these talents. Specifically and prophetically speaking, **the talents to multiply ARE the mysteries of the Kingdom of Heaven.** It has been given to you to unravel the "mysteries." Jesus said in Matthew's Gospel 16:19, *"And I will give you the keys of the Kingdom of Heaven, and whatever you bind on earth will be bound in heaven, and whatever you loose on earth will be loosed in heaven."* You have in your possession the keys and the authority to unlock the Kingdom of Heaven.

If we are left with this legacy, this ability to solve the mysteries of the Kingdom, why do so many Christians have no clue that there are mysteries; what these mysteries are; or even what the Kingdom of Heaven is?

Why haven't they accepted their rightful inheritance and place of authority? Jesus said to us in John's Gospel that we would do even "greater works" than He did. In Galatians 3:29, Paul tells us, *"And if you are of the Messiah, then you are the seed of Abraham, and heirs according to the promise."* This sounds wonderful. We get saved and we inherit the promises, all the authority, solve all the mysteries, and do greater works than Jesus, right? Not so fast! Paul clarifies in the very next verses. *"And I say, for as long as the heir is a child, he is no different from a slave, though he is master of all, but is under guardians and trustees till the time prearranged by the father"* (Galatians 4:1-2).

When we are born again, we are like a little baby with a big trust account. A newborn can't tell the difference between a dollar and a candy wrapper. Nevertheless, once born again, we become *"masters of all"* and owners of a huge fortune. Unfortunately, there is one major complication. We must grow up first in order to use it. Much like a son inheriting a fortune from his earthly father, if he is too young and immature to manage the responsibilities, his father places the inheritance in a trust account for him. It remains in trust until a time prearranged by the father, and when older and more mature, the son receives his full inheritance. When is the time prearranged by our heavenly Father for us to receive our full inheritance? The clue is found a few verses later, when in Galatians 4:19 Paul writes, *"My little children, for whom I labor in birth again until Christ is formed in you."* When Christ is formed in you and you grow up to look like Him, then you will be ready to receive your full inheritance. Later in this book, we will complete a detailed exploration into the mysteries of being conformed into His image and the Kingdom of Heaven. These are mysteries that we cannot fully understand until we begin to grow out of spiritual childhood and towards our full inheritance. But for now, let's deal with the heart issue.

Christian Vascular Disease (CVD)
The Dull Heart

If we are being offered a new heart and are promised the eyes to see and the ears to hear, why do so many Christians suppress their full inheritance? Why do we reject our rights to know the mysteries of the Kingdom of Heaven? What is it about human nature that causes us to reject what is new, unusual, or "mysterious" and call it untrue before we investigate it fully? Why does the Christian's heart remain "dull"?

I believe one source of this dullness is that many Believers have a tendency to think that salvation is all there is. In their hearts, "getting saved" is the high calling. Others believe they know as much as necessary already. Even those deep in the faith oftentimes believe that everything that would be known has already been expounded upon by Biblical "scholars" and "theologians." They place their trust in the words of these scholars to teach them "all truth" without searching the Scriptures for themselves (under the guidance of the Holy Spirit); and so their own hearts remain dull. For example, should we readily accept someone else's interpretation of Paul's writings, or even our own surface understanding, without searching the Scriptures for their deeper meaning by the leading of the Spirit? In Acts 17:11, the Bereans were considered more noble because they received the word with all readiness and then *searched the Scriptures daily to see if what Paul was saying was true.* Shouldn't we do the same?

This "dull" heart problem was the same disease suffered by many of the Pharisees in the first century. Jesus said of them in Mark 7:6-7: *"Well did Isaiah prophesy of you hypocrites, as it is written: 'This people honors Me with their lips, **but their heart is far from Me**. And in vain they worship Me, teaching as doctrines the **commandments of men**.'"*

If you trust in the words and teaching of the scholars of the day, without searching the Scriptures yourself, you face the same risks that you would have 2000 years ago. You may get "doctrines and commandments of men" in lieu of truth. In Luke's Gospel 12:1, Jesus says, *"Beware of the leaven of the Pharisees, which is hypocrisy."* In Matthew chapter 16 He calls the leaven *"the doctrine of the Pharisees."* Jesus says beware! I am in no way saying that every modern-day teacher or scholar can be likened to a Pharisee. What I am saying, however, is that there is no way to tell if what they are saying is true unless you search the Scriptures for yourselves.

If you naively rely on the words of scholars and teachers who ultimately prove to possess hard hearts, distant from God's truth, they will shut up the Kingdom of Heaven to you just as they did to them in Matthew 23:13. *"But woe to you, scribes and Pharisees, hypocrites! For you shut up the Kingdom of Heaven against men; for you neither go in yourselves, nor do you allow those who are entering to go in."* What could cause Believers to remain ignorant to the mysteries of the Kingdom of Heaven? They might put their faith and ultimate trust in men, and their hearts would remain dull and hard.

In John 16:12-13, Jesus told His disciples before He left them that He still had many more things to say to them, but that they were not able to bear them or comprehend them at that time. He said that the Spirit of truth, when He comes, shall lead or guide them into all truth. This is definitely an indication that Jesus did not reveal all that would be revealed. There are mysteries to be uncovered that are mentioned well after His death, burial and resurrection, and all the way into the book of Revelation chapter 10, when Jesus, through John, says in verse 7 that when the seventh angel shall sound his trumpet, *"the mystery of God would be finished."* This indicates that, at least up until the very end of days, there are still mysteries to unravel.

In *The Heart of David,* we hope to unravel some of the deepest mysteries of God, the mysteries of the Kingdom. We can do this by developing a thorough comprehension of "Biblical Blueprints," "The Wilderness Prophet," and the "Prayer of David." The question, however, remains for you, the reader: Are you willing and open to discovering the secrets of the Kingdom? The Bible instructs us that if we seek we shall find, and if we knock the door will be opened.

Jesus said that the Father has hidden the secrets of the Kingdom from those who think they are wise and has revealed them to babes. Matthew 11:25 reads: *At that time Jesus answered and said, "I thank You, Father, LORD of heaven and earth, that You have hidden these things from the wise and prudent and have revealed them to babes."* This Scripture uses babies as a metaphor, alluding to the open heart of a child, which is soft and pure. Jesus says in Mark 4:11: *"To you it has been given to know the mystery of the Kingdom of God; but to those who are outside, all things come in parables."* Are YOU inside or outside?

Are you willing to be called into the Wilderness? Are you willing to have your heart softened and eventually transplanted? Are you willing to develop eyes to see and ears to hear God's high calling on your life? Are you willing to seek and knock? Do you want to know the mysteries of the Kingdom of Heaven? Are you a forerunner? My experience in discovering truth and unraveling these mysteries is that it always comes down to an issue of the heart. If your heart is soft and open, you will be more capable of accepting truths that challenge your current thinking process and belief system. If your heart remains hard and closed, the truth will not penetrate it because God will not impose His will on anyone.

If you remember our fathers in Israel who walked the desert sands in Sinai for 40 years, you will recall that it was a hard heart that kept them in the Wilderness. Many years later, David said in Psalm 95:7-10, *"Today, if you will hear His voice, do not harden your hearts as in the rebellion, in the day of trial in the Wilderness, where your fathers tested Me, tried Me, And saw My works forty years."*

God led them around the Wilderness for four decades, a trip that should have taken only two to three weeks had it not been for their hard, rebellious hearts. Many Christians are astounded at how these people could have been so rebellious after all the miracles they witnessed: the plagues, the parting of the sea, the water from a rock, manna and quails from heaven, the cloud by day and fire by night, the voice of God from the mountain, etc. There was an endless intercession by God on behalf of His people, yet they still hardened their hearts.

Many years later, the writer of the book of Hebrews quotes David when he writes to born again Believers in Hebrews 3:12-15:

> ➤ *Beware, brethren, lest there be in any of you an **evil heart** of unbelief in departing from the living God; but exhort one another daily, **while it is called "Today,"** lest any of you be hardened through the deceitfulness of sin. For we have become partakers of Christ if we hold the beginning of our confidence steadfast to the end, while it is said: "Today, if you will hear His voice, do not harden your hearts as in the rebellion."*

While it is called **"Today."** Wow! The writer brings the warning right into the present day. The same warning that went out to the rebellious sons of Israel 3,500 years ago also went out to the Believers in the First Century Church. Sadly enough, I can echo the same warning **"Today,"** two thousand years later. "While it is called **"Today,"** if you hear His voice, do not harden your hearts!"

Amazingly, we have less of an excuse now than those who witnessed, first-hand, all those miracles in the Wilderness thousands of years ago. We have had the indwelling of the Holy Spirit for 2,000 years, yet the Church is no closer to understanding the mysteries of the Kingdom of Heaven today, than we were back in the days of Paul. The reason: The Church suffers the same hard heart disease as Israel did while it wandered aimlessly through the Wilderness 3,500 years ago and the same disease that blinded many of the Pharisees 2,000 years ago.

We must find a cure for this heart disease before the Church suffers a fatal heart attack. The prophet Amos spoke of a people at the End of the Age who were longing for the return of the Lord, but His return was not a happy day for them. They had been bound up in doctrines and commandments of men and did not even know it. Amos 5:18-21 reads:

> **"Woe to you who desire the day of the Lord!**
> **For what good is the day of the Lord to you?**
> **It will be darkness, and not light.**
> *It will be as though a man fled from a lion,*
> *And a bear met him! Or as though he went into the house,*
> *Leaned his hand on the wall, And a serpent bit him!*
> *Is not the day of the Lord darkness, and not light?*
> *Is it not very dark, with no brightness in it?*
> **I hate, I despise your feast days,**
> **And I do not savor your sacred assemblies."**

Men who desired to see the "Day of the Lord" were involved in feast days and assemblies that God despised. Are you? (See Appendix A for resources on this topic.) Amos 6:5 portrays the people for whom this warning tolls. They are those *"who are singing to the sound of the harp having composed songs for themselves like David"* (The Scriptures © 1998). What people on earth today can be described as those who compose songs to God like David, while they eagerly anticipate the Day of the Lord? Amos prophesied of a people who Paul later described as those *"who are fervent for God, but not according to knowledge."* They loved the Lord, but had poor spiritual practices and faulty doctrines. We could say that this prophecy is being fulfilled by the modern-day Church, which is composed of thousands of denominations, each with differing and even contrasting doctrines. Many Churches are filled with people *"who are fervent for God, but not according to knowledge."* They can't all be right and, in fact, EVERY denomination probably has a number of doctrinal beliefs that are wrong. We should, **"Search the Scriptures daily to see if what we are hearing or reading is true!"** We are of one faith and should insist on truth and unity, settling for no less. And in fact, this is precisely what the Scripture predicts. Unity is inevitable, so let's start working towards unity today.

Why however, will the day of His return be darkness and not light for those longing for it? Because He returns to a large group of professing Believers who have heart disease, and only a small remnant who are actually prepared. Jesus said in Matthew 7:13-14: *"Enter by the narrow gate; for wide is the gate and broad is the way that leads to destruction, and there are many who go in by it. Because narrow is the gate and difficult is the way which leads to life, and there are few who find it."*

The Remedy

To remedy this disease, we must begin our journey of exploration in the field of open-heart surgery. Explore, if you wish, while you remain in Captivity. But know this; the remedy requires a journey into the Wilderness. The disease: Hardening of the heart or "Christian Vascular Disease." The treatment: A circumcision surgery that begins with a small incision on the foreskin of your heart with a spiritual scalpel, the Word of God. Be careful, for this scalpel is sharp and is no respecter of flesh. *For the word of God is living and powerful, and sharper than any two-edged sword, piercing even to the division of soul and spirit, and of joints and marrow, and is a discerner of the thoughts and intents of the heart (Hebrews 4:12).* If a skillful surgeon handles this precision surgical instrument, then the circumcision will be successful. If not, your heart will remain dull and your eyes and ears will remain closed, though you may be bruised and bloodied from the experience.

So, before we even hear the words echoed through *The Heart of David*, or pray the model prayer that God is waiting for His people to pray, we must hearken to the voice of the one crying in the Wilderness. He will guide us through the rough terrain and prepare us for a small incision on the foreskin of our hearts. Remember, he must be a skillful surgeon because the surgery is critical and his scalpel is sharper than a two-edged sword.

Chapter Two

The Circumcised Heart

Circumcise yourselves to the Lord,
and take away the foreskins of your hearts.
Jeremiah 4:4

I n this chapter you will learn what a circumcised heart looks like and, more importantly, determine if you have one. If you don't, you must decide if you are willing to enter the Wilderness to have the circumcision surgery performed. You must decide if you are a forerunner.

Moses was the first to introduce the notion of the circumcised heart in Deuteronomy 10:12-16. *"And now, Israel, what does the LORD your God require of you, but to fear the LORD your God, to walk in all His ways and to love Him, to serve the LORD your God with all your heart and with all your soul, and to keep the commandments of the LORD and His statutes which I command you today for your good? Indeed heaven and the highest heavens belong to the LORD your God, also the earth with all that is in it. The LORD delighted only in your fathers, to love them; and He chose their descendants after them, you above all peoples, as it is this day. **Therefore circumcise the foreskin of your heart, and be stiff-necked no longer."***

Jeremiah later prophesied about the new (renewed) covenant. In Jeremiah 31:31-34, he writes that the commandments of God would one day be written on our hearts.

"Behold, the days are coming, says the LORD, when I will make a new covenant with the house of Israel and with the house of Judah—not according to the covenant that I made with their fathers in the day that I took them by

the hand to lead them out of the land of Egypt, My covenant which they broke, though I was a husband to them, says the LORD. But this is the covenant that I will make with the house of Israel after those days, says the LORD: **I will put My Law in their minds, and write it on their hearts;** *and I will be their God, and they shall be My people. No more shall every man teach his neighbor, and every man his brother, saying, 'Know the LORD,' for they all shall know Me, from the least of them to the greatest of them, says the LORD. For I will forgive their iniquity, and their sin I will remember no more."*

Moses and Jeremiah both allude to a time when man's heart would be turned back towards God. Ezekiel confirmed this when he recorded these words from the LORD, *"I will give you a new heart and put a new spirit within you; I will take the heart of stone out of your flesh and give you a heart of flesh."* This is the heart surgery that must take place in the Wilderness before you pray the Prayer of David. Before the masses will follow, a remnant of Believers, acting as forerunners, must pave the way in the Wilderness. We must make the message of the Gospel of the Kingdom clear, and then the rest will follow. My prayer is that *The Heart of David* will then open the doors so that *"the Gospel of the Kingdom is preached in all the world."*

Resistance to Obedience

Many in the Christian world today believe that their hearts are already circumcised. They feel that the circumcision takes place the moment they confess Jesus as Lord and Savior. I see a different picture. Jeremiah reports that God will put His Law in our minds and write it on our hearts, and then it would **NOT** be necessary to teach men about God, for they would all know Him. Clearly this is a future event, not simply future to the time Jeremiah wrote the words, but future to you reading the words today. We must still evangelize so that people, who don't know God, will know Him. Also, at the beginning of Jeremiah 30, it tells of the time these things will occur. Jeremiah 30:3 states, *'For behold, the days are coming,' says the LORD, 'that* **I will bring back from captivity My people <u>Israel</u> and <u>Judah</u>,***' says the LORD. 'And I will cause them to return to the land that I gave to their fathers, and they shall possess it.'* Judah began to return to the Land in the first part of the twentieth century and continues to return till this day. In 1948, Israel became a nation again in one day, as prophesied would happen in Isaiah 66:8.

> ➤ NIV *Who has ever heard of such a thing? Who has ever seen such things? Can a country be born in a day or a nation be brought forth in a moment? Yet no sooner is Zion in labor than she gives birth to her children.*

The remaining lost Tribes of Israel have yet to return to the Land. (See Appendix C for a detailed explanation of Israel's full identity and future union). Christianity connects deeply with the Jeremiah 31 covenant, as it describes the circumcision of the heart; a covenant Christians believe has already been **completed** in Jesus. However, this is only partially true. This prophecy has not yet been entirely fulfilled and the renewed covenant spoken of in Jeremiah 31 has only just begun. It will not be complete until the Law is totally written on the hearts of all Believers and it is no longer necessary to teach men about God.

We also see in Deuteronomy 10 that when we love God with all our hearts we will keep His commandments and statutes. This, unfortunately, is not the predominant mindset in today's Christianity. Instead of looking for commandments that they can keep, most Christians are looking for theological reasons why they no longer need to keep commandments. Whenever I speak to Christians about the details of many of the commandments in the "Old Testament," the common responses I get include: "Oh that's legalism or bondage," or "that's for Jews, not for Christians," or "Jesus died on the cross so we don't have to keep the Law." It is rare for me to hear a response like, "Whatever God says, I will hear and obey." The reason for the negative responses is because the Law is not yet written on their hearts. Their hearts are only partly circumcised. And please understand I am not only talking about the Ten Commandments and tithing, but every commandment that applies to you as a disciple of Christ.

For a point of reference, the book of Deuteronomy was a sermon preached in **ONE** day before Israel entered the Promised Land. It highlights the importance of obedience. Moses used that day to reemphasize the commandments of God before the people crossed into the Promised Land to enter God's rest. Anywhere in the Book of Deuteronomy where you see the phrase, *"all the commandments which I command you today"* (which appears no less than 23 times), Moses' emphasis that day was on all of God's commandments, not limited to tithing and the Ten Commandments written on stone tablets.

The Prophetic Significance of Obedience

Think, about it!   (Note: If you are not familiar with this "Think about it!" symbol, please go back to the Prologue and read about its significance throughout this book. If you want the most for your time invested in *The Heart of David*, be diligent and do it!) Let's take a look at the blueprint or prophetic overlay of a circumcised heart. Circumcision of the flesh was given as a sign of a covenant. *"This is My covenant which you shall keep, between Me and you and your descendants after you: Every male child among you shall be circumcised"; "and you shall be circumcised in the flesh of your foreskins, and it shall be a sign of the covenant between Me and you"* (Genesis 17:10-11). Circumcision of the flesh itself, however, confers nothing on the recipient. Paul teaches that without obedience circumcised flesh may as well be uncircumcised flesh. Romans 2:25 states: *"For circumcision is indeed profitable if you keep the Law; but if you are a breaker of the Law, your circumcision has become uncircumcision."* And faith in God that leads to obedience counts as circumcision, even in those who are uncircumcised in the flesh. *Therefore, if an uncircumcised man keeps the righteous requirements of the Law, will not his uncircumcision be counted as circumcision? (Romans 2:26).*

As patterns predict, if obedience to God's commandments is a sign of circumcision of the flesh, it should also be an indication of a circumcised heart. Paul makes this vital connection in Romans 2:14-15: *For when Gentiles, who do not have the Law, by nature **do the things in the Law**, these, although not having the Law, are a Law to themselves, who show the work of the Law **written in their hearts...*** Becoming more obedient to God's commandments indicates what is happening in your heart.

Love & Obedience

What does it look like when a heart of stone has been replaced with a heart of flesh? In Deuteronomy 30, Moses describes the attitude of a people whose circumcision is complete. And Deuteronomy 30:3-4, just like Jeremiah 30:3, points to our future. *"That the* LORD *your God will bring you* **back from captivity**, *and have compassion on you, and gather you again from all the nations where the* LORD *your God has scattered you. "If any of you are driven out to the farthest parts under heaven, from there the* LORD *your God will gather you, and from there He will bring you."* Again, to the present day, only part of this prophecy has been fulfilled so it still points to our future.

Jesus understood obedience when He taught about loving God; *"If you love Me, keep My commandments."* This type of obedience describes a circumcised heart of flesh. And let's be perfectly clear; when Jesus says, *"Keep my commandments,"* he is talking about all His Father's commandments. He clarifies this when He teaches in 1 John 5:2-3; *"By this we know that we love the children of God, when we love God and keep* **His** *commandments. For this is the love of God, that we keep* **His** *commandments.* **And His commandments are not burdensome.**" Jesus did not have a different set of commandments than His Father. Jesus' message was 100% consistent with the words of Moses in Deuteronomy 30 when he taught that if you loved God with all your heart, you would keep His commandments; and you would not complain that they were too difficult. This of course makes perfect sense, since Jesus did not come with a new doctrine. Jesus said in John 7:16, *"My doctrine is not Mine, but His who sent Me."* And in John 12:49-50, He said He came with the words of His Father, *"For I have not spoken on My own authority; but the Father who sent Me gave Me a command, what I should say and what I should speak. "And I know that His command is everlasting life. Therefore, whatever I speak, just as the Father has told Me, so I speak."* He also said in reference to Moses in John 5:46-47, *"For if you believed Moses, you would believe Me; for he wrote about Me. But if you do not believe his writings, how will you believe My words?"*

On the other hand, disobedience to God is a sign of a lack of faith. In other words, disobedience is a sign of an uncircumcised heart.

And to whom did He swear that they would not enter His rest, but to those who did not obey? So we see that they could not enter in because of unbelief (Hebrews 3:18-19). Hebrews 11:6 says that without faith it is impossible to please God.

Jesus Taught the Doctrine of Moses

Jesus made an allusion to Moses' words in Deuteronomy 30 when He taught about the attitude people should have towards God's commandments. Remember, this was not His own doctrine, but the doctrine of His Father. He said in John's Gospel 14:15, *"If you love Me, keep My commandments"*; and in 14:21, *"He who has My commandments and keeps them, it is he who loves Me. And he who loves Me will be loved by My Father, and I will love him and manifest Myself to him"*; and in John 15:10, *"If you keep My commandments, you will abide in My love, just as I have kept My Father's commandments and abide in His love."* Jesus also told us that these commandments are not burdensome. He taught us in Matthew 11:29-30, *"Take My yoke upon you and learn from Me, for I am gentle and lowly in heart, and you will find rest for your souls. For My yoke is easy and My burden is light."* Jesus said it this way in 1 John 5:3, *"For this is the love of God, that we keep His commandments. And His commandments are not burdensome."* It should not be difficult to keep His commandments.

The Significance of Moses' Words

What do Jesus' words above have in common with Moses' words in Deuteronomy 30:6-20, and how might they reveal the condition of your heart? Let's take a close look at the words of the LORD through Moses and confirm from them that Jesus did not teach His own doctrine, but the doctrine of His Father.

"And the LORD your God will circumcise your heart and the heart of your descendants, to love the LORD your God with all your heart and with all your soul, that you may live. Also the LORD your God will put all these curses on your enemies and on those who hate you, who persecuted

46

you. And you will again obey the voice of the LORD and do **all His commandments which I command you today.** The LORD your God will make you abound in all the work of your hand, in the fruit of your body, in the increase of your livestock, and in the produce of your land for good. For the LORD will again rejoice over you for good as He rejoiced over your fathers, if you obey the voice of the LORD your God, to keep His commandments and His statutes which are written in this Book of the Law, and if you turn to the LORD your God with all your heart and with all your soul."

"For this commandment which I command you today **is not too mysterious** (difficult) for you, nor is it far off. It is not in heaven, that you should say, 'Who will ascend into heaven for us and bring it to us, that we may hear it and do it?' Nor is it beyond the sea, that you should say, 'Who will go over the sea for us and bring it to us, that we may hear it and do it?' But the word is very near you, in your mouth and in your heart, that you may do it."

"See, I have set before you today life and good, death and evil, in that I command you today to love the LORD your God, to walk in His ways, and to keep His commandments, His statutes, and His judgments, that you may live and multiply; and the LORD your God will bless you in the land which you go to possess. But if your heart turns away so that you do not hear, and are drawn away, and worship other gods and serve them, I announce to you today that you shall surely perish; you shall not prolong your days in the land which you cross over the Jordan to go in and possess. I call heaven and earth as witnesses today against you, that I have set before you life and death, blessing and cursing; **therefore choose life,** that both you and your descendants may live; that you may love the LORD your God, that you may obey His voice, and that you may cling to Him, **for He is your life and the length of your days;** and that you may dwell in the land which the LORD swore to your fathers, to Abraham, Isaac, and Jacob, to give them."

Excellent! As we expect, Jesus' words are perfectly consistent with Moses' words which are the doctrine of the Father. With a circumcised heart you will not say that God's commandments are too difficult, too mysterious, too burdensome or too far off. They will be near to you in your mouth and in your heart to obey them. Now, how does this apply to you as a New Testament Believer? The answer, although profound, is quite simple. **If your heart was truly circumcised, you would believe that you could keep ALL God's commandments without difficulty.** Please do not overlook this concept. It is a vital component that needs to be established in your heart and in your mind. This concept will further come into focus as we explore Paul's teaching about Deuteronomy 30 from the Book of Romans.

Paul Teaches the Doctrine of Moses

I'd bet you didn't know there was a specific area of teaching (doctrine) in the Book of Romans on this subject. Yes, the most famous area in all of Scripture that contains the call to salvation, (the Sinner's Prayer), is taken right from the words of Moses in Deuteronomy 30. We must interpret Paul's words correctly if we desire to be consistent with our Lord's decree that He did not come with His own doctrine, but the doctrine of His Father. When teaching from the words of Moses, Paul also did not invent his own doctrine about salvation, but referred directly to the "doctrine of the Father." Likewise, we must not interpret Paul's words in Romans by inventing our own doctrine or, worse yet, fall victim to the doctrines and commandments of other men. We should understand the call of salvation in light of the Scripture from where it came; and in so doing, we will unveil one of the mysteries of the Kingdom of Heaven, which is the circumcised heart. Let's explore and compare Deuteronomy 30 and Romans 10.

Deuteronomy 30 & Romans 10

I find it fascinating that the prayer of confession quoted from Romans 10 is generally only seen as a call to salvation. Also curious is that the Scripture is not cited beginning from verse 1, but rather from verse 9. "*That if you **confess with your mouth** the Lord Jesus and **believe in your heart** that God has raised Him from the dead, you will be saved. For with* *the heart one believes unto righteousness and with the mouth* **confession is made unto salvation.** *For the Scripture says, "Whoever believes on Him will not be put to shame." For there is no distinction between Jew and Greek, for the same Lord over all is rich to all who call upon Him.* **For "whoever calls on the name of the LORD shall be saved"** *(Romans 10:9-13).*

Whoever calls on the name of the LORD shall be saved. This is the bottom line in Christian evangelism. Call out to God; confess your sins and that Jesus is Lord and Savior. Confess He is who He says He is and your sins are forgiven, and you are saved to spend eternity in the presence of God. I believe this just as you do. I know that Jesus is the only way to the Father. However, **confessing** that He is who He says He is, is only part "A" of the call. Faith perfects itself in you when you also **believe you are** who He says **YOU ARE** in Him. This is part "B." *"For with the* **heart one believes unto righteousness."** Righteousness is the state of being right in God's eyes. It comes from the Hebrew word that means "Lawful" and the Greek word that means "observant of divine Laws." Part "B" of the call is demonstrated in Romans 10, verses 1-8 when, at its core, the condition of the heart is paramount and Paul's masterful use of Deuteronomy 30 comes into play. So, for our purpose in understanding Romans 10, and the confession of our faith as Christians, we are going to begin starting in verse 1.

Paul Teaches Righteousness

Brethren, my heart's desire and prayer to God for Israel is that they may be saved. For I bear them witness that they have a zeal for God, but not according to knowledge. For they being ignorant of God's righteousness, and seeking to establish their own righteousness, have not submitted to the righteousness of God. For Christ is the end of the Law for righteousness to everyone who believes. For Moses writes about the righteousness which is of the Law, "The man who does those things shall live by them." But the righteousness of faith speaks in this way, "Do not say in your heart, 'Who will ascend into heaven?' " (that is, to bring Christ down from above) or, " 'Who will descend into the abyss?' " (that is, to bring Christ up from the dead). But what does it say? "The word is near you, in your mouth and in your heart" (that is, the word of faith which we preach) (Romans 10:1-8).

There is a lot to cover here so please stick closely and reread this section over and over if necessary. **This section is a "must understand" prerequisite before you can go on to the rest of the book.** Before you move on, learn it well enough that you could **EXPLAIN** it to your Christian brothers and sisters. Spend time in prayer and meditation on this information. In God's timing, you will see it. At some point, you will have an "ah hah" moment, an epiphany. The lights will go on and you will have a level of excitement that begins to build in you. The comparison of Deuteronomy 30 and Romans 10 is actually the foundation of our faith as Believers in Jesus. When you realize the profound lesson being alluded to by Paul, and you grasp the depth of the calling on your life, you will be ecstatic. You will cross over into the Wilderness and be one step closer to the Prayer of David with a heart like David's.

Romans Chapter 10

Brethren, my heart's desire and prayer to God for Israel is that they may be saved. For I bear them witness that they have a zeal for God, but **not according to knowledge** *(Romans 10:1-2).* Paul refers to the people of Israel as having a zeal for God, but there is something wrong with their knowledge. It would be likened to a modern-day Believer who is "on fire" for God, but has wrong doctrines. We explored this problem briefly in Chapter 1 using the prophet Amos. What was Israel's bad doctrine? *For they being ignorant of God's righteousness, and* **seeking to establish their own righteousness,** *have not submitted to the righteousness of God (Romans 10:3).* They somehow thought they could be good enough or Lawful enough to be righteous on their own, and they did NOT submit to the righteousness of God. Paul explained the distinction between self-righteousness and faith earlier in the same book. *"For the promise that he would be the heir of the world was not to Abraham or to his seed through the Law, but* **through the righteousness of faith** *(Romans 4:13).*

How then do we submit to the righteousness of God? How do we demonstrate the righteousness of faith? *For Christ is the* **end** *of the Law* *for righteousness to everyone who believes (Romans 10:4).* Through the power of God, and with faith in Christ and His work done on the cross, we can achieve a right standing in front of a Holy God. (For those who predated Christ's first coming, a right standing required faith in the promises of God.)

We need to clarify a vital point in verse 4 before we move on. The English word "end" is chosen as the translation for the Greek word "telos." *For Christ is the end {tel'-os} of the Law for righteousness to everyone who believes.* It is an interesting choice here, perhaps even purposeful. To the English speaking western mind, the word "end" suggests Christ **ended or terminated the Law for everyone who believes.** This makes no sense considering that righteousness actually means "Lawfulness." You cannot terminate the Law and still have Lawfulness. A better translation is the word "goal or outcome." *Christ is the goal or Messiah is the outcome of the Law for righteousness to everyone who believes. For with the heart one believes unto righteousness.* This is easily demonstrated in another verse using the same Greek word "telos," also translated into the English word "end." *Receiving the end {tel'-os} of your faith, even the salvation of your souls (1 Peter 1:9).* Clearly we do not terminate our faith and then receive the salvation of our souls. The **outcome** of our faith is the salvation of our souls, not the termination of our faith. So the mistake Israel made was in seeking their own righteousness. The correction is found by seeking the righteousness of faith which we find in Christ.

Now for the meat! *For Moses writes about the righteousness which is of the Law, "The man who does those things shall live by them." But the righteousness of faith speaks in this way, "Do not say in your heart, 'Who will ascend into heaven?'* "*(that is, to bring Christ down from above) or, "'Who will descend into the abyss?' "(that is, to bring Christ up from the dead). But what does it say? "The word is near you, in your mouth and in your heart" (that is, the word of faith which we preach) (Romans 10:5-8).*

Follow closely now. If Christ is the goal, target or outcome of the Law for righteousness and Moses writes about the righteousness of the Law, then Moses is writing about Christ. Remember, we have already established, and we can be certain Moses understood, that there is no

51

righteousness in the Law outside of faith. Let me remind you what Jesus said in John 5:46-47: *"For if you believed Moses, you would believe Me; for he wrote about Me. But if you do not believe his writings, how will you believe My words?"* When Moses wrote, he was writing about Christ.

What follows Romans 10:4 (*Christ is the goal of the Law*) are two very profound "Old Testament" references; both were written by Moses, both about Christ. This is critical to your understanding! The first is in verse 5: **"The man who does those things shall live by them."** This statement appears seven times through all of Scripture. Only **ONE** time is it written by Moses and that is in the book of Leviticus 18:5. It appears in Nehemiah once, Ezekiel three times, and twice by Paul, once here in Romans and once in Galatians. The second is in verses 6-8 and refers directly to Deuteronomy 30:11-14. We will explore verses 6-8 in a few moments. Keep in mind, both Old Testament references are from the Books of Moses. Let's start with Leviticus 18.

Is Moses simply relating the consequences of violating God's commandments or does Paul see something more?

> ➤ **(Leviticus 18:1-5)** *Then the LORD spoke to Moses, saying, "Speak to the children of Israel, and say to them: 'I am the LORD your God.' According to the doings of the land of Egypt, where you dwelt, you shall not do; and according to the doings of the land of Canaan, where I am bringing you, you shall not do; nor shall you walk in their ordinances.* **(The warning!)** *'You shall observe My judgments and keep My ordinances, to walk in them: I am the LORD your God. 'You shall therefore keep My statutes and My judgments,* **which if a man does, he shall live by them** (The blessing): *I am the LORD.*

Moses declares "a man shall live by them" as both an admonition and an endorsement. He is warning the people of the curse for following the way of the pagans and teaching them of the LORD'S blessing of abundant life for keeping His commandments. The context here is that within **God's commandments** exists blessing and life and outside **His commandments** lies death. Wouldn't you agree to this statement if I substituted "Christ" for "God's Commandments"? Within **Christ** exists blessing and life, and outside **Christ** lies death. Moses was writing about Christ.

Leviticus 18:5 is **NOT**, as some would like it to mean, a warning for those who want to keep God's commandments, and if this is not what Moses meant, then certainly it is not what Paul meant either. It is **NOT** a warning that if you want to diligently observe God's Laws, you better keep all of them or else you will have to live by the consequences. It is **NOT** a reference for anyone trying to get saved by keeping the commandments of God. It simply teaches that God's commandments contain blessings and life, and Paul knows that Christ exemplifies God's commandments. *For when Gentiles, who do not have the Law, by nature **do the things in the Law**, these, although not having the Law, are a Law to themselves, who show the work of the Law **written in their hearts** (Romans 2:14-15).* This is faith in Christ.

Understanding this, we can go on to the details of Romans 10:6. It is generally translated using what I consider to be "inherited bias"; not the entire verse, simply the first word. This word creates sharp contrast between **Law and Faith**; a contrast that I will prove was clearly not intended by Paul. I believe the bias was inherited from generations past and that there was absolutely no evil intent by translators.

Somewhere, a long time ago, the Church lost its understanding of the critical relationship between Law and Faith. Paul, in the book of Romans, is the master teacher on this relationship. *But Israel, pursuing the Law of righteousness, has not attained to the **Law of righteousness**. Why? Because they did not **seek it** (or keep it) **by faith**, but as it were, by the works of the Law. For they stumbled at that stumbling stone (Romans 9:31-32).* They stumbled not knowing the Messiah. They did not apply faith in the Messiah (to come or who came) to the Law of righteousness. That was their excuse starting over 3,500 years ago. What excuse does the Body of Christ have today? How do we apply faith to the Law? Space in this book does not permit elaboration on how we lost this critical understanding, but you can research Church history and early anti-Semitism to discover when and why this took place. Coming up in this chapter, you will see that God's Law is not replaced with faith. God's Law is kept with faith.

A Short Grammar Lesson

For continuity, let me repeat Romans 10:5. *For Moses writes about the* ***righteousness which is of the Law,*** *"The man who does those things shall live by them.* Verse 6 then begins with the coordinating conjunction "BUT." ***But the righteousness of faith speaks in this way…*** In translation, **"But"** is used to show a definite contrast between **"the righteousness of the Law"** and **"the righteousness of faith."** In verse 6, it is the Greek word "deh" {deh} that is translated to the English word "but." It is commonly translated as "and" or "moreover" when a comparable point is being made, a point where two similar ideas are being joined together. And it is commonly translated as "but" when an adversative or opposing point is being made, a point where two contrasting ideas are being joined together. When a definite contrast is intended, the Greek primary particle {men} is found along with {deh}. In this combination, although "men" is often not translated, "deh" always has adversative force and must denote contrast between the two consecutive thoughts. In combination, they would be correctly translated as "but" or "but on the other hand." However, when no definite contrast can be determined by the grammar, it is the context that decides which is appropriate. "Men" {men} **DOES NOT** appear in Romans 10:6. So when translating the word "deh" between the continuous thoughts of Romans 10:5 and 10:6, which conjunction should it be? Should it be "and," which equates **"the righteousness of the Law"** and **"the righteousness of faith,"** or "but" which contrasts them? We will let the context of the Scripture answer this question.

Context

If Christ is the goal or target of the Law for righteousness to all who have faith (Romans 10:4), and Moses writes about the righteousness of the Law bringing life, then Moses is writing about Christ and the life that comes from faith. This is exactly what Jesus said Moses did! *"For if you believed Moses, you would believe Me;* ***for he wrote about Me.*** *But if you do not believe his writings, how will you believe My words?"* (John 5:46-47). *Philip found Nathanael and said to him,* ***"We have found Him*** *of whom Moses in the Law, and also the prophets, wrote* — Jesus of Nazareth, the son of Joseph" (John 1:45). And beginning at Moses and all the Prophets, He (Jesus) expounded to them in all the Scriptures the things concerning Himself" (Luke 24:27).

Considering these facts, we can conclude that the righteousness of the Law in Romans 10:5 *is* the righteousness of faith in Romans 10:6. This is because there can be no righteousness of the Law other than **keeping it by faith.** The righteousness of the Law is established by faith. That is why Paul wrote, *do we then make void the Law through faith? Certainly not! On the contrary, we establish the Law (Romans 3:31).* This interdependent relationship between Law and faith necessitates that the first word of verse 6 be translated as the comparable conjunction "and" or "moreover," **NOT** the contrasting conjunction "but." Moreover means: "in addition, likewise, furthermore, what is more, besides, also, additionally." Paul is not contrasting the concepts of Law and faith; he is unifying them. **Moses writes about the righteousness which is of the Law. Moreover (likewise) the righteousness of faith speaks in this way.** Paul is quoting Moses in both verse 5 (Leviticus 18:5) **and** in verses 6-8 (Deuteronomy 30:11-14), and he is teaching about the critical relationship between **Law and Faith** in a way that few others could do. Unfortunately, his words have been twisted over the centuries. Paul said that the only way to attain to the Law of righteousness is by faith, for there is no promise of life if the Law is not done with faith, for Christ is the goal of the Law for righteousness to everyone who believes; and *that the righteousness of the Law might be fulfilled in us, who walk not after the flesh, but after the Spirit (Romans 8:4* ᴷᴶⱽ).

And now for deeper revelation, let's directly compare the Scriptures from Romans 10:6-8 to Deuteronomy 30:11-14.

Romans 10:6-8

But (moreover) the righteousness of faith speaks in this way, "Do not say in your heart, 'Who will ascend into heaven?'" (that is, to bring Christ down from above) or, "'Who will descend into the abyss?'" (that is, to bring Christ up from the dead). But what does it say? "The word is near you, in your mouth and in your heart" (that is, the word of faith which we preach).

Deuteronomy 30:11-14

"For this commandment which I command you today is not too mysterious (difficult) for you, nor is it far off. It is not in heaven, that you should say, 'Who will ascend into heaven for us and bring it to us, that we may hear it and do it?' Nor is it beyond the sea, that you should say, 'Who will go over the sea for us and bring it to us, that we may hear it and do it?' But the word is very near you, in your mouth and in your heart, that you may do it."

Now let's blend them together so we can reveal the mystery.

(Deuteronomy 30:11) *"For this commandment which I command you today is not too mysterious* (difficult) *for you, nor is it far off.* All the commandments of God were commanded that day before Israel entered the Promised Land and Moses says they are not too difficult or mysterious. Paul said in **Romans 10:6** that *the righteousness of faith speaks in this way.* That's right; the righteousness of faith says that God's commandments are **NOT** too difficult. Jesus said, *"If you love Me, keep my commandments"* and *"My yoke is easy and My burden is light"* and *"For this is the love of God, that we keep His commandments. And His commandments are not burdensome."*

    (Deuteronomy 30:12) *It is not in heaven, that you should say, 'Who will ascend into heaven for us and bring* **it** *to us, that we may hear it and do it?'* Bring what to us? The commandments, the Law. Paul says in **Romans 10:6**: *"Do not say in your heart, 'Who will ascend into heaven?'* (that is, to bring Christ down from above). Here Paul makes the clear connection that Christ equals the Law. The Law is not unreachable that you must ascend to heaven in order to get it before you can do it. It is in the Person of Jesus Christ, and He already came to show us how.

    (Deuteronomy 30:13) *Nor is it beyond the sea, that you should say, 'Who will go over the sea for us and bring it to us, that we may hear it and do it?'* Paul says in **Roman 10:7**: *"'Who will descend into the abyss?' (that is, to bring Christ up from the dead)."* Again he makes it very clear.

Moses says "it" is the Law and Paul says "it" is Christ.

*(Deuteronomy 30:14) But the word is very near you, in your mouth and in your heart, **that you may do it.*** Paul says in **Roman 10:8:** *But what does it say? "The word is near you, in your mouth and in your heart"* **(that is, the word of faith which we preach)."** Moses says "that you may do it." Do what? The word or the Law! Paul says *"that is, the word of faith which we preach."*

The word of faith that Paul is preaching during the prayer that we call the "Prayer of Salvation" or the "Sinner's Prayer" is that the commandments are near you in your mouth and in your heart to do them and they are not too difficult. Both Paul and Jesus teach a message consistent with Moses. God's commandments are not burdensome. The degree of resistance that you have to this idea is directly proportionate to how uncircumcised your heart is and how long you will remain in the Wilderness.

What follows is the famous prayer of repentance in Romans 10:9-13, *that if you confess with your mouth and believe in your heart...* Again, the word of faith that Paul is preaching is that with a circumcised heart you will no longer say that God's commandments are too difficult. In Christ we can do it. The word will be near you, in your mouth and in your heart to DO IT!

So if our attitude is that we cannot or should not keep all of His commandments, or if we say in our hearts that the commandments are too difficult, or if we call them a burden and treat them with complaint; are our hearts completely circumcised? Certainly not! We must **confess with our mouth** unto salvation **AND** we must **believe in our hearts** unto righteousness. We need both parts A and B. Do you C (see)?

When we declare our faith and confess our salvation, the circumcision ceremony begins. *For circumcision is indeed profitable if you keep the Law; but if you are a breaker of the Law, your circumcision has become uncircumcision. Therefore, if an uncircumcised man keeps the righteous requirements of the Law, will not his uncircumcision be counted as circumcision? (Romans 2:25-26).*

However, the Scriptural evidence shows that the circumcision will not be completed until the very end of days, and that it will take place in the Wilderness. This is the circumcised heart of faith that we also see prophesied about in Ezekiel when the LORD says, "I will take out your heart of stone and give you a heart of flesh." *For he is not a Jew who is one outwardly, nor is circumcision that which is outward in the flesh; but he is a Jew who is one inwardly; and* **circumcision is that of the heart,** *in the Spirit, not in the letter; whose praise is not from men but from God* (Romans 2:28-29). The debate over the Law and circumcision was one that became all too familiar to the First Century Church, and Paul was the key figure smack in the middle of the controversy. Let's diverge for a moment to examine Paul's opinion on the subject.

Paul was a Law keeper even after Christ

Many doctrines inside of Christianity depict Paul as the anti-Law disciple of Jesus. Scholars use Paul's own writings to prove that Christ made the Law of nil effect. They especially use his letter to the Galatians to prove this doctrine. Let me put Paul's words in perspective for you so you won't fall victim to those who twist his words to their own destruction. *Therefore, beloved, looking forward to these things, be diligent to be found by Him in peace, without spot and blameless; and consider that the longsuffering of our Lord is salvation — as also our beloved brother Paul, according to the wisdom given to him, has written to you, as also in all his epistles, speaking in them of these things, in which are* **some things hard to understand, which untaught and unstable people twist to their own destruction, as they do also the rest of the Scriptures.** *You therefore, beloved, since you know this beforehand, beware lest you also fall from your own steadfastness, being led away with the error of the wicked* (2 Peter 3:14-17).

As with all Scripture, interpretation should not be approached casually. In Matthew 22:29 Jesus said, *"You are mistaken, not knowing the Scriptures nor the power of God."* Paul was a brilliant man who wrote in complex thought patterns mixed with deep prophetic inspiration. Concerning Paul's words, we are especially warned that they are "hard to understand." Interpretation is a complex and serious undertaking and errors by the untaught are imminent and grievous. Peter says that if you are not steadfast you may be led astray by the wicked who twist Paul's words. It is interesting to note that the word wicked is derived from the word "wick," a cord or strand of loosely woven, twisted, or braided fibers. Wicked conjures up the idea of something being horribly twisted. Those who twist Paul's words were and are wicked. The admonition: Don't fall into the same trap!

Let's observe Paul's actions when he is confronted directly regarding his belief concerning the Law of Moses. In Hebrew, the Law of Moses is called the Torah. Be mindful that the following event took place approximately 25 years after the resurrection.

> (Acts 21:17-24) *And when we had come to Jerusalem, the brethren received us gladly. On the following day Paul went in with us to James, and all the elders were present. When he had greeted them, he told in detail those things which God had done among the Gentiles through his ministry. And when they heard it, they glorified the Lord. And they said to him, "You see, brother, how many **myriads** of Jews there are who have believed, and they are all zealous for the Law; "but they have been informed about you that you teach all the Jews who are among the Gentiles to forsake Moses, saying that they ought not to circumcise their children nor to walk according to the customs. "What then? The assembly must certainly meet, for they will hear that you have come. "Therefore do what we tell you: We have four men who have taken a vow. "Take them and be purified with them, and pay their expenses so that they may shave their heads, and that all may know that those things of which they were informed concerning you are nothing, **but that you yourself also walk orderly and keep the Law."***

The accusation against Paul is that he is no longer observing God's commandments and that he is teaching the Jews to forsake circumcision and the Law of Moses. Wow! This is a serious allegation. Ironically enough, this was the same allegation against Stephen. *They also set up false witnesses who said, "This man does not cease to speak blasphemous words against this holy place and the Law"* (Acts 6:13). Stephen was falsely accused and paid the ultimate price. Before his belief in Jesus, Paul oversaw the murder of innocent Stephen who was accused of "teaching against the Law." Under the watchful eye and authority of Paul, Stephen's life was taken for "blasphemy." During the events of Acts 21 years later, Paul, now reaping the consequences of his actions against Stephen, faces the same false accusation. He is accused of teaching against and breaking the Laws of Moses. Paul has the opportunity to set the record straight. If the doctrine of Christ truly nullifies the Law of Moses, this is the occasion for Paul to defend that position. He is challenged by the myriad of Jews who have believed in Christ, yet still maintain fervency for God's commandments. The word "myriad" means thousands upon thousands, an innumerable multitude, or an unlimited number. There was a huge community of Jewish Believers in the first century who fervently kept the Law, and they wanted to know Paul's position. James solves the dilemma by asking Paul to take a vow to prove that he still *walks orderly and keeps the Law.* Paul can reject the offer and declare that Christ has set us free from circumcision and the Law. Instead, Paul takes the vow and pays a large sum to support four other men and, in so doing, declares that, to him, the Law still has a standing. Paul completes the vow of a Nazirite, which is a vow of separation instructed in the book of Numbers chapter 6. Paul spent many years with the false accusation of being a "Law breaker" following him and every step of the way he defended his faith and his upkeep of the Law of Moses. *When he had come, the Jews who had come down from Jerusalem stood about and laid many serious complaints against Paul,* **which they could not prove,** *while he answered for himself, "Neither* **against the Law of the Jews,** *nor against the Temple, nor against Caesar have I offended in anything at all"* (Acts 25:7-8). Is Paul wrong? Does he have bad doctrine? Is the apostle to the Gentiles twisted in his faith? Has he become a hypocrite? Would he compromise his faith in Jesus for man's approval? Maybe, just maybe, he knows something of which modern-day Christianity has lost sight.

Back in Acts 15, about five years earlier, Paul had a dispute with some Jewish Believers about the doctrine of circumcision. It's roughly 20 years after the resurrection and Paul is in Antioch. *And certain men came down from Judea and taught the brethren, "Unless you are circumcised according to the custom of Moses, you cannot be saved"* (Acts 15:1). Paul was certain that you could mix nothing with the shed blood of Jesus in order to earn salvation, so he argued with them vehemently. In a moment, when we look

at this event in Antioch as recorded in the letter to the Galatians, we will
see that it was probably Peter, who was one of the men who came down
from Judea, who was caught away in this hypocrisy. Paul decided to take
this issue to James and the Church leadership in Jerusalem to find a remedy for this heretical doctrine. But there he was met with even more
resistance. *But some of the sect of the Pharisees who believed rose up, saying,
"It is necessary to circumcise them, and to command them to keep the Law of
Moses" (Acts 15:5).* Now faced with the claim that it was necessary to
mix the entire Law of Moses with the shed blood of Jesus to earn salvation, the Church was forced to rule on its first great doctrinal challenge.
You have learned thus far in this chapter that the Law has saving value
only if mixed with faith. Paul knew that the Law alone could not save,
and that requiring anything other than faith in Christ unto salvation was
blasphemy. Paul understood that the Law could never save him and that
his obedience to the Law was **BECAUSE** he was saved (the byproduct);
not so that he would be saved (the cause).

This doctrine must be firmly established or the early Church is headed for the same mistakes as their Israelite ancestors.

*Now the apostles and elders came together to consider this matter. And when
there had been much dispute, Peter rose up and said to them: "Men and
brethren, you know that a good while ago God chose among us, that by my
mouth the Gentiles should hear the word of the Gospel and believe. "So God,
who knows the heart, acknowledged them by giving them the Holy Spirit, just
as He did to us, "and made no distinction between us and them, purifying their
hearts by faith.* **"Now therefore, why do you test God by putting a yoke
on the neck of the disciples which neither our fathers nor we were able to
bear?** *"But we believe that through the grace of the Lord Jesus Christ we shall
be saved in the same manner as they" (Acts 15:6-11).* Peter obviously con-
victed of his error in Antioch by Paul's rebuke, ultimately defended Paul's
position. However, to clarify, Peter was not referring to the Law as the
yoke around the neck; but rather the impossible burden the Law would

present if required for salvation. This is a key distinction.

No man or woman of Israel was ever able to bear the burden of keeping the Law as a requirement for salvation. Father Abraham "believed" God and it was accounted to him as righteousness, and so it would be for his seed that follows. Also, what Believers who came from the sect of the Pharisees meant by, *"It is necessary to circumcise them, and to command them to keep the Law of Moses,"* was a formal conversion to Judaism and the necessity of keeping, not just the written commandments of God as a prerequisite for salvation, but obedience to the oral commandments compiled by religious leaders as well.

James, the leader of the early Church, through the inspiration of the Holy Spirit, made an official ruling in the controversy in Acts 15:19-20. *"Therefore I judge that we should not trouble those from among the Gentiles who are turning to God, but that we write to them to abstain from things polluted by idols, from sexual immorality, from things strangled, and from blood."* There is nothing that can mix with the blood of Jesus to cause anyone to obtain eternal life. But it seemed good that the Holy Spirit would guide those new in the faith towards a "Torah observant" (Law abiding) lifestyle. At first, Gentiles are instructed in the basics of the Law and nothing else. Because of their newfound faith, the Gentiles were guided to immediately start by removing idolatry and sexual immorality from their lives, as well as adopting a "clean" diet. Abstaining from blood and things that were strangled is a reference to kosher eating. Crazy, isn't it? I bet you never knew that the New Testament made reference to new Believers adopting kosher eating habits. However, the basic instructions given to Gentile Believers in Acts 15 were so they would sufficiently cleanse themselves of these abominable practices in order to enter the Synagogues, as implied in verse 21, the next verse following the ruling. *"For Moses has had throughout many generations those who preach him in every city, being read in the synagogues every Sabbath."*

The Jerusalem Council of Acts 15 was actually advocating Synagogue attendance for new Gentile converts in order for these non-Jewish Believers to join their Jewish brethren on the Sabbath to learn the Law. In the first century, all that was available in the Synagogues on the Sabbath was teachings from the Law and the Prophets, and James was encouraging new Gentile converts to attend these services. It is profound to contemplate that there was no "New" Testament yet, and that Peter, James, John, Paul, and any other first century disciple of Christ could teach only from the "Old" Testament. As they progressed in their faith, Gentile converts would be instructed more and more about the lifestyle choices commanded in the Law of Moses. Over time, new converts were expected to become progressively more obedient to God's commandments as a natural consequence of being saved. However, no amount of obedience was required to get saved. Faith forever remains the only requirement for salvation.

Don't Twist Galatians

While in Antioch, before his journey to Jerusalem to address the heresy being desseminated by believing Jews who did not yet fully comprehend the free gift of salvation, Paul composed a letter to the Churches in Galatia to shed light on this very issue.

> ➤ *(Galatians 2:11-14) Now when Peter had come to Antioch, I withstood him to his face, because he was to be blamed; for before certain men came from James, he would eat with the Gentiles; but when they came, he withdrew and separated himself, fearing those who were of the circumcision. And the rest of the Jews also played the hypocrite with him, so that even Barnabas was carried away with their hypocrisy. But when I saw that they were not straightforward about the truth of the Gospel, I said to Peter before them all, "If you, being a Jew, live in the manner of Gentiles and not as the Jews, why do you compel Gentiles to live as Jews?"*

It seems that Peter was carried away in this hypocrisy, but by the time the Jerusalem Council met in Acts 15, he had adjusted his heretical doctrine and had come into agreement with Paul. If Peter could be carried away with erroneous doctrines, don't be so sure it hasn't happened to you! Many Believers inherit false doctrines even while attempting to understand Paul's very letter to the Galatians, written to expunge the belief in false doctrines. Ironic, isn't it? However, the modern-day Christian is guilty of quite the opposite doctrinal error as Peter. Whereas Peter was guilty of misapplying the Law of Moses, modern-day Christianity is guilty of nullifying it. The letter to the Galatians was written to clarify the idea that adding anything to the blood of Jesus in order to be justified is utter nonsense. I could exhaust the contents of an entire book to explore the intricacies of this letter, and perhaps in the future I will, but here I will simply compose a brief explanation.

In Galatians, Paul records his testimony and proclaims that he received his inspiration and authority directly from God. He is astound-ed that those who received the Holy Spirit by faith are now compelled to become circumcised and keep the Law **to be saved**. Paul's letter focuses on clarifying the error in this doctrine. On the contrary, the letter **SHOULD NOT** compel the reader to disdain the Law of Moses, but instead award the Law its correct standing. The Law is a tutor unto Christ; it is a handbook to become like Him.

> ➢ *(Galatians 3:24-29) Therefore the Law was our tutor to bring us to Christ, that we might be justified by faith. But after faith has come, we are no longer under a tutor. For you are all sons of God through faith in Christ Jesus. For as many of you as were baptized into Christ have put on Christ. There is neither Jew nor Greek, there is neither slave nor free, there is neither male nor female; for you are all one in Christ Jesus. And if you are Christ's, then you are Abraham's seed, and heirs accord-ing to the promise.*

This may be the most profound area of this difficult-to-understand letter. Let's untwist Paul's most commonly twisted words. The Law is our tutor to bring us to Christ. But what does Paul mean by "bring us to Christ"? Does he simply mean "until we believe Jesus is Messiah"? Do we aban-don the Law once we accept Jesus as Lord and Savior? Once we believe, we certainly become heirs, but does this act of faith instantly negate the value of the Law?

> ➢ *(Galatians 4:1-2) Now I say that the heir, as long as he is a child, does not differ at all from a slave, though he is master of all, but is under guardians and stewards until the time appointed by the father.*

Paul's answer is clear. Even as a Believer in Christ, the Law remains your guardian and steward until the time appointed by the Father. When is that time? Later in verse 19, Paul writes that the time is when *Christ is formed in you.* When does that happen? Christ is fully formed in you when you attain the stature of Messiah. Think about it. If Christ is fully formed in you already, then you would be the image of Christ. Are you? Perhaps the work is not yet done.

The Confusion around Circumcision

Just like in Antioch, there was an issue in the Churches throughout Galatia regarding the value and necessity of circumcision. Those who had twisted the Gospel were bringing immature Believers into bondage, teaching them that circumcision was required for salvation.

> ➤ *(Galatians 2:3-4) Yet not even Titus who was with me, being a Greek, was compelled to be circumcised. And this occurred because of false brethren secretly brought in (who came in by stealth to spy out our liberty which we have in Christ Jesus, that they might bring us into bondage)...*

Was Paul calling circumcision bondage? No! Circumcision was not bondage, any more than any of God's commandments are bondage. Bondage only enters the equation when anything at all is added to the requirements for justification. There is no reason to be compelled to do anything other than confessing faith in the shed blood of Jesus, in order to secure eternal life. Nonetheless, we should explore what impact this fact has on the practice of physical circumcision.

Circumcision is Profitable

The reality that faith alone brings justification does not devalue physical circumcision. Paul makes this point remarkably clear. *What advantage then has the Jew, or what is the profit of circumcision? Much in every way! Chiefly because to them were committed the oracles of God (Romans 3:1-2).* Being raised in the understanding of God's oracles, His Word and commandments, is an advantage. You should recognize as Christians that understanding the deep meaning of physical circumcision will give you an edge to understanding the circumcised heart.

Jewish Tradition

To the Jew, the act of circumcision suggests a change of state, like water baptism to the Christian. It is symbolic of a cut through the known to reveal the unknown. This is exactly what happens with a circumcised heart. As we learned in Chapter 1, and will see later on, we have been given keys to the mysteries of the Kingdom of Heaven. A circumcised heart allows you to uncover those mysteries. The act of circumcision is the removal of the foreskin. When used in Scripture, the word refers to a barrier in the way of a beneficial result. It also has the connotation of something that is uncontrolled. The removal of the foreskin then symbolizes the idea of control. Through the act of circumcision one indicates that he can control the pattern of his life. We have choices to make. As we learned in Romans, we confess our faith for salvation **AND** we believe in our hearts unto righteousness. Salvation is free. Growing in the faith is a choice and comes with a price. Circumcision is the removal of the defilement or barrier that could restrict spiritual development. The rabbinic notion of salvation is symbolized by the blood of circumcision. The foreskin is the offering with which the people of Israel seal the covenant with the LORD. What perfect symbolism for the blood of Christ. Can you see how being raised with the oracles of God can lead to a deeper understanding of our faith as Christians? Can you now recognize that Scripture works in patterns and blueprints? Look here at some excerpts from Romans chapter 4 to learn the lesson that connects circumcision with faith.

*For what does the Scripture say? "Abraham believed God, and it was accounted to him for righteousness." Does this blessedness then come upon the circumcised only, or upon the uncircumcised also? For we say that **faith was accounted to Abraham for righteousness** (belief in his heart). How then was it accounted? While he was circumcised, or uncircumcised? Not while circumcised, but while uncircumcised. **And he received the sign of circumcision, a seal of the righteousness** of the faith which he had while still uncircumcised, that he might be the father of all those who believe, though* *they are uncircumcised, that righteousness might be imputed to them also, and the father of circumcision to those who not only are of the circumcision, but who also walk in the steps of the faith which our father Abraham had while still uncircumcised (Romans 4:3, 9-12).*

Abraham had to walk in the steps of faith. Faith is action. You have to confess with your mouth unto salvation AND believe in your heart unto righteousness. Belief in the heart is the action component of faith. James says it this way in James 2:18: *But someone will say, "You have faith, and I have works." Show me your faith without your works, and **I will show you my faith by my works.*** Paul understood that salvation is free. We don't get saved by obedience to God's commandments (works). However, we are obedient to God's commandments because we are saved. *For by grace you have been **saved through faith**, and that not of yourselves; it is the gift of God, **not of works**, lest anyone should boast. For we are His workmanship, **created in Christ Jesus for good works**, which God prepared beforehand that **we should walk in them** (Ephesians 2:8-10).* We were prepared beforehand to walk in God's commandments. However, if you believe the circumcision of your heart is complete, yet you are not eager to obey all of His commandments, put down the book. You're finished. You may not have eyes to see and ears to hear your higher calling. On the contrary, if you are eager to learn radical, faith-based obedience then carry on; your new heart is on the horizon.

If you can't decide whether or not your circumcision is complete, you can calculate it one of two ways. The first way uses a very complex formula. Take the number of years you are a Believer and break that down in seconds. Then calculate the size of the New Jerusalem in square cubits from Revelation chapter 21. Divide the number of minutes into the square cubits and multiply that by the number of times you sin each day. If the number is below 100, you have a circumcised heart. The second method is much easier; look at yourself in the mirror.

Just a bit of humor to lighten the mood while we take a sobering look at ourselves and admit that the evidence points to a partially uncircumcised heart in all of us. More than likely, no matter how long you have been a Believer, you probably consider radical, faith-based obedience to ALL of God's commandments too difficult, too far off, or worse yet, simply not necessary. You have to admit that your change of heart is just not finished. **If you get this, if you truly get the major points made in this chapter, you are being called into the Wilderness.** You are one step (and one chapter) closer to discovering and praying the prayer that is this book's namesake and purpose.

Whether we look at this on an individual or corporate level, the evidence of a completely circumcised heart will be a voluntary willingness to obey God in all that He commands. Before we will be able to effectively pray the single most important prayer we will ever pray as Believers, we need to enter the Wilderness and have heart surgery. Can you now understand what needs to occur in your heart and the heart of the Body of Christ?

As forerunners, when we step out into the Wilderness as living examples, the rest of the Church will eventually follow; and life as you know it will be changed forever. It's time to till the soil of your heart. Jeremiah 4:3-4 says:

> *Break up your fallow ground,*
> *And do not sow among thorns.*
> *Circumcise yourselves to the LORD,*
> *And take away the foreskins of your hearts.*

Moses said that the "Word", the commandments of God, would be near you in your heart that you would do them. Paul demonstrated that faith should yield a desire to obey God in all that He commands and should inspire a confession that His commandments are not too difficult. It is no coincidence that Paul's teaching about willing obedience is connected with the prayer of salvation in Roman 10:9-13. The result of a confession in Jesus will ultimately lead to pure righteousness that comes from an unwavering faith. This affirms you are who He says you are and you can do what He says you can do. It's all a matter of the heart. *Then I will give them a heart to know Me, that I am the LORD; and they shall be My people, and I will be their God, for they shall return to Me with their whole heart (Jeremiah 24:7).*

Everyone has a call. In the days ahead, all Believers will be faced with a choice. Today, **YOU** are faced with a choice. Are you a forerunner? Today, if **YOU** hear His voice, do not harden your hearts as in the rebellion as in the day of trial in the Wilderness. Today, if you hear His voice, I pray you would answer; "LORD, here am I! Send me."

Chapter Three

The Call

*Also I heard the voice of the LORD, saying: "Whom shall I send,
And who will go for Us?" Then I said, "Here am I! Send me."*
Isaiah 6:8

I n the beginning God created the heavens and the earth. We can't
even get past the first verse in the Bible without significant lessons.
We learn that "God created" and we learn that "God separated" heavens
and earth. Separation is God's plan for holiness or "set-apartness." He
separated light and darkness, day and night, land and sea. God sets one
thing apart from the other. The idea of "holy" is one that weaves its way
throughout the pages of the "Holy Bible." However, everything that is
good is not necessarily holy. He separated the six days that were good
from the seventh day that was holy. The Bible is holy because it is set-
apart from all other books. We are called to be holy because we are set-
apart from all other people. *But you are a chosen generation, a royal priesthood, a holy nation, His own special people, that you may proclaim the praises of Him who called you out of darkness into His marvelous light (1 Peter 2:9).*
You have an extraordinary call. In whatever you do, be set-apart from the
world. *But as He who called you is holy, you also be holy in all your conduct,
because it is written, "Be holy, for I am holy" (1 Peter 1:15-16).*

If you make that vital and personal decision to join me in the
Wilderness, to become a forerunner, you will discover what we must
accomplish together. Upcoming, we will meet the Wilderness prophet,
learn his message, and explore the Prayer of David. But, before we go
there, I will tell you a personal story about how I discovered that I was

called into the Wilderness as a forerunner, and that I must reach out for others to join me.

I'll start by going back to the beginning. The revelation came to me at a special time in September of 2004. It was during that season when the vision finally made sense to me. The journey to discovery actually began more than 15 years earlier when, in a moment's time, I had a vision. It lasted only a second or two, but was as vivid as if I had lived it out in real time. I was standing in a massive stadium and I was speaking to a jam-packed crowd. The place was crammed, not an empty seat in sight. I could not hear what I was saying, but I could tell that the response of the people was dramatic. They were moved. I could sense that their lives were changing in an instant. I knew deep inside that these people would never be the same. Their lives had been changed forever.

Did you ever just know something inside, deep inside? It really is unexplainable. When I came back to reality, I did not know what to think. Part of me wanted to write it off like it hadn't happened or chalk it up to a temporary ego attack; while the other part of me could not deny the almost daunting reality of it. The interesting thing about that time in my life is that I WAS NOT yet a Believer. I was definitely searching and I was definitely on the right track, but I had not yet given my life over to Christ. I decided to file the vision in the back of my mind, concluding that the man in the picture could not have been me. How could I have such an impact on people and in such a supernatural way?

Soon afterwards, sitting alone in my room, the Holy Spirit got hold of me. I was raised Catholic and always had a healthy fear of God. I knew *about* Jesus, but certainly did not *know* Jesus. As I grew from a youth, I separated further from the Catholic Church, but I never forgot my spiritual roots. I always had a deep yearning for spiritual things. I was searching for God and it landed me smack in the middle of the New Age movement. I even toyed with the idea that the vision in the stadium had something to do with my spiritual growth. I felt that I could do extraordinary things for God. Ironically, I did not even know Him, yet the seeds of truth were planted in me from childhood and one day the seeds finally took root.

The New Age movement sees Jesus as a "great evolved master," so it was safe to still hold the memory of Him in my new belief system. As a matter of fact, this eventually led me to search the Scriptures to learn more about Him. I got myself a Bible and began to read the Gospels. I started in Matthew. By the time I had finished a few days later, I found myself sitting on my bed coming to some very important conclusions. I determined that Jesus had it all right. He had what I wanted. I determined that I believed everything the Gospels said about Jesus and His life. I believed He was who He said He was and He did what He said he would do. And then I asked myself the question: "What does this belief make me?" I answered myself; "I believe I am a born again Christian." My life from that precise moment has never been the same. I have been on fire for the faith ever since. As you know, life as a Believer is rich and exciting. There is never a dull moment as you grow as a disciple of Christ.

It was years later that I moved to South Florida with my wife and new child. Isaiah was eight months old at the time and we were relocating by faith. Through prayer and fasting, God had confirmed to my wife and me that South Florida was the spot. I practice Chiropractic as a profession and I was sure God was leading us to Ft. Lauderdale to serve His people. I had been in practice for many years and had been through a long Wilderness experience before meeting my wife, Andrea. That story alone is a topic for an entire book. But to summarize, I met her on a mission trip, fell in love with her after just a few days, told her she was my wife, and married her a few months later. I relocated from Connecticut to Georgia to be with her while she completed her education in nutrition and Chiropractic. Andrea had always planned on leaving Georgia *immediately* after her education and moving back to South Florida to be with her family. That was great for me as I had been praying, for an entire year before I met Andrea, for God to take me out of the cold Northeast and bring me some place warm, like South Florida or Southern California. So the sun and warmth of Fort Lauderdale was an answer to prayer.

I was sure that the decision to relocate to South Florida was God's plan, and I knew that the safest place for me and my young family was in the center of His will. So with no money and a lot of faith, we made the move from Atlanta to Ft. Lauderdale. However, the certainty of that decision was not without trial. I knew that anything God asked of me was not unreasonable, so I followed His leading. In Romans 12:1, Paul tells us that even the most radical call from God is merely our reasonable service to Him. *I beseech you therefore, brethren, by the mercies of God, that you present your bodies a* **living sacrifice***, holy, acceptable to God,* **which is your reasonable service***.* So in God-style, after packing the entire apartment in Atlanta to relocate, the Lord gave me the sudden feeling that we needed to "hold." Our entire apartment was in boxes and I had to tell my wife… not yet! She was devastated and depressed for weeks, but as soon as she surrendered to the idea, she had peace. She agreed, "If we have to hold, we will."

During this "hold" time, I had a vivid dream in which God instructed me to go into the mountains of Tennessee (the Wilderness) and fast for ten days. He assured me He would confirm our next move. It was a life changing experience. The most memorable part of that intense and intimate time with God in the mountains took place beginning on the morning of the sixth day. I had this undeniable feeling (although I tried to fight it) that I was to drive further north into Kentucky and go to the city of Lexington. I had driven from Atlanta to Tennessee and I was a bit worn out after five days of fasting, and the thought of going further from home was not appealing. I had never even been in Kentucky before and I was not interested to go there now.

As the morning waned, the sense that I had to go was growing ever stronger. I felt that God wanted me to go to Lexington and deliver a message to a pastor at a Church on that evening. What pastor and what Church, I did not know. I simply told God that it was not enough information for me and that without more clarity, I would not go! Pretty bold of me, wouldn't you agree? Within moments of that miniature rebellion, I had the worse burning feeling in my stomach and chest than I had ever felt. Now, I had fasted before and never have I felt anything like that. So I prayed. "Father, take this pain from me and I will go." Within moments of surrender, I was pain free and packing my bags. Good bye Tennessee; hello Lexington, Kentucky and pastor whoever-you-are.

On the road, I had to take care of some unfinished business. I had, of course, to figure out where I was going and I only had a few hours. So, with my trusty map and newfound faith, I made my way north. I figured that as I neared the Lexington exits, God would give me some type of indication of where to get off and where to go. The info I did have was that I needed to find a Church with a Friday night service and I needed a place to sleep. With no other directions than that, I exited at the second exit in town and made my way to a service station. I found a phonebook and looked up Churches.

The Church that we attended in Atlanta was a Church of God and our congregation DID have a Friday night service so I started with that. I looked up Churches of God and I located about five or six numbers and called each. No answers and no indication of service times. Tired and a bit discouraged I decided to get a room. I found a local motel and checked in. It was about 6:45pm and I knew that if I was going to find a Friday night service, I'd better do it soon. I lay on the bed exhausted and contemplated the idea of just going to sleep. I thought, "I can't have come this far and just give up," so I sat up and took out the phonebook. It was January of 2000 and the phonebook in my room was a 1999 edition. I distinctly remembered that the phonebook at the station had 2000 on the cover. I opened it and there, to my surprise, was a listing that was not in the newer book at the station. It was a Church of God, it had a Friday 7:00 pm service listed, and it was two blocks away.

I arrived at the Church just minutes after the service started and it was wild, singing and dancing and banners worshiping the Lord. I broke into tears as I found a seat. I felt the presence of God so strongly that I knew I had come to the right place. I just didn't know how I was going to get the message to the pastor. Oh yes, and I didn't know the message. As the worship began to wind down and people were finding their seats, some-thing extraordinary happened. It became quiet and the pastor walked right up to me, handed me a microphone and asked me why I was there. I was shocked (and relieved). I knew God was orchestrating the whole thing. I told the congregation that I had been fasting in the mountains in Tennessee and that God told me to come here and deliver a message to their pastor. The pastor said, "See me after the service."

We met in his office afterwards and all of a sudden I knew what to say. God showed me that He did not want his people playing Church any-more. *"These people draw near to Me with their mouth, and honor Me with their lips, but their heart is far from Me"* (Matthew 15:8). It was time for them to grow up. The pastor confirmed that God was dealing with him on this exact issue and that I was His messenger. It was all very surreal to me. The experience changed me. I was serious about my faith before this, but now I knew He was calling me to a higher level. *"Here am I LORD! Send me."* At the time, I never actually connected this calling to the vision in the stadium. That would happen later.

In addition to the miraculous mission in Kentucky, God also answered my question about relocating to South Florida, or so I thought. After fasting for ten days in the mountains of Tennessee to seek God's will in our lives, I arrived home only to explain to Andrea that we were staying in Georgia for now. She was a real trooper, a true helpmate. Not one gripe.

It was the beginning of February 2000, and we had spent the last few weeks organizing our "renewed" life in Georgia when we got the call. Andrea's brother and sister-in-law had their first baby. Nikolas was born and we decided to take the opportunity to go down to Florida for a few weeks to visit and meet the new arrival. We had been establishing plans to open a chiropractic office in Georgia and were planning a mid-March opening. My thoughts were that if we don't visit now, it would be a long time before we could leave a new practice once it opened. Andrea agreed and we packed for a **VISIT** to South Florida. On the drive, I counseled my wife, guarding her from temptation to develop expectations about moving to Florida while we were visiting. She understood.

Just as God would have it, every plan we had to stay in Georgia dissolved while we were in Florida. We were planning on opening with a partner and, before we left for Florida, we were in agreement on everything; this included the office build out, marketing plan, and services we intended to offer. Suddenly, in one phone call, the agreement turned to conflict and the plans were off. At first, I was very angry. I was mad at God for about an hour. But as I surrendered my understanding, I felt a release from God; almost as though we were being tested. We never wanted to stay in Georgia in the first place, but we were willing to stay because God had given us the "hold sign." And now I felt He was releasing us to go. It was all a test of faith and obedience. *"Well done, good and faithful servant; you were faithful over a few things, I will make you ruler over many things. Enter into the joy of your Lord."* We were released to pursue our dreams and about to enter a new season of our lives; *I will make you ruler over many things.*

Now that our mission was confirmed, we were moving to Florida. We stayed an extra week to set the plans in motion. Every move we made after that seemed inspired. The hand of God was in every detail of our relocation, from the condo we rented to the office space we leased. It all flowed effortlessly.

Because my wife's family lives in South Florida, we had a support system waiting for us. Having visited her family a number of times after we were married, we also knew which Church we would attend, Calvary Chapel Ft. Lauderdale. The decision in which area to live and practice was simple. I needed to live close enough to Church and the office, so there was no "South Florida - Interstate 95 commute." My brother-in-law owned a condo nearby, but it was already rented. His current tenant was moving out and he had already made an agreement with a new tenant for rental. The woman preparing to move in approached my sister-in-law the very same day God released us to come to Florida and told her, "I cannot rent the condo from you. God told me it is for someone else." First problem solved.

We located an office space by making a serendipitous stop at an office park. Really, the stop was only unanticipated by us. God had it all planned. We stopped in front of one of the offices. I asked the gentlemen out front if he knew anything about the spaces or availability. He replied, "I am the property manager. What size space are you looking for?" I told him that I needed to start small, no more than 1000 square feet. He turned and pointed to the space we had stopped in front of and said, "This is 1000 square feet and it's available." My wife and I went inside and it was perfect. It needed nothing other than new carpet and paint. Not one wall had to be changed.

The manager said that there was just one complication. He said that the realtor who offers the leases had someone interested and was already negotiating with him for the space. He called the realtor from his office next door and put me on with him. The realtor called himself by his initials "J.C." He asked me if I liked the space. I told him it was perfect. He asked why. I told him it was the exact size and layout I needed and, more importantly, that it was very close to the Church I will attend when I relocate. (I always like to throw in a comment about Church or faith when I meet new people. It's like throwing a hook in the ocean and seeing if you get a bite. Sometimes it creates an evangelical opportunity. At least, it reveals what kind of person you are dealing with. Try it, it elicits a definite response. In this case it offered no opportunity for outreach, but it did show me that God had arranged for me to deal with a brother in the Lord.) He asked what Church that was. I told him Calvary Chapel, and he replied, "That's my Church." I asked who had the final decision on who gets the lease. He told me, on the spot, that he did, and that I could have it if I wanted it. He also assured me that he could guarantee the best price possible. It's great when God arranges for us to find favor with a brother. Second problem solved.

Wow! It was clear to me that God had intervened on our behalf and that this was a God-ordained move. We returned to Georgia to gather our things and one month later, in April of 2000, we relocated and started our life in South Florida, with nothing but vision and faith. It has been a beautiful testimony ever since. Not that it has been without significant challenges. In between having our three boys, my wife and I suffered through two ectopic pregnancies, but God has always been faithful to carry us through. We have emerged stronger and even more faithful. In our office, we have served thousands of people and have virtually turned our practice into a ministry. It has become a place where spiritual healing happens along side the physical. Salvation is preached to the lost and maturity in the faith is preached to the saved. We have never been wanting since. The new season in our lives was taking shape; *I will make you ruler over many things.*

As a man, the only concern that I had in relocating was the need to connect on a deep level with other strong Christian men. I knew that I could never be the husband and father I should be without other men in my life. I voiced my concern to my brother-in-law Jerry, and asked if he could help organize a men's Bible study. The first one took place in the reception area at my new office a few months later. I am eternally grateful for what was birthed at that study.

Even though everything was going along smoothly and life was great,

I developed a sense that I was missing something. There was an empty spot inside. This feeling persisted in me for months. My friends prayed for me about it, and I also prayed that God would reveal what this feeling was. What was I missing? God did answer that prayer on one faithful day, in the beginning of 2001, months after he planted the seed of emptiness. I knew immediately on that day what was missing.

All through the years that led to that moment, I would periodically have the vision of me speaking in the giant packed stadium. It was always the same, always very vivid and real. Most of the time, I would shrug it off, mostly because I had no explanation. I could not see why God would use me in such a capacity. What had changed over the years, however, was that I no longer considered the vision impossible. I came to realize through my experience in the mountains of Tennessee, that if God wants to use me for something big, He could. Hey, if He used a donkey, He could use me. Besides, I was sure I was willing to serve Him in any way He called. *"Here am I! Send me."*

Now in one day, in the beginning of 2001, the emptiness began to fade away. Something big was happening. I didn't know how or if this directly connected with the vision, but it was a start. It wouldn't be until almost four years later, at that extraordinary moment in September of 2004, that I'd know exactly how. It was in 2004 that I knew exactly what I was saying in that stadium in the midst of thousands of people. I knew why they were responding in such a dramatic and emotional way. He revealed what the vision was all about. Everything that I came to realize in September 2004 was part of a work God was doing in me over the previous 15 years. And now, in one prophetic moment, it was finally making sense. However, birthing this revelation was not without labor pains.

It took over four years from the time God planted the seed of emptiness in me, in April 2000, to receive the full revelation in September 2004. At the beginning of that four year journey, which was really the final stretch of a fifteen year journey, I realized that I had an empty spot inside. I had missed something. I had missed one of the most beautiful and revealing sides of my faith as a Christian; and at the beginning of 2001, I came to realize what it was. I had missed **the Feasts of the Lord.**

Through educational materials produced and distributed by a

Messianic Hebrew Roots organization based in Israel, I was exposed to the Feasts of the LORD. The Feasts are talked about throughout the Old Testament and lived out by Jesus throughout the New Testament. I had discovered that they should still be an integral part of my faith as a Christian. Christianity is a faith that has grown from "Hebrew Roots," but I knew nothing about these Hebrew roots. I learned over the next months and years that the work and life of Jesus ("Y'shua" in Hebrew) could be beautifully portrayed in all the Feasts of God. They have deep prophetic meaning for us as Christians and I wanted to know as much as possible. I read, watched, and listened to everything I could regarding the Feasts of the LORD from a Messianic perspective (as a Believer in Christ). *"A Rood Awakening!"* is the organization that first inspired my search. They produce a variety of excellent educational materials for Christians seeking their "Hebrew Roots." I learned many truths from them and other good resources mentioned in Appendix A. In Appendix B, I've included an outline of all the Feasts of the LORD, with a brief description of each.

We began to keep and celebrate the Feasts and the weekly Sabbath in our home. We invited many friends and family to join us. It has been a rich and rewarding experience ever since, but not without its challenges. Some people call it "bondage" to celebrate "Old" Testament Feasts and the Sabbath. I pray that this book will revolutionize that attitude throughout Christianity. As you have already learned in Chapter 2, calling God's commandments "bondage" or treating them with complaint is a sign of an uncircumcised heart.

One of my desires is that at some point, while reading this book, you will be called to join me in search of your "Hebrew Roots." As a forerunner, you first must cry out to the LORD to release you from the political, economic and religious systems that enslave you. *Then the children of Israel groaned because of the bondage, **and they cried out**; and their cry came up to God because of the bondage (Exodus 2:23b).* Then you will make an Exodus to freedom in the Wilderness. After your journey through the Wilderness, you will find yourself facing the Promised Land from across the Jordan. As a forerunner, you will complete your personal journey before you come back to call the masses out to join you. Remember, as a Christian, your inheritance is the Promised Land, not some piece of real estate. It is a spiritual inheritance, "the Kingdom of Heaven." This being so, realize that your Exodus is also spiritual in nature. You don't necessarily leave one place to go to another. The Exodus is a "coming out" or "separation" from what is not holy. And let me remind you, holy is not the opposite of evil or bad. Something can be good, yet not holy. God is the only one who defines what is holy, and He is calling us to "come out and be holy!"

In the Wilderness, your heart will be transformed and you will be drawn to pray the Prayer of David. This revelation will change everything for you. You will realize the true power and authority bestowed on you through Christ. Then, together, we can go back into "Egypt" and say for God, "Let My people go!" Be warned, the world systems are not eager to let them go. God had to use ten plagues to persuade the "hard hearted" to let His people go in the past, and He will do whatever it takes again. The final and most devastating plague is the death of the firstborn. The stench will fill the earth and God's people will be freed.

God's call will ultimately prevail. The future Bride of Christ will make a massive Exodus to freedom and move one step closer to her rightful place of authority. When the masses cross over in the "Greater Exodus" they too will have a change of heart. This will usher in an age of maturity and unity in the faith throughout the world, an age of radical obedience. This massive Exodus is the beginning of the Day of the LORD and is represented prophetically by the Biblical Feast of Passover. Again, what a beautiful overlay. *"And this Gospel of the Kingdom will be preached in all the world as a witness to all the nations, and then the end will come."* As forerunners, we are charged with making the message of this Gospel of the Kingdom clear and understandable. The forerunners will be few in number compared to the masses who will emerge from the Greater Exodus. The masses will then become the laborers who preach the Gospel of the Kingdom to the entire world.

But a journey of a thousand miles begins with just one step. For me, personally, the journey began with keeping the Feasts. It was while celebrating the Feast of Tabernacles in September of 2004 that led to the revelation about my reoccurring vision. It was the second day of the Feast when my good friend, Stephen, was speaking at the Church we began attending earlier that year. He was teaching from Deuteronomy 12 where God instructs His people to seek out a place **that He chooses to build the Tabernacle.** God says that it will be a place "where the LORD your God **will make His Name abide."** It struck me at that moment that if we are the "Living Temple" (2Co 6:16), there must be a pattern or prophetic overlay that shows that His name will abide in us. Then I recalled that in the Book of Revelation, God places His name on the foreheads of His faithful (Rev 22:4).

It all seemed to gel together as the Feast progressed. The Feast of Tabernacles is an eight day festival, and I was teaching the closing service on the last day. The eighth day is referred to as the "Last Great Day" and has deep prophetic implications in both the Old and New Testaments. In Chapter 12 of this book, I cover details about the Last Great Day. But for now I will tell you that it was during the last few days of the Feast, while I was preparing my study for the last day, that God revealed to me what He truly meant by the vision He had given me for all those years.

In the Scriptures, the Feasts are called "Holy Convocations." A convocation is a calling together for rehearsal or an appointment. When you keep the Feasts, you are keeping appointments with God on His prophetic calendar. Miraculous things happen when you align yourself with God's spiritual calendar. He shows up and we are there waiting. I understand that, as Believers, we have personal access to God all the time, but I am talking about a prophetic moment. These prophetic moments are not guided by "personal relationships" with God. They are **pre-established times** when God will show His people His next prophetic move. God has His calendar set and He has predetermined when He will reveal His plans. You can't pray for these prophetic moments to be forthcoming, on *your* schedule, or that they be delayed because you are tied up doing your own thing. You do not want to miss God in the day of His visitation. We must be aware of His times and seasons. *Therefore let us not sleep, as do others; but let us watch and be sober (1 Thessalonians 5:6).* If your lamp is not trimmed with oil, you may miss the wedding supper.

God's plans are revealed on His schedule and His Feasts; not our own, or those set by other men. If you are not in attendance, you miss it. Attendance is not a place, but a state of preparation. For example, while contemplating the events of the Feast during the long drive home from a campsite in Georgia where we celebrated the Feast of Tabernacles in 2001, I realized, by revelation, the fundamental relationship between Romans 10 and Deuteronomy 30. (I revealed this **mystery of the Kingdom** to you in Chapter 2.) I had never been taught this deep significance before that time, and I have never heard it taught by anyone else since. Yet, it is the very foundation of our faith. God revealed it to me in a prophetic moment because I was prepared to receive it. I did not miss His visitation. I was keeping the Feast. Keeping the Feasts are rehearsals or shadows of good things to come.

I now knew that I was to write this book and God would use it to begin the heart transplant in His set-apart people. And I knew that it was this change of heart in the people that was happening in the vision of the stadium 15 years earlier. My call was that of the spirit of Elijah, or at least to make a way for Elijah. The message to the world; "Let my people go!" The message to the people; "Repent, the Kingdom of Heaven is at hand!"

The book I was to write needed to establish how we can achieve unity of faith and reveal the mystery of this prayer of David's heart. I needed to write a book that was simple enough to touch the masses inside Christianity, yet profound enough to inspire a hunger for more. He taught me that at the time of King David, He was waiting for a man to arrive on the scene who would be sensitive enough to understand the heart of God, yet bold enough to ask if he could do the unbelievable. He revealed to me that David was such a man. *"But now your (Saul's) kingdom shall not continue. The LORD has sought for Himself **a man after His own heart** (David), and the LORD has commanded him to be commander over His people, because you (Saul) have not kept what the LORD commanded you"* (1 Samuel 13:14). Because David had a heart that was aligned with the heart of God, and he had the eyes to see and ears to hear what God wanted of him, David was bold enough to pray for what his contemporaries would have thought to be blasphemous. As you will see shortly, this prayer may be the boldest prayer in all of Scripture. You almost get the sense that David is overstepping his authority. Yet it turns out that it was just what God Almighty was waiting for.

He opened my eyes to David's prayer during the Feast and showed me that **I needed to be bold enough to pray the same prayer.** I needed to teach the Church about this prayer and invite my Christian brothers and sisters to pray this prayer with me. This prayer is the Believer's equivalent to the sinner's prayer, and is the ultimate declaration that we are who God says we are.

The vision in the stadium is God's people hearing & praying the prayer that David prayed!

They are inviting the spirit of Elijah to do a work on their hearts and now it is changing their lives forever. They do not want to "play Church" anymore. It is time to grow up and they are stepping out in faith "one more time." In unity and with power, they are declaring to the world that "the time is now!" It is time to mature. *For everyone who partakes only of milk is unskilled in* **the word of righteousness,** *for he is a babe. But solid food belongs to those who are of* **full age,** *that is, those who by reason of use have their senses exercised to discern both good and evil (Hebrews 5:13-14).*

As we approach the End of the Age, there will be many who mock us as we stand boldly in the faith. But know this first: *Scoffers will come in the last days, walking according to their own lusts, and saying,* **"Where is the promise of His coming? For since the fathers fell asleep, all things continue as they were from the beginning of creation."** *For this they willfully forget: that by the word of God the heavens were of old, and the earth standing out of water and in the water, by which the world that then existed perished, being flooded with water (2 Peter 3:3-6).* Many will not recognize the "signs of the time." They will not acknowledge the hand of God in the events around them.

As I edit this section of the book, we have just experienced the greatest single national disaster in the history of the United States of America. Hurricane Katrina poured out her wrath on the Gulf Coast and destroyed the entire city of New Orleans, and the surrounding areas, affecting three States. This massive tragedy in the US followed on the heels of a great injustice in the Land of Israel, where Israeli Jews were forced to leave their homes in the Gaza Strip, yielding their land (presumably) forever; land that was given to Israel by the LORD Himself. *Remember the word which Moses the servant of the LORD commanded you, saying, 'The LORD your God is giving you rest and is **giving you this land'** (Joshua 1:13)*. The US backed and even encouraged the unlawful surrender of this Land, God's Land, in the name of "peace." "Land for peace" seems to be the motto of the Roadmap to Peace (as it was for the Oslo Accords) fostered by the US, as well as by the UN and EU, on Israel. Paul says, *for when they say, "Peace and safety!" then sudden destruction comes upon them, as labor pains upon a pregnant woman. And they shall not escape (1 Thessalonians 5:3).*

When you are party to dividing God's Land, you are subject to God's judgment. The LORD, speaking through Joel the prophet says, *"And I will enter into judgment with them there on account of My people, My heritage Israel, whom they have scattered among the nations; they have also divided up My Land" (Joel 3:2b)*. We cannot escape the righteous judgment of a holy and righteous God.

The morning after Hurricane Katrina passed over, many in New Orleans proclaimed, "Wow! It wasn't as bad as it could have been." Then, just hours later, the levees broke devastating the entire city. Still the nation did not repent, but instead proclaimed, "We can rebuild: bigger, better, stronger!" This nation lives as if God is not watching. **"Where is the promise of His coming? For since the fathers fell asleep, all things continue as they were from the beginning of creation."** Yet the LORD says of Israel, *"I will bless those who bless you, and I will curse him who curses you; and in you all the families of the earth shall be blessed" (Genesis 12:3)*. Please hear my heart. I am not singling out the people of the Gulf Coast (Louisiana, Alabama, and Mississippi); they are no more guilty than anyone else in the USA. We will all inherit the punishment of our unrighteous nation. God seemingly chose that area because it is a strategic area that affected the entire country. Every American filling their gas tank was reminded of the tragedy within days of the disaster and this reminder continued for months. But to this day, "arrogant men" leave God out of the equation and blame it on the "Global Warming" or some other natural causes. Yet those (like me) who proclaim Katrina and other natural disasters like it to be the judgment of God are considered, by most, to be religious whackos.

And (God) did not spare the ancient world, but saved Noah, one of eight people, a preacher of righteousness, bringing in the flood on the world of the ungodly; and turning the cities of Sodom and Gomorrah into ashes, condemned them to destruction, making them an example to those who afterward would live ungodly (2 Peter 2:5-6). In both Sodom and Gomorrah and Hurricane Katrina, we have examples of what God does to the ungodly, yet will our nation repent before it is too late? Katrina means "pure." The Greek word in the Scriptures for pure is "katharos" and for purify it is "katharizo." God used Katrina to purify a nation. Did you hear His warning?

There is only one way to avoid the impending judgment of a holy and righteous God on this nation. If the leadership of the United States of America and Sovereign States, which includes the President and his administration, the high courts, and leaders at the State level, repent of their anti-Biblical management of this land and reverse their Godless policies concerning Israel, abortion, gay rights, etc. (and there are many others), God may spare us. *If My people who are called by My name will humble themselves, and pray and seek My face, and turn from their wicked ways, then I will hear from heaven, and will forgive their sin and heal their land (2 Chronicles 7:14).*

My belief is that America will not turn, and judgment will be inevitable. I heard little mention of repentance or even the recognition of God's judgment following Katrina, even from our Evangelical Christian President. All the focus was on how we can rebuild and who was to blame for the poor response time to bring help to those left stranded. Even from the Christian and Jewish communities, there was little cry for repentance (though there were some voices crying in the wilderness). The humanitarian efforts by the Body of Christ were necessary and impressive as always, but there was no cry for repentance or warning of judgment in any significant way. We daily examined the President's approval ratings, but we continue to ignore the warnings of a righteous God.

Less than one month after Katrina, Hurricane Rita smashed into the Gulf Coast again, this time a little west of New Orleans. The storm caused massive damage in Texas and Louisiana. Some of the recently repaired levees gave way and parts of New Orleans were under water again. Rita is short for Margarita which comes from the Greek "margarites" which means "pearl" or "a word of great value." Here is the **Word** of great value: "Don't just rebuild, **REPENT!**"

In order to NOT be named in the judgment, our only hope as children of God is to "come out and be holy." Do not touch what is unclean! We need to separate ourselves from ungodly institutions. We need an Exodus.

> ➤ *(2 Peter 3: 7, 10) But the heavens and the earth which are now preserved by the same word, are reserved for fire until the day of judgment and perdition of ungodly men. ... But the day of the Lord will come as a thief in the night, in which the heavens will pass away with a great noise, and the elements will melt with fervent heat; both the earth and the works that are in it will be burned up.*

We are entering an era when it is not just the lost who need to be evangelized. It is the House of the LORD that needs to be "born again" again. It's time for a heart transplant in the Church. Scripture warns in 1 Peter 4:17-18: *For the time has come for judgment to begin at the house of God; and if it begins with us first, what will be the end of those who do not obey the Gospel of God? Now "If the righteous one is scarcely saved, where will the ungodly and the sinner appear?"* The ungodly have an inheritance from which we as Believers want to separate. Come out and be holy.

The vision that had followed me over the last 15 years was to teach the world about the Prayer of David. If I could just invite enough Christians from around the world to boldly pray this prayer, we could establish unity of the faith and usher in God's Kingdom on earth. *Behold, how good and how pleasant it is for brethren to dwell together in* **unity!** *(Psalm 133:1).*

With a transformation in the hearts of the people who are called to serve the living God, the Body of Christ can become the living stones that build the Spiritual Temple. David was given the plans to build and made provision for the items within the physical Temple. Solomon, his son, took his father's plan and actually had the stones cut and set in place. Solomon laid those stones in place according to his father's plan. The members of the Body of Christ are living stones and will build the Spiritual Temple according to our Father's plan. *You also, as living stones, are being built up a spiritual house, a holy priesthood, to offer up spiritual sacrifices acceptable to God through Jesus Christ (1 Peter 2:5)*. I literally believe that it will be the children of today who will ultimately lay the "living stones" in place and build the Spiritual Temple. As the David generation, we get the plans, make the message clear, and pave the way. To accomplish our critical task, we must unify as Believers, reflect the vision of David, and pray with boldness. It is the perfect prophetic overlay. *Then the LORD replied: "Write down the revelation and make it plain on tablets so that a herald may run with it. For the revelation awaits an appointed time; it speaks of the end and will not prove false. Though it linger, wait for it; it will certainly come and will not delay" (Habakkuk 2:2-3 NIV)*.

What God had shown me in the Wilderness, while I was fasting in the mountains, was a microcosm of the vision in the stadium. He did not want his people playing Church anymore. It was time for them to grow up. It was time for a heart transplant. It was time for the people who draw near to God with their mouths and honor Him with their lips, whose hearts remain far from Him, to come out and be holy. *Therefore "Come out from among them and be separate, says the Lord. Do not touch what is unclean, and I will receive you" (2 Corinthians 6:17)*. It was time for unity of the faith. It was time for maturity. It was time to build the Spiritual Temple. It was time to say, *"Here am I! Send me."* He showed me that true restoration takes place in the Wilderness; and without a trip through the Wilderness, there is no Promised Land. God will raise up a remnant to help purify His people, a royal priesthood to help lead the way in the Wilderness. Do you believe you can be part of that remnant? Will you leave the world behind and press toward what lies ahead? Will you join me as forerunners in the Wilderness?

It was an Exodus to the Wilderness that prepared both John the Baptist and Jesus for their calling. The Wilderness experience equipped them both with the same message. John's message is recorded in Matthew 3:1-2: *In those days John the Baptist came preaching in the **Wilderness** of Judea, and saying, **"Repent, for the Kingdom of Heaven is at hand!"*** After John's Wilderness experience, *Jesus was led up by the Spirit into the Wilderness to be tempted by the devil (Matthew 4:1)*. After 40 days of fasting in the Wilderness, He was tempted and found victory over the enemy.

Then the Lord left the Wilderness with a message to the people, the same message that John found in the Wilderness. Matthew 4:17 records Jesus' first words after leaving His Wilderness; *Jesus began to preach and to say,* **"Repent, for the Kingdom of Heaven is at hand."** Soon after His trials in the Wilderness, *Jesus went about all Galilee, teaching in their synagogues, preaching* **the Gospel of the Kingdom,** *and healing all kinds of sickness and all kinds of disease among the people (Matthew 4:23).* The Gospel of the Kingdom, the "good news" of the Kingdom is that the Kingdom of Heaven is at hand.

In Chapter 5, we will define and discuss the good news of the Kingdom of Heaven in detail. What is it? Is it a thing? Is it a place? It is a state of being? And what does repentance have to do with getting it, going there, or being it? In Chapter 11, we will discuss how this Gospel of the Kingdom will be preached to the entire world. Stay tuned!

"Again, the Kingdom of Heaven is like treasure hidden in a field, which a man found and hid; and for joy over it he goes and **sells all that he has** *and buys that field. "Again, the Kingdom of Heaven is like a merchant seeking beautiful pearls, "who, when he had found one pearl of great price,* **went and sold all that he had and bought it"** *(Matthew 13:44-46).* Are you willing to sacrifice everything to discover the mysteries of the Kingdom of Heaven that lie ahead of you in the Wilderness?

As a forerunner, you must cross into the Wilderness, find your way to the Promised Land, and then come back for the others. Then and only then can you come preaching, "Repent, the Kingdom of Heaven is at hand." To encapsulate the Kingdom of Heaven, Jesus taught, **"Therefore you shall be perfect, just as your Father in heaven is perfect."** And this Gospel of the Kingdom will be preached to all the world, as a witness to all the nations, and then the end will come.

As Jesus went about and taught the Gospel of the Kingdom, He later commissioned His disciples to preach the same message; however, He informed them that at the time of His earthly ministry there were simply too few laborers available to reap the harvest of preaching the Gospel of the Kingdom to the entire world. *Then He said to His disciples, "The harvest truly is plentiful,* **but the laborers are few.** *Therefore pray the Lord of the harvest to send out laborers into His harvest"* (Matthew 9:37-38). In

Matthew chapter 10, Jesus sends them out to preach the Kingdom of Heaven, the same message that both He and John learned in the Wilderness. He instructs them NOT to go into the nations, but to focus on the "House of Israel." There simply are not yet enough laborers to preach the Gospel of the Kingdom to the world as a witness to all the nations. *These twelve Jesus sent out and commanded them, saying:* **"Do not go into the way of the Gentiles,** *and do not enter a city of the Samaritans.* *"But go rather to the lost sheep of the house of Israel.* *"And as you go, preach, saying,* **'The Kingdom of Heaven is at hand.'** *"Heal the sick, cleanse the lepers, raise the dead, cast out demons (Matthew 10:5-8).*

Because of the work of forerunners, at the End of the Age there will be enough laborers to preach the Gospel of the Kingdom to the entire world. *"And this Gospel of the Kingdom will be preached in all the world as a witness to all the nations, and then the end will come" (Matthew 24:14).* The good news of the Kingdom being preached to all the world is a sign of the end. But first, we must make sure the House of the Lord understands this Gospel of the Kingdom. As forerunners, we must equip the laborers to preach it to all the world. Will you join me on this mission?

God needs a small army of laborers, a remnant, to go into the Wilderness first and emerge with a true understanding of the Gospel of the Kingdom. Then together we can say to the rest of His people, "Repent, the Kingdom of Heaven is at hand" and teach them what that means. We will tell the world to, "Let My people go!" When the rest of God's people leave the world behind and join us in the Wilderness, we will fashion a mighty army to preach this Gospel of the Kingdom to the rest of the world as a witness to all the nations.

If you will acknowledge your call and the work needed to be done on your own heart, then we can search for the heart surgeon to **complete the restoration**. *And His disciples asked Him, saying, "Why then do the scribes say that Elijah must come first?" Jesus answered and said to them, "Indeed, Elijah is coming first and* **will restore all things** *(Matthew 17:10-11).* Recall the words of the LORD as revealed to the Prophet Malachi: *"Remember the Law of Moses"* and *"Behold I send you Elijah the Prophet."*

Chapter Four

The Spirit of Elijah

Behold, I send My messenger, And he wil prepare the way before Me.
Malachi 3:1

A nd His disciples asked Him, saying, "Why then do the scribes say that Elijah must come first?" Jesus answered and said to them, "Indeed, *Elijah is coming first and **will restore all things.*** Recall the words of the LORD as revealed through the Prophet Malachi: *"Remember the Law of Moses"* and *"Behold I send you Elijah the Prophet."*

In this chapter, we will discuss the identity and role of the Wilderness Prophet, as well as discover the mechanism of change for you as a fore-runner and for the Body of Christ as a whole.

Let us pray...
> *Search me, O God, **and know my heart;***
> *Try me, and know my anxieties;*
> *And see if there is any wicked way in me,*
> *And lead me in the way everlasting. Selah*
> **Psalm 139:23-24**

God has searched your heart and knows your ways. Do you acknowledge the work needed to be done on your heart? You have heard the voice of the one crying in the Wilderness. Are you feeling called? Are you will-ing to go? Who is drawing you into the desert and who will prepare the soil of your heart for the Promised Land? Who will ultimately lead the greater Exodus and guide us all in the Wilderness? It's time for a heart transplant, but who is the spiritual surgeon who will **complete the restoration**?

It's the moment of truth. You have arrived at the shore of the Red Sea. Are you personally ready for the changes that will take place once you cross over? Are you ready for the call of the forerunner? The Wilderness is a place of testing and dependence. Like Israel, you must depend on the LORD one hundred percent for everything. Every provision is Divine because the world around you can offer nothing for your survival; all provision of man ceases.

> ➤ *(Deuteronomy 8:2-4) "And you shall remember that the LORD your God led you all the way these forty years in the Wilderness, **to humble you and test you, to know what was in your heart,** whether you would keep His commandments or not. So He humbled you, **allowed you to hunger, and fed you** with manna which you did not know nor did your fathers know, that He might make you know that man shall not live by bread alone; but man lives by every word that proceeds from the mouth of the LORD. **Your garments did not wear out** on you, nor did your foot swell these forty years."*

The Wilderness may seem like a scary place, but really it is the safest place you will ever be. You will be in the palm of God's hands and in the center of His will, depending on His provision and His provision alone. Are you being drawn into the Wilderness? Are you being called as a forerunner? Step toward the water and the LORD will part the sea. Pass over on dry ground.

Face to Face with God

The LORD spoke to Moses face to face, as a man speaks to his friend (Exodus 33:11). Moses was a prophet like no other who came before him. The LORD said, speaking in Numbers 12:6-8: *Then He said, "Hear now My words: If there is a prophet among you, I, the LORD, make Myself known to him in a vision; I speak to him in a dream. **Not so with My servant Moses; He is faithful in all My house. I speak with him face to face,** even plainly, and not in dark sayings; and he sees the form of the LORD.* Moses stood face to face with a loving God. The people of Israel were not prepared for the level of intimacy that Moses experienced with the LORD. They were afraid of this intimacy and did not want to hear the Words of God directly. Other than Adam, no man but Moses had experienced the privilege of this face to face relationship. (And you know what Adam did with the privilege.)

The LORD did, however, tell Moses that He would raise up another prophet like him in the future. In Deuteronomy 18:18 the LORD said, *'I will raise up for them a Prophet* **like you** *from among their brethren, and will put My words in His mouth, and He shall speak to them all that I command Him.*

At the end of his life, in Deuteronomy 34:9-10, we see Moses passing authority to Joshua; *Now Joshua the son of Nun was full of the spirit of wisdom, for Moses had laid his hands on him; so the children of Israel heeded him, and did as the LORD had commanded Moses.* ***But** since then there has not arisen in Israel a prophet like Moses, whom the LORD knew face to face.*

You may not be a prophet like Moses, but you can have something he had. *The LORD spoke to Moses face to face, as a man speaks to his friend.* Jesus told His followers in John 15:14-15: *"You are* **My** *friends if you do whatever I command you. No longer do I call you servants, for a servant does not know what his master is doing; but* **I have called you friends,** *for all things that I heard from My Father I have made known to you."* In Chapter 2 we discussed the importance of obedience to everything that God commands. Jesus calls you friend if you do what He commands. His commandments should not feel burdensome, for they should be near to you in your heart. Think about it. If God's commandments are near to us in our hearts through Messiah, yet we still feel that obeying them is a burden, then this burden must come from our inner struggle to REMOVE the holiness that has "invaded" us. Our carnal struggles reflect our enmity towards the purity within us. *Because the carnal mind is enmity against God; for it is not subject to the Law of God, nor indeed can be (Romans 8:7).*

The Prophet Like Moses

God calls Moses "friend." Jesus calls you "friend." But who is that prophet like Moses who is coming again and will know the LORD face to face? Who will lead the Greater Exodus? Who is the Wilderness Prophet that calls us into the Wilderness, circumcises our hearts, and then leads us to the edge of the Promised Land? And what is the spirit that calls, inspires, and animates the forerunner?

The Blueprint of the Wilderness Prophet

John the Baptist, in the spirit of Elijah, came as a forerunner to Messiah's first coming to prepare the hearts of man. He called the people into the Wilderness. Elijah must come again to call God's people into the Wilderness where he will complete the restoration. However, the spirit of Elijah is already at work in the world today, and may be stirring your heart at this very moment. The spirit may be crying out to you to cross over as a forerunner. In the first century, John, in the spirit of Elijah, was the prophet who prepared a way in the Wilderness. John's role was, and Elijah's role will be, to restore the hearts of the people and to prepare a way in the Wilderness for the Lord's return. The spirit of Elijah is the spirit of the circumcised heart.

If prophetic overlays are predictive, the Scriptures should show John and Elijah to be Wilderness Prophets just like Moses. They call the people INTO the Wilderness. *A voice of one calling: "In the desert prepare the way for the LORD; make straight in the Wilderness a highway for our God (Isaiah 40:3 NIV)*. Make straight a highway for our God. Straight is a reference to righteousness. The incision on the foreskin of your heart takes place the moment you step into the Wilderness. This purification or heart transplant is completed in the Wilderness before you enter the Promised Land. Hasn't the Wilderness been the place of growth for you in your personal life as a Christian?

John the Baptist called out from the Wilderness, warning the people to turn back from their wicked ways. Repent! *In those days John the Baptist came preaching in the Wilderness of Judea, and saying,* **"Repent, for the Kingdom of Heaven is at hand!"** *For this is he who was spoken of by the prophet Isaiah, saying: "The voice of one crying in the Wilderness: 'Prepare the way of the LORD; Make His paths straight'"* (Matthew 3:1-3).

In Matthew 11:11-15, Jesus speaks so plainly regarding John's calling.

"Assuredly, I say to you, among those born of women there has not risen one greater than John the Baptist; **but he who is least in the Kingdom of Heaven is greater than he.** *And from the days of John the Baptist until now the Kingdom of Heaven suffers violence, and the violent take it by force. For all the prophets and the Law prophesied until John.* **And if you are willing to receive it, he is Elijah who is to come. He who has ears to hear, let him hear!"**

The question is: Do you have ears to hear? Jesus said seek and you shall find, knock and the door will be opened. If you are willing to receive it, if you are willing to look for the answers to these mysteries, they will be revealed to you. "If you are willing to receive it!" This is a proposition to separate those who want to go deeper from those not interested in seeking and knocking.

John was the greatest of those born of women, yet he is less than the least in the Kingdom of Heaven. All the prophets and the Law pointed towards John because he was the key prophetic forerunner for the coming of the Messiah. And if you are willing to accept it, he is Elijah *who is to come.* The mystery revealed here is that John is the prototype of the Elijah who will come before the second coming of Messiah. Jesus is using the Scriptural pattern and overlay that we have seen numerous times thus far.

John, as a forerunner to Christ and a foreshadow of Elijah who is to come, was calling people out of their religious and political systems into the Wilderness with the message of, *"Repent, the Kingdom of Heaven is at hand!"* When Elijah comes, he will call you out of your comfortable world of religion, politics, and economics. He will call you into the Wilderness. And what do you think his message will be? Yes, you guessed it, *"Repent, the Kingdom of Heaven is at hand!"* But in these days to come, Elijah will word it in a slightly different way. As you will soon learn in this chapter, Elijah, who is coming again, will use the phrase **"Remember the Law of Moses."** This, by the way, is the same message as **"Repent!"** which is "tshuva" in Hebrew. Tshuva means **turn back** towards God. Remember His ways. And the most exciting thing about this is that when we turn towards God, we will establish the Kingdom of Heaven on earth. And in God's economy, the least of us in the Kingdom will be greater than John the Baptist.

But even John did not fully understand the mystery that he was the intermediate fulfillment of this prophecy. He did not see the overlay. He denied being Elijah, although he knew he fulfilled the role of a Wilderness Prophet. He knew he was not "The Prophet," and it was actually Christ who taught that John had come in the spirit of Elijah. Elijah who comes before the second coming of our Lord is "The Prophet." *Now this is the testimony of John, when the Jews sent priests and Levites from Jerusalem to ask him, "Who are you?" He confessed, and did not deny, but confessed, "I am not the Christ." And they asked him, "What then?* **Are you Elijah?" He said, "I am not." "Are you the Prophet?" And he answered, "No."** *Then they said to him, "Who are you, that we may give an answer to those who sent us? What do you say about yourself?"* **He said: "I am 'The voice of one crying in the Wilderness: "Make straight the way of the LORD,"'** *as the prophet Isaiah said"* (John 1:19-23).

John understood, from Isaiah, that before the Lord could come, the people needed to be called into the Wilderness to prepare a way before Him. He also recognized from the Prophet Malachi that Elijah was the Prophet who would appear on the scene before the *"great and dreadful Day of the LORD."* John was not quite sure about his role. He knew he would prepare a way in the Wilderness, but he did not see the overlay with the prophecy from Malachi, which I will show you in a moment. He did not recognize that he was a shadow of the Elijah to come. *John had heard in prison about the works of Christ, he sent two of his disciples and said to Him, "Are You the Coming One, or do we look for another?"* (Matthew 11:2-3). Of course, Jesus tells John's disciples about the Messianic prophecies that He fulfills. John knows he has prepared a way for the Lord in the Wilderness. He knows he has prepared the hearts of men and that his mission is completed. And now he must decrease.

As a point of interest, the lack of understanding of these overlay patterns is what holds back many Jews today from recognizing that Jesus (Y'shua) is the Messiah. They cannot see that He is Messiah "who has come and is coming." They have been blinded in part, by God, until the fullness of the Gentiles has come in. You, however, have no excuse to be blinded.

Perhaps as you work through the pages of this book, you are feeling the same calling; the voice of one crying, in the Wilderness prepare a way for the Lord. Take notice that in all four Gospels this Scripture is written in a similar way: *The voice of one crying in the wilderness: Prepare the way of the LORD; Make His paths straight.* However, in Isaiah 40:3, from where this Scripture comes, it says: *The voice of one crying in the wilderness: "Prepare the way of the LORD; Make straight **in the desert** a highway for our God."* This passage is even more accurately translated in the NIV: *A voice of one calling: "**In the desert** prepare the way for the LORD; make straight **in the wilderness** a highway for our God."* The voice is not crying out to you **from the Wilderness.** The voice is crying out for you to **come into the Wilderness** and prepare a way for the Lord.

Preparation for the Lord's coming always takes place in the Wilderness. If this is your calling, soon you may be crying out to God's people, "Repent, the Kingdom of Heaven is at Hand! Come into the Wilderness and help prepare a way for the Lord's return." And you will be exclaiming to the world, "Let My people go! The Kingdom of Heaven is advancing." Matthew 11:12 best describes the expansion of God's Kingdom; *NIV from the days of John the Baptist until now, the Kingdom of Heaven has been forcefully advancing, and forceful men lay hold of it.* Now let's complete the picture of Elijah.

It was before conception that John's father received a message from an angel.

> ➤ (Luke 1:13-17, 67, 76) *But the angel said to him, "Do not be afraid, Zacharias, for your prayer is heard; and your wife Elizabeth will bear you a son, and you shall call his name John. And you will have joy and gladness, and many will rejoice at his birth. For he will be great in the sight of the Lord, and shall drink neither wine nor strong drink. He will also be filled with the Holy Spirit, even from his mother's womb. **And he will turn many of the children of Israel to the LORD their God.** He will also go before **Him in the spirit and power of Elijah, 'to turn the hearts of the fathers to the children,'** and the disobedient to the wisdom of the just, to make ready a people prepared for the Lord." ...*
> *Now his father Zacharias was filled with the Holy Spirit, and prophesied, saying:... "And you, child, will be called the prophet of the Highest; **For you will go before the face of the Lord to prepare His ways...***

Jesus, in His own words in Matthew 11:9-10 said, *"But what did you go out to see? A prophet? Yes, I say to you, and more than a prophet. For this is he of whom it is written: 'Behold, I send My messenger before Your face, Who will prepare Your way before You.'"*

Jesus, referring to Malachi 3:1, knew that there needed to be a restoration prophet before His first coming. He also knows that there needs to be restoration prophet before His second coming. Elijah has come, and is coming again, just like the Messiah.

It was common knowledge in the first century that Elijah must come before the Messiah. In Matthew 17:10-13, the disciples asked, **"Why then do the scribes say that Elijah must come first?"** *Jesus answered and said to them,* **"Indeed, Elijah is coming first** *and* **will restore all things.** *But I say to you that* **Elijah has come already,** *and they did not know him but did to him whatever they wished. Likewise the Son of Man is also about to suffer at their hands." Then the disciples understood that He spoke to them of John the Baptist.* If Elijah hadn't come first, then Jesus could not be the true Messiah. In the future, until Elijah comes again and restores all things, Messiah CANNOT come again. But 2 Corinthians 11:4 says beware, *for if he who comes preaches another Jesus whom we have not preached, or if you receive a different spirit which you have not received, or a different gospel which you have not accepted — you may well put up with it* **(if you are not prepared)!** Anyone claiming to be the Messiah, who comes BEFORE Elijah, is a false christ. Anyone claiming Messiah can come, BEFORE Elijah comes again, is a false prophet preaching a false gospel. *"For false christs and false prophets will rise and show great signs and wonders to deceive, if possible, even the elect"* (Matthew 24:24). Beware!

Old Testament scribes understood from Malachi 4:5 that Elijah must come before the Lord. *Behold, I will send you Elijah the prophet* **before** *the coming of the great and dreadful day of the LORD.* Nevertheless, they did not recognize that Elijah would come two times, a first and a second coming. Consequently, many Christians today also do not realize that Elijah must come first, to prepare the way, before **each** coming of the Lord. Most of the evangelical Church believes that the next event on God's prophetic calendar is the Rapture of the Church. They believe He is coming to get His people before the Tribulation. But instead of calling His coming for

His people the "second coming," they treat it more like a "secret coming," which does not count as His second coming. If it did, they would have to account for a third coming when He returns again at the end of the Tribulation. The reality, however, is that the Rapture takes place at the second coming. They are parts of the same event. Any way you slice it, Elijah must come first. There will be no coming of the Lord, of any kind, unless Elijah comes first. Space does not permit a full dissertation on this topic, but I have included some resources in Appendix A to which you can refer. Perhaps this entire subject will be the topic of a future book.

Before John's birth, the angel spoke to Zacharias (his father) and showed him that John would go before the Lord in the spirit and power of Elijah, and turn many of the children of Israel to the LORD their God. His calling would be to transform the disobedient hearts of the people and to make ready, "in the Wilderness," a people prepared for the Lord. In Luke, the angel refers directly to the prophecy in Malachi that I have included on the next page.

It is obvious that this Malachi prophecy is concerning the End-of-Days, the great and dreadful Day of the LORD (the second coming), and the role Elijah will play. When the Lord came in the first century, it was not the great and dreadful Day of the LORD so the angel said that John would come in "the spirit of Elijah." John is not "The Prophet." Elijah himself is "The Prophet" who will return before the great and dreadful Day of the LORD (the second coming). Malachi prophesied that Elijah would turn the hearts of the fathers to their children and the hearts of the children to their fathers. The Wilderness Prophet is a heart specialist. In the spirit of Elijah, John would play the same role. The angel is displaying the Scriptural technique of overlay. Can you recognize the blueprint? Clearly John the Baptist, in the spirit of Elijah, was NOT the Elijah who would fulfill the role of the prophet Elijah on the Day of the LORD. He is an intermediate fulfillment that overlays the prophecy. Elijah is coming again and will precede the Lord's second coming. Before Jesus can come again, Elijah must come first, just as Jesus said. *"Indeed, Elijah is coming first and will restore all things. But I say to you that Elijah has come already."* Before Jesus' return, God's concern is for the hearts of His children. This prophecy in Malachi is a shadow of the spiritual heart transplant that will someday transform the hearts of God's children before He returns. Elijah is the surgeon who performs the transplant. Elijah is coming again and will restore all things.

Elijah must come again and restore all things.
Pay extremely close attention to his message and his ministry:

*"**Remember the Law of Moses**, My servant,*
Which I commanded him in Horeb for all Israel,
With the statutes and judgments.
Behold, I will send you Elijah the prophet
Before the coming of the great and dreadful day of the LORD.
And he will turn the hearts of the fathers to the children,
And the hearts of the children to their fathers,
Lest I come and strike the earth with a curse."
Malachi 4:4-6

His Message: "Remember the Law of Moses!"

His Ministry: He will turn the hearts of the fathers to the children and the hearts of the children to their fathers.

The Prophet Who Restores All Things

Think about it!

Elijah is the prophet who **always** precedes the coming of the Lord. His role at the end-of-days is to restore all things, just as taught to us by the Messiah Himself and emphasized by Peter in the book of Acts. We can see in the prophecy from Malachi that the restoration of all things has to do with turning our hearts toward the Father. Jesus answered and said to them, "Indeed, Elijah is coming first and will **restore all things**."

Peter teaches us in the book of Acts 3:19-23 that the prophet who comes to "restore all things" is the prophet "like Moses" whom we have been looking for. *Repent therefore and be converted, that your sins may be blotted out, so that times of refreshing may come from the presence of the Lord, and that He may send Jesus Christ, who was preached to you before, whom heaven must receive until the times of restoration of all things, which God has spoken by the mouth of all His holy prophets since the world began. For Moses truly said to the fathers, 'The LORD your God will raise up for you a Prophet like me (Moses) from your brethren. Him you shall hear in all things, whatever He says to you. And it shall be that every soul who will not hear that Prophet shall be utterly destroyed from among the people.'*

Peter makes the clear link between Elijah, the Prophet who will restore all things, and his reference to Moses. Jesus taught us that it is Elijah who restores all things, and God promised to raise up another prophet like Moses; another Wilderness Prophet. Peter now links the prophet who "restores all things" with the "prophet like Moses." A prophet must come first to restore all things, and according to Peter, Messiah **must remain in heaven until this happens.** Jesus does not restore all things, Elijah does. Is the spirit of Elijah calling you to be part of the restoration?

Following his instruction that the Messiah must remain in heaven until the restoration of all things, Peter paraphrases Moses from Deuteronomy 18:15-19. **In the future, the Lord will raise up a Prophet like Moses.** Him you shall hear. God will put His words in this prophet's mouth, and He shall speak to the people all that He has commanded them and it shall be that whoever will not hear the words of this Prophet (like Moses), which He speaks in the LORD'S name, *shall be utterly destroyed from among the people!* In other words, if the hearts do not turn (Elijah's ministry), *the LORD will strike the earth with a curse (Malachi 4:6).* If you don't listen to the prophet like Moses, you shall be utterly destroyed. If you don't listen to Elijah, God will strike the earth with a curse. Although Christian theology teaches that Jesus is the future prophet of whom Moses speaks, the Scriptural evidence actually points to Elijah being this "prophet like Moses."

Let's confirm with yet another Biblical Blueprint that it is Elijah who is the prophet like Moses who will come first. Jesus CANNOT be the prophet who comes first. He must remain in heaven until the restoration of all things. The next prophetic date on God's calendar CANNOT be the "imminent return" of the Lord, secret or otherwise.

Why do the scribes say Elijah must come first? *"Indeed Elijah is coming first and will restore all things."* The Wilderness Prophet must come to lead the Greater Exodus into the Wilderness for a complete heart restoration in God's people **before the coming of the great and dreadful Day of the LORD.** If you believe the Lord will appear in the clouds at any moment to snatch away the Church before the restoration of all things, you have conceded to the doctrines of men.

Again, who is this prophet like Moses?

Moses is the Wilderness Prophet. He leads the Exodus of the people out of bondage (Egypt, the world) into the Wilderness. Moses DOES NOT lead the people into the Promised Land. He passes his mantle to Joshua whose name means *"YAHWEH is salvation."* Elijah is the future prophet who will restore all things. He will restore the hearts of the children and lead another Exodus out of Captivity (an uncircumcised heart) and into the Wilderness. This is the place of purification and heart restoration which precedes the Promised Land. However, Elijah DOES NOT lead the people into the Promised Land. But like Moses, he passes his mantle to another servant of the LORD. As a pattern, the first Elijah (9th century BCE) passed his mantle to Elisha, whose name means *"Elohim (God) is my salvation"* (not a coincidence). John the Baptist, in the spirit of Elijah, had to transfer his ministry (pass his mantle) to make a way for the Lord's first coming. Likewise, in the end, Elijah will come again and make a way for the Lord's second coming. At the second coming, Elijah will pass his mantle to the Lord Jesus, whose name in Hebrew is "Y'shua" which means, like the others, *"YAHWEH is salvation."* Is this not the most beautiful picture? Scriptural patterns of overlay are striking. Are you now learning to read the blueprints?

> *"Remember the Law of Moses, My servant,*
> *Which I commanded him in Horeb for all Israel,*
> *With the statutes and judgments.*
> **Behold, I will send you Elijah the prophet**

Before the coming of the great and dreadful day of the LORD.
*And he will **turn the hearts** of the fathers to the children,*
And the hearts of the children to their fathers,
Lest I come and strike the earth with a curse."
Malachi 4:4-6

Malachi words it this way; "Remember the Law of Moses," "Behold, I will send you Elijah the prophet," "Turn your hearts," "Lest I come and strike the earth with a curse." Can you feel in the depth of your being the vast significance of getting your heart right? It's Elijah who is the prophet, and the spirit of Elijah that is charged with the role of restoring all things, restoring the hearts. This is major heart transplant surgery. When he comes, he comes with a clear message as witnessed above in Malachi 4: **Remember the Law of Moses** with the statutes and judgments. God said to Moses in Deuteronomy 18:18, *"I will raise up for them a Prophet like you from among their brethren, and will put My words in His mouth, **and He shall speak to them all that I command Him."*** It is Elijah the Prophet who restores all things and speaks to them **(to us)** all that God has commanded. Remember the Law of Moses! This is the restoration that needs to begin in the hearts of men.

Do you understand the magnitude of what needs to occur in your heart? Entering the Wilderness is the beginning of a heart restoration that makes praying the Prayer of David possible. As a Believer, it will be the single most important prayer you will ever pray? The Word is near you; it is in your heart to do it! It's the moment of truth. God has lifted you to the summit of change in your life. It is all a matter of the heart.

The Forerunner: Your Personal Transformation

Where does the change begin? Change begins as a small seed planted deep within the chambers of your heart, and ready to burst forth in a harvest of transformation. In the dark, this tiny seed waits impatiently. The seed was planted the moment you surrendered your life to Christ, and tarries only for the soil of your heart to become fertile. The change begins when we turn back towards God and remember His ways. How fast this transformation occurs depends only upon your willingness and how much living water you will allow in to enrich the soil of your heart.

The Veil

Your natural disposition as a human being is to have a veil covering your face and your heart. The foreskin over your heart acts as a veil which creates a barrier between you and God. This veil will hinder the transformation that God has in store for you. You cannot understand the depth of God's will for your life with this barrier shielding your heart. Jeremiah 4:3-4 says, break up your fallow ground and do not sow among thorns. Circumcise yourself to the LORD and **take away the foreskins of your hearts**. In Christ, you have no excuse to remain "veiled" in your obedience to God.

In 2 Corinthians 3, Paul describes a veil over our face and heart. The face is an external indicator which acts as a reflection or index of the condition of your inward thoughts and feelings. The heart denotes the center of spiritual life and is the fountain or seat of our thoughts, passions, desires, appetites, affections, purposes, and endeavors. From the heart springs forth the will or character of a man. Inside a man's heart, he lies naked and exposed. With inspiration from the Holy Spirit, you can have God's commandments written on your heart. But first, to gain a full appreciation of them, you will need the veil or "foreskin" of your heart removed. In this process, it is best if you are a willing participant. If not, the Spirit will do it anyway. The Word says, "Every knee **will** bow and every tongue **will** confess."

2 Corinthians 3:14-18

But their minds were blinded. For until this day the same veil remains unlifted in the reading of the Old Testament, because the veil is taken away in Christ. **But even to this day, when Moses is read, a veil lies on their heart. Nevertheless when one turns to the Lord, the veil is taken away.** *Now* *the Lord is the Spirit; and where the Spirit of the Lord is, there is liberty. But we all, with **unveiled face**, beholding as in a mirror the glory of the Lord, are being transformed into the same image from glory to glory, just as by the Spirit of the Lord.*

With an **unveiled face** you start becoming transformed into the image of Christ. The complete transformation does not take place at the moment you believe. As the veil is lifted off your face, the Spirit of the LORD begins to transform you from glory to glory. At some point, you will look in the mirror and see only the refection of Christ. Until then, some part of the veil remains over your heart. This veil will quench the Spirit and encourage a more fleshly understanding of the Law given to Moses, and the words of the prophets. You will see them as letters, and not Spirit. *For when we were in the flesh, the sinful passions which were aroused by the law were at work in our members to bear fruit to death. But now we have been delivered from the law, having died to what we were held by, **so that we should serve in the newness of the Spirit and not in the oldness of the letter.** What shall we say then? Is the Law sin? Certainly not! On the contrary, I would not have known sin except through the Law* (Romans 7:5-7).

A Ministry of Death

Think about it!   The veil over your heart, or the uncircumcised heart, is an obstacle to a deeper, more spiritual appreciation of the Mosaic Covenant. In pursuit of the high calling, the veil will be completely taken out of the way and you will be **transformed, by the Spirit, into the image of Christ.** Without this transformation by the Spirit through faith, the Law of God remains a "ministry of death." However, *do we then make void the Law through faith? Certainly not! On the contrary, we establish the Law* (Romans 3:31).

The Law is a "ministry of death" to anyone who does not walk by the Spirit. *But if you are led by the Spirit, you are not under the Law* (Galatians 5:18). "Under the Law" is a term used in Scripture to describe the concept of being under the **penalty** of the Law. In short, you sin you die! It is NOT a term used to devalue God's commandments or to differentiate God's Laws from His Spirit. Remember, in God's eyes, the only way to correctly keep His commandments, was, is, and always will be by faith.

*But when the fullness of the time had come, God sent forth His Son, born of a woman, **born under the Law**, to redeem those who were under the Law, that we might receive the adoption as sons (Galatians 4:4-5).* Jesus was born under the penalty of the Law; you sin you die. *Now we know that whatever the Law says, it says to those who are under the Law, that every mouth may be stopped, and all the world may become guilty before God (Romans 3:19).* Yet, Jesus was sinless and still paid the penalty as if He was guilty of sin. It had to be this way. In order for His sacrifice to be a substitute for our deaths, He had to be born with the same risk as we; if we sin, we should surely die. But because He died **without** sin, He was able to transfer the penalty we deserved to Himself and, as a result, we are redeemed from our sins. *But now having been set free from sin, and having become slaves of God, you have your fruit to holiness, and the end, everlasting life. For the wages of sin is death, but the gift of God is eternal life in Christ Jesus our Lord (Romans 6:22-23).*

Paul teaches one of the most difficult to understand concepts in all of Scripture. He explains how the Spirit of God relates to the Law of God. He walks this delicate tightrope throughout the book of Romans. Just when you think he is becoming disparaging about the Law, he swings in the opposite direction displaying masterful balance. Paul is careful to never fall off the rope, and you would be wise to walk carefully in his footsteps on this issue. *But sin, taking opportunity by the commandment, produced in me all manner of evil desire. For apart from the Law sin was dead. I was alive once without the Law, but when the commandment came, sin revived and I died.* **And the commandment, which was to bring life, I found to bring death.** *For sin, taking occasion by the commandment, deceived me, and by it killed me. Therefore **the Law is holy, and the commandment holy and just and good.** Has then what is good become death to me?* **Certainly not!** *But sin, that it might appear sin, was producing death in me through what is good, so that sin through the commandment might become exceedingly sinful. For we know that the **Law is spiritual**, but **I am carnal**, sold under sin (Romans 7:8-14).* The Law is capable of exposing the carnal man, who without it would never need a Savior, and this makes the Law *holy* and *just* and *good*. Paul's verdict is that the Law is spiritual and that the problem lies with his personal carnality, not the Law itself.

Paul describes the great conflict that wars inside a man who wills to submit himself to the Law of God, but battles with his flesh to do so. Romans 7:15-25 says is best. *For what I am doing, I do not understand. For what I will to do, that I do not practice; but what I hate, that I do. If, then, I do what I will not to do,* **I agree with the Law that it is good.** *But now, it is no longer I who do it, but sin that dwells in me.* **For I know that in me (that is, in my flesh) nothing good dwells;** *for to will is present with me, but how to perform what is good I do not find. For the good that I will to do, I do not do; but the evil I will not to do, that I practice. Now if I do what I will not to do, it is no longer I who do it, but sin that dwells in me. I find then a law, that evil is present with me, the one who wills to do good.* **For I delight in the Law of God according to the inward man.** *But I see another law in my members, warring against the Law of my mind, and bringing me into captivity to the law of sin which is in my members. O wretched man that I am! Who will deliver me from this body of death? I thank God — through Jesus Christ our Lord! So then,* **with the mind I myself serve the Law of God, but with the flesh the law of sin.**

Paul says, "*For I delight in the Law of God according to the inward man.*" The spirit man within him delights in the Law of God, the commandments; but his flesh serves the law of sin. It has often puzzled me how "spiritual" men and woman of God so often, and so glibly, dismiss the Law of God as "old," "done away with," or "nailed to the cross." They categorize it as "bondage," "legalism," or a "burden." However, we see from the passages above that Paul sees the Law as holy, spiritual, just, and good. Paul's inward, redeemed man loves the Law. He is simply confessing his weakness according to his flesh. Praise God that *there is therefore now no condemnation to those who are in Christ Jesus, who do not walk according to the flesh, but according to the Spirit. For the Law of the Spirit of life in Christ Jesus has made me free from the* **law of sin and death** (Romans 8:1-2).

So, without the Spirit, the Law is a "ministry of death" because of the weakness of the flesh, not because of any fault of the Law. The propensity of the flesh to sin, this "evil inclination" as described in Judaism, must be subdued by the "Spirit" as described by Paul. If not, to remain carnally minded is death. (Note: Judaism also recognizes this battle between our Spirit and the flesh, but comes from the angle of physically mastering our flesh by keeping commandments. Paul understood that this capability was a byproduct of the Spirit working in you.) *For what the Law could not do in that it was weak **through the flesh**, God did by sending His own Son in the likeness of sinful flesh, on account of sin: He condemned sin in the flesh, that the righteous requirement of the Law might be fulfilled in us who do not walk according to the flesh **but according to the Spirit**. For those who live according to the flesh set their minds on the things of the flesh, but those who live according to the Spirit, the things of the Spirit. For to be **carnally minded is death**, but to be spiritually minded is life and peace. Because the carnal mind is enmity against God; for it is not subject to the Law of God, nor indeed can be (Romans 8:3-7).*

The righteousness of the Law can only be fulfilled by those walking according to the Spirit. This is because those who walk according to the flesh are subject to their carnal mind, which will always express hatred toward God and disobedience to His commandments. The carnally minded are incapable of submitting to God's Law, as opposed to those whose minds have been quickened by the Spirit. Therefore, it is those who are "in Christ," and only those "in Christ," who are actually given the power, by the Spirit, to keep the Law of God. If God has empowered us to be the only people on earth able to completely keep His commandments, wouldn't it make sense that we are also the very same group of people He expects to keep them?

Unveiled Face

When Moses met with the LORD to receive His Word in Exodus 34, it was so glorious that the esteem of God lit up Moses' face. Moses, with an unveiled face, would then relay to the people all that God had commanded. He'd then immediately cover his face with a veil because the glory was passing away. Anytime he went before the LORD, he would let down the veil to stand before God, face to face. The temporary glory of the Law revealed to Moses pales in comparison to the permanent glory of the Law written on our hearts that was later revealed in Christ. The former remains veiled, and is the only glory available to the uncircumcised heart. The latter, so much more glorious, is reserved solely for the heart that is circumcised. The former is passing away and the latter is everlasting.

Moses had a unique and special calling in the Wilderness, and so does Elijah. Now that you have learned that Elijah is the prophet, like Moses, who will be raised up as we near the end of the age, you will be looking for the coming of Elijah before the Lord's return. He will have the LORD'S words in his mouth, and will proclaim to the people all that God commands him. Those who are alive for the return of Elijah will have something available to them that no generation could previously attain. In Christ, the Holy Spirit begins to lift the veil off your heart, and when the Wilderness Prophet "like Moses" comes, the circumcision will be complete. This time, we will not crucify the messenger as we once crucified the Messiah. They (or possibly we) will enter an era when it will be possible to attain a heart that is completely circumcised, just as I described in Chapter 2. The generation that is alive at that time can and will become like Christ. We are each living stones joined with Him to become the Spiritual Temple. The glory that shown on Moses' face was passing away. The glory that shines from us is everlasting and is growing ever brighter.

Remember, we should not simply consider these prophetic events from a corporate point of view. While it is true that the greater Exodus is best understood from the perspective of what will happen to the Body of Christ, my conviction is that God is calling a remnant of forerunners to come out first and lead the way.

The spirit of Elijah is being unleashed into the world today and is calling forerunners into the Wilderness. Three thousand five hundred years ago, God used a series of plagues to proclaim "Let My People Go!" I believe the massive destruction and widespread catastrophes that we are witnessing in the world today may be a sign of His plagues that will ultimately release His people into the Wilderness. When you hear the Gospel of the Kingdom being preached, come out! Don't wait for the death of the firstborn (especially if you are a firstborn). If the words of these pages are calling you to cross over, the spirit of Elijah may already be at work in you and may be calling you as a forerunner. Hearken unto the calling and be extraordinary. In the Wilderness, we will receive a new heart and pray the prayer that David prayed. Elijah will follow and call every other Christian into the Wilderness to do the same. "Why then do the scribes say that Elijah must come first?" Jesus answered and said to them, "Indeed, Elijah is coming first and will restore all things!"

Again, this transformation takes time. Through the Spirit of the Lord, a child of God is changed *"from glory to glory."* How much and how fast you change is up to you. The more you resist, the more likely you are to pull the veil back over your heart. The less you resist, the thinner the veil becomes until you fully surrender. When the barrier is completely removed, you will be transformed from glory to glory. Israel entered the Wilderness with a veil over their hearts, and it remained that way. You have the option to travel in the Wilderness with your heart unveiled. Today if you hear His voice, do not harden your hearts.

Personal Transformation Matches Biblical Blueprints

Your transformation from glory to glory will be accomplished by a similar pattern of events that we see corporately in the lives of God's chosen people. Again, we will rely on patterns or the blueprint of God's plan. Israel was called and delivered out of Egypt. They entered the trials in the Wilderness and then reached the Promised Land 40 years later. Similarly, God has a call on your life. He wants to deliver you from bondage and, ultimately, set you down in the Promised Land. He wants the veil removed completely, but you must enter the Wilderness first. The Wilderness is where the soil of your heart is cultivated.

God wants change. He wants to deliver you from something. It may be as vital as delivering your eternal soul; as crucial as freeing you from addiction; or as practical as placing you in a new job. Your first stop after deliverance, however, is a season of trial. This season is referred to as a Wilderness experience. Only after cultivation do you then reach the

Promised Land, the place to where God is leading you. You will notice that these types of patterns repeat over and over in your life. You may perceive that the length of the trial in the Wilderness is exactly proportionate to how long you remain rebellious in your heart to God's plan. In Hebrews 3, God told his people, *"Do not harden your hearts as in the rebellion, in the days of trial in the Wilderness."* They marched around in the desert for 40 years because they did not have faith enough to enter the Promised Land and would not trust God for their provision. Their hearts were rebellious.

Today in the Church, members of the Body of Christ are suffering a similar type of heart disease. We are held back from our full inheritance, from the manifestation of the "Sons of God," and from understanding the mysteries of God, because our hearts remain hard. We simply do not have complete faith in His promises. We do not fully believe we are who He says we are. Corporately, the Church must have a change in heart. This heart overhaul in the body of Messiah is mentioned throughout the Scriptures. Change will happen in the future according to the same pattern of events as in the past. This is how our Creator works.

Let's review for a moment what brought us to this point.

In Christ, it is the Spirit of the LORD that is leading you towards God and His Commandments. The Spirit liberates you from the bondage of being conformed into the image of imperfect man and frees you to be conformed into the image of Christ. In the Wilderness, those in Christ will have the veil completely removed, allowing for the heart transplant. The Wilderness Prophet performs the surgery and reveals the circumcised heart. With a circumcised heart you will not say that, "the Law of God is too mysterious or difficult." It will be near you in your mouth and heart to do it. Jesus calls you "friend," and will speak to you face to face as a man speaks to his friends. This is if you do all that He commands. Once transformed, we will behold in the mirror the face of the Lord as if we see Him **face to face**. We will see His image when faced with our reflection.

Let us move one step closer to attaining a heart like David's by exploring the Gospel of the Kingdom and mysteries of the Kingdom of Heaven. How can we develop and deliver a clear message to the Church about unity of the faith and how to become conformed into the image of Christ? It is in the Wilderness that these institutions of God are established. It is in a desolate place where we can cultivate a clear message about the Gospel of the Kingdom. All of nature is in anticipation for the "manifestations of the sons of God." So get manifesting!

Now is the time to press on to the high calling and move one step closer to discovering the daring prayer that David prayed. You have been diligent up to this point to work through this book and develop a strong foundation to support what lies ahead. When prayed, this prayer will be a bold declaration to the world. And be ever watchful because the LORD says, *"Behold, I send My messenger, And he will prepare the way before Me."*

Section Two:

A Voice in
the Wilderness

Chapter Five

Making the Message Clear

*"But seek first the Kingdom of God and His righteousness,
and all these things shall be added to you."*
Matthew 6:33

Y ou have endured many things to arrive at this point in the book. *"We must through many tribulations enter the Kingdom of God (Acts 14:22b)."* I am certain that you have been challenged as a Believer in many ways. In the Wilderness, however, God will determine how much He can trust you. *"And you shall remember that the LORD your God led you all the way these forty years in the Wilderness, to humble you and test you, to know what was in your heart, whether you would keep His commandments or not (Deuteronomy 8:2).*

For many of you, reading this book has exposed a higher calling. The LORD is using it during this season of your life to call you out. I am sure some of you know that you are one of the "remnant" being called into the Wilderness to prepare the way for the others. You know who you are. You have a burning feeling in your gut and an unyielding pull on your heart. It is undeniable. You are a forerunner!

Many of you have been challenged concerning your doctrines. You have discovered passages in the Scriptures that have given new meaning to your faith. You've also seen many Scriptures in a new light. You have a more concrete goal toward which to aim. You are developing an expanded purpose or deeper level of commitment. You are now certain that there is a high calling, after salvation, and you have become inspired to "press on."

I am sure you are eager to finally find out what this Prayer of David is, to which I have been referring since the Introduction. You may be thinking, "What exactly are the words uttered by King David, and what will they mean to me?" I want to commend you on your patience thus far. It will take every ounce of your commitment and concentration, on the material contained in Chapters 1-7, for you to experience the full impact of David's words, and acquire the heart from which they spring forth. Without all the necessary preparation, his words will be practically meaningless to you. If you cheated, against my advice in the Introduction, and skipped ahead to Chapter 8, you undoubtedly walked away from the passage disappointed and confused. (Really, you only cheated yourself.) Having worked through much of the foundation, you now undoubtedly feel more excited and certain. Having come this far, you are just three chapters away from understanding the depth and impact of David's words. Please continue to be diligent and patient for *the plans of the diligent lead surely to plenty, but those of everyone who is hasty, surely to poverty (Proverbs 21:5).*

Before you can reap the full harvest of David's words, we must first define and discuss the Gospel of the Kingdom and the Kingdom of Heaven, and how they differ from the Gospel of salvation. To this end, we will explore the essential call to unity of the faith in Christianity, uncover the secrets of building the Spiritual Temple, and unravel some of the mysteries of the Kingdom of Heaven itself. We must have a firm grasp on these concepts in order to understand the full impact of David's bold proclamation, and to follow our charge to make this message clear to the world.

> ➤ NIV *(Habakkuk 2:2-3) Then the* LORD *replied: "Write down the revelation and make it plain on tablets so that a herald may run with it. For the revelation awaits an appointed time; it speaks of the end and will not prove false. Though it linger, wait for it; it will certainly come and will not delay.*

The Gospel of the Kingdom

The Kingdom of Heaven & The Kingdom of God

Before I define the "Good News of the Kingdom of Heaven" or help uncover its mysteries, I must clarify the phrase itself. Do not be confused with the alternate use of the phrases "the Kingdom of Heaven" and "the Kingdom of God," as they are identical in meaning. Matthew is the only writer to use "the Kingdom of Heaven"; he also uses "the Kingdom of God" in five places as well. Mark, Luke, and John all use "the Kingdom of God" exclusively. Luke uses it in Acts, as well as in his Gospel. Paul also uses "the Kingdom of God" in five of his letters. I have included two corresponding verses in two Gospels, and two contiguous verses in the same Gospel to demonstrate how these phrases are interchangeable. However, there are many other examples that I have not included.

> ➤ *(Matthew 13:11) He answered and said to them, "Because it has been given to you to know the mysteries of* **the Kingdom of Heaven**...

> ➤ *(Luke 8:10) And He said, "To you it has been given to know the mysteries of* **the Kingdom of God**...

Here are consecutive verses in Matthew that alternate the phrases to show that they mean the same thing.

> ➤ *(Matthew 19:23-24) Then Jesus said to His disciples, "Assuredly, I say to you that it is hard for a rich man to enter* **the Kingdom of Heaven**. *"And* **again I say** *to you, it is easier for a camel to go through the eye of a needle than for a rich man to enter* **the Kingdom of God**.*"

One phrase is an exact substitute for the other. Understanding this, let's move on.

The Gospel of the Kingdom of Heaven

What is the Kingdom of Heaven and what is the Gospel (good news) about it? Is it a thing? Is it a place? It is a state of being? And what does repentance have to do with getting it, going there, or being it? As you learned earlier in Chapter 4, both John the Baptist and Jesus came preaching, *"Repent, the Kingdom of Heaven is at hand!"* After that admonition, Jesus went about teaching in the synagogues, preaching the Gospel of the Kingdom. The Gospel of the Kingdom is the "good news" that the Kingdom of Heaven has "drawn near" *(Luke 8:1)*. *Now it came to pass, afterward, that He went through every city and village, preaching and bringing the* **glad tidings** *(Gospel) of the Kingdom of God. And the twelve were with Him.*

When asked the pointed question about when the Kingdom would come, Jesus gave an important clue for us to understand the Kingdom of God. *Now when He was asked by the Pharisees when the Kingdom of God would come, He answered them and said, "The Kingdom of God does not come with observation; nor will they say, 'See here!' or 'See there!' For indeed, the Kingdom of God is within you" (Luke 17:20-21)*. The Kingdom is within you. It is NOT a place. It is not heaven. It is not something you see or touch. It is something else. Paul writes in 1 Corinthians 4:20, *For the Kingdom of God is not in word but in* **power**. Power for what? In Matthew 18:3 Jesus says it is the power to be converted. *"Assuredly, I say to you, unless you are* **converted** *and become as little children, you will by no means enter the Kingdom of Heaven."* He is not talking about entering a place. He is teaching about becoming converted into something. **We need power to become converted.** The clue to understanding this conversion is revealed as Jesus summarizes His teaching about the Kingdom at the end of Matthew 5. In the midst of the Sermon on the Mount, Jesus encapsulates His great dissertation about the Kingdom of Heaven, with one verse, *"Therefore you shall be perfect, just as your Father in Heaven is perfect."*

The conversion represented by the concept of the Kingdom of Heaven is that of a Believer being conformed into the perfect image of Christ. The Kingdom of God is within you. As prophesied by Moses in Deuteronomy 30, it is near you in your heart and in your mouth to do it. You have the ability to become exactly like Christ Jesus. Yes, you read right. You have the ability to become **exactly like Christ Jesus!** This is the Kingdom of Heaven. To better understand this conversion, look through corporate eyes. It is not **"I"** who will be like Christ; it is **"We"** who will be like Christ. Each of us is an **individual** stone in the **corporate** Spiritual Temple.

So, entering the Kingdom of Heaven is not the same as "going to heaven" when you are saved. You can sin or "fall short" and still go to heaven. However, any sin at all will prevent you from being conformed into the image of Christ or having the Kingdom of Heaven within you. When John and Jesus taught, *"Repent, the Kingdom of Heaven is at hand,"* they were saying, "Turn away from sin!" The opportunity to become sinless is at hand or nearly available. The "good news" of the Kingdom was that sinlessness would some day be possible. This was not simply a New Testament teaching. We get this same teaching directly from the mouth of God all the way back in Genesis.

> NIV *(Genesis 4:6-7) Then the LORD said to Cain, "Why are you angry? Why is your face downcast? If you do what is right, will you not be accepted? But if you do not do what is right, sin is crouching at your door; it desires to have you, **but you must master it."***

Sinlessness

Think about it!

And you know that He was manifested to take away our sins, and in Him there is no sin (1 John 3:5). Jesus was a master over sin. He also commanded us to stop sinning. *No one who is born of God will continue to sin, because God's seed remains in him; he cannot go on sinning, because he has been born of God (1 John 3:9* NIV*).* Jesus said it this way in Matthew 5, *"Be perfect, just as my Father in heaven is perfect."* In human form, Jesus was made perfect by remaining sinless, even though He was challenged like each one of us. *For we do not have a High Priest who cannot sympathize with our weaknesses, but was in all points tempted as we are, **yet without sin** (Hebrews 4:15). And having been perfected, He became the author of eternal salvation to all who obey Him (Hebrews 5:9).* Being without sin defines perfection. To understand perfection more clearly, let's define sin. *Whoever commits sin also commits lawlessness, and **sin is lawlessness** (1 John 3:4).*

If sin is lawlessness, then lawful**ness** must be sin**lessness**. Jesus was perfect because He was sinless. Therefore, by definition He must have been lawful. If He calls us to be perfect, *"Be perfect, just as My father in heaven is perfect,"* He is asking us to become sinless. If He is asking us to become sinless, then He must be asking us to be lawful as well.

If:
Sin = Lawlessness = Imperfection
Then:
Sinlessness = Lawfulness = Perfection
Conclusion:
Perfection is the state of "Sinlessness"
achieved by "Lawfulness"!

Perfection is sinlessness. Sinlessness is lawfulness. Therefore perfection is lawfulness. Upholding what Law, you might ask? Follow the subsequent verses carefully to determine to which Law you must be obedient in order to be perfect.

Whoever transgresses and does not abide in the doctrine of Christ does not have God. **He who abides in the doctrine of Christ has both the Father and the Son** *(2 John 1:9).* However, is the doctrine of Christ a new set of "Christian commandments"? *Jesus answered them and said, "My doctrine is not Mine, but His who sent Me" (John 7:16). "For if you believed Moses, you would believe Me; for he wrote about Me" (John 5:46).* Jesus said it best while teaching about the Kingdom of Heaven in Matthew 5:17. *"Do not think that I came to destroy the Law or the Prophets. I did not come to destroy but to fulfill."* Fulfill DOES NOT mean, "He did it for you so you don't have to," as you may believe from modern Christian teachings. Be a Berean; look it up! "Fulfill" means: *"give true meaning to, to make full, to fill up, or to cause to abound, to render perfect, with reference to the will of God- to carry out, perform, accomplish, or to cause God's will (as made known in the Law) to be obeyed as it should be, and God's promises (given through the prophets) to receive fulfillment.* He came to give true meaning to His Father's Law; the Law of Moses. He did not come to destroy or abolish it, but to be a living example of how to obey it. Not obeying Christ's commandments is the same as not obeying the Father's commandments.

Again, upholding **what** Law will make you lawful or perfect? Answer: The doctrine of Christ —*which* is the doctrine of the Father — *which* is the Law of Moses. Sin is lawlessness to God's commandments. Perfection or being conformed into the image of Christ is obedience to God's commandments. Isn't that simple?

Jesus taught in 1 John 5:3, *For this is the* **love** *of God, that we keep* **His commandments.** *And His commandments are not burdensome,* and in John 14:15, *"If you* **love** *Me, keep My commandments.* Jesus says that to show love for the Father, you should keep the Father's commandments. And to show love for the Son, you must keep the Son's commandments. He further testifies that the Father's and the Son's commandments are the same commandments, and that they are not a burden. Paul eventually teaches that the love demonstrated by this obedience defines perfection. *But above all these things put on* **love,** *which is the bond of perfection (Colossians 3:14).* The love of the Father and of the Son, demonstrated by lawfulness to God's commandments, is the bond of perfection. In other words, love equals lawfulness equals sinlessness equals perfection.

Those who do not practice keeping God's commandments, with faith of course, are lawless. The Kingdom of Heaven is perfect, Christ-like obedience to all of God's commandments. Sound impossible? Paul says that with the power of Him who is working in you it is not impossible. *Christ in you, the hope of glory. Him we preach, warning every man and teaching every man in all wisdom, that we may present every man* **perfect in Christ Jesus.** *To this end I also labor, striving according to His working which works in me mightily (Colossians 1:27b-29).* It is not uncommon for a Believer in need of inspiration and encouragement to evoke the power of one of modern Christianity's favorite verses. *I can do all things through Christ who strengthens me (Philippians 4:13).* Consider it in your pursuit of perfect, Christ-like obedience to all of God's commandments.

Works of Law or Obedience by Faith

Please do not confuse this radical obedience with legalism. I am in no way saying that keeping the Law perfectly will get you saved. But, as a Believer, you should WANT to keep God's commandments because you ARE saved. Giving your life as a living sacrifice is your reasonable service to God, is it not? You should recall (as we covered in Chapter 2) that the only legitimate way to attain the *"righteousness of the Law"* is by faith. In Romans, Paul, with the masterful use of similar yet contrasting terms, reveals the eternal difference between obedience by faith and legalism.

> ➤ *(Romans 2:13)* *For not the hearers of the Law are just in the sight of God, but the **doers of the Law will be justified.***

> ➤ *(Romans 3:20)* *Therefore by the **deeds of the Law no flesh will be justified** in His sight, for by the Law is the knowledge of sin.*

Sound contradictory to you? You're not alone. All the way back in the time of Paul, many found his complex teachings hard to grasp. Peter writes about this when he states that in Paul's letters there are *"some things hard to understand, which untaught and unstable people twist to their own destruction" (2 Peter 3:16)*. So let's work through this step by step.

Paul says that by "doing the Law" you will be justified, but by "deeds of the Law" no flesh will be justified. The suggestion that justification comes by **doing the Law** is Paul's way of describing obedience that comes from faith. "Doing the Law" represents the idea of faithfully guarding or keeping watch over God's commandments. To demonstrate these points, Paul wrote: *Circumcision is nothing and uncircumcision is nothing, but keeping the commandments of God is what matters (1 Corinthians 7:19)*. "Deeds of Law," however, is the opposite of faith. *Therefore we conclude that a man is justified by faith apart from the deeds of the Law (Romans 3:28)*.

Trying to be justified by **deeds of the Law** is Paul's way of describing legalism (keeping commandments to get saved). This burden of having to perform something to get saved was a common doctrinal error among first century Jewish Believers.

> ➤ *(Acts 15:1, 5)* *And certain men came down from Judea and taught the brethren, "Unless you are circumcised according to the custom of Moses, you cannot be **saved."**... Some of the sect of the Pharisees who believed rose up, saying, "It is necessary to circumcise them, and to command them to keep the Law of Moses."*

Peter rose up in response and confirmed that all men are purified in the same way, by faith. He called it an unbearable burden to add anything to the free gift of grace as a requirement for salvation. *"Now therefore, why do you test God by putting a* **yoke on the neck of the disciples which neither our fathers nor we were able to bear?"** *But we believe that through the grace of the Lord Jesus Christ* **we shall be saved** *in the same manner as they"*(Acts 15:10-11). On the other hand, Paul made certain that no one would mistake this free gift as an excuse to **SIN** or **nullify God's Laws.**

> ➢ **(Romans 6:1-2)** *What shall we say then?* **Shall we continue in sin that grace may abound?** *Certainly not! How shall we who died to sin live any longer in it?*

> ➢ **(Romans 3:31)** *Do we then* **make void** *the Law through faith? Certainly not! On the contrary,* **we establish the Law.**

Paul contrasts "doing the Law," which brings justification, with "deeds of the Law" by which no flesh will be justified. James describes the delicate relationship between faith and obedience this way: *But someone will say, "You have faith, and I have works." Show me your faith without your works, and I will show you my faith by my works (James 2:18).*

Therefore, anytime you see the phrase "deeds of the Law" or "works of the Law" in the New Testament, keep in mind that they mean the same thing, and that Paul is describing legalism, which is actually a form of lawlessness itself. As evidenced by Paul's words in Galatians 3:10, those practicing "works of Law" are NOT genuinely keeping the Law. *For as many as are of the* **works of the Law** *are under the curse; for it is written, "Cursed is everyone who* **does not** *continue in all things which are written in the book of the Law, to do them."*

Wow! That's another tough one from Brother Paul. Those who are "of the works of the Law" are cursed BECAUSE they are NOT "doing all that is written in the Torah (the book of the Law)." What Paul is saying is that those who practice **"works of the Law"** are cursed, **NOT** because they are trying to keep God's commandments, but because they are **SEEKING RIGHTEOUSNESS** by a **FAITHLESS**

ATTEMPT to obey God's commandments. Essentially, they are under the curse because they ARE NOT *"continuing in all things which are written in the book of the Law, to do them,"* by faith. Therefore, we conclude that the term "works of the Law" identifies those NOT keeping the Law. In this case, they are considered uncircumcised in God's eyes. *For circumcision is indeed profitable if you keep the Law; but if you are a breaker of the Law, your circumcision has become uncircumcision (Romans 2:25).*

Those practicing works of Law are breaking the Law and are acting contrary to faith. *Therefore we conclude that a man is justified by faith apart from the deeds of the Law (Romans 3:28). For not the hearers of the Law are just in the sight of God, but the **doers of the Law** will be justified (Romans 2:13).* The Scriptures say we are justified by both faith AND by doing the Law. By linking these concepts, we must conclude that the only legitimate way to do or keep the Law is by faith. **This is faith-based obedience!** On the other hand, "works of the Law" is a form of breaking the Law which must be identified as a lack of faith.

Works of the Law was never, and will never be, of saving value to anyone. Remember, to be of saving value, the Law must be practiced with faith. And this "Law done in faith" is what Paul describes as "doing the Law" in Scripture. In this book, I call doing the Law, "faith-based obedience." Either before or after Jesus' death on the cross, to have justification power, obedience to God's commandments must always be by faith.

> ➤ *(Romans 9:31-32) But Israel, pursuing the Law of righteousness, has not attained to the Law of righteousness. Why? Because **they did not seek it by faith, but as it were, by the works of the Law.***

> ➤ *(Romans 3:28) Therefore we conclude that a man is justified by* **faith** *(doing the Law) apart from the **deeds of the Law.*** And that is why Paul said: *"For not the hearers of the Law are just in the sight of God, but the **doers of the Law will be justified"** (Romans 2:13).*

Believers are justified in the same manner as our father Abraham. *For if Abraham was **justified by works** (of Law), he has something to boast* *about, but not before God. For what does the Scripture say? "Abraham believed God, and it was accounted to him for righteousness."... For the promise that he would be the heir of the world was not to Abraham or to his seed through the Law* (works of Law), *but through the righteousness of faith (Romans 4:2-3, 13).* What is *the righteousness of faith?* Faith-based obedience (doing the Law) is the righteousness of faith.

To perfect our faith, we need faith working with obedience, or in other words, *faith working through love (Galatians 5:6).* This is the very definition of doing the Law or faith-based obedience. *Was not Abraham our father justified by works when he offered Isaac his son on the altar? Do you see that faith was working together with his works, and by works faith was made perfect? And the Scripture was fulfilled which says, "Abraham believed God, and it was accounted to him for righteousness." And he was called the friend of God (James 2:21-23).*

"Works/deeds of the Law" describes a legalist who keeps a checklist of God's commandments and feels that every time he obeys one, he becomes more righteous. As Christians, we know that performance based righteousness is impossible. This is the same mistake Israel made in the Wilderness. Paul described them as "seeking to establish their own righteousness," thereby forsaking the righteousness of God. Unfortunately, the lifestyle of someone performing "works of the Law" and someone performing "faith-based obedience" looks pretty much the same to the outside world. It is the inner condition of the heart that determines "WHY" they are obeying God. So legalism is separated from faith-based obedience by only one thing: The condition of the heart.

> *(Ephesians 2:8-10) For by grace you have been saved **through faith**, and that not of yourselves; it is the gift of God, **not of works**, lest anyone should boast. For we are His workmanship, **created in Christ Jesus for good works**, which God prepared beforehand that we should walk in them.*

> *(James 2:18) But someone will say, "You have faith, and I have works." Show me your faith without your works, and **I will show you my faith by my works**.*

When the veil over your heart is removed, and you see the blueprint for the forerunner, you will most likely be compelled toward radical, faith-based obedience. When this happens, your desire to be obedient to the LORD'S commandments will, in all likelihood, earn you the title of "Legalist" or "Judaizer" from other Believers. Even though your actions are motivated by your love for God and not to gain righteousness, don't be surprised when you are falsely accused by the brethren. Jesus told us in Mark 13:12 that in the last days *"brother will betray brother to death."*

Faith-based obedience is the race to perfection. Becoming like Jesus is the ultimate goal of that race. Believing that you can become like Jesus, and with perfect ministry do even greater works than He, is a monumental leap of faith. The chief purpose of this book is to guide you out of your comfortable world, draw you into the Wilderness, and lead you towards this confession of faith. As you will soon learn, David's prayer is this exact confession.

The Prayer of David will focus our attention beyond salvation as we press on to the high calling, which is being conformed to the image and likeness of Christ. However, as mentioned earlier, this high calling differs greatly with the salvation of our souls. For most of our lives as Believers, we have been focused solely on the Gospel of salvation, a confession of faith that secures our eternity with God. Let's take a moment to define and differentiate this Gospel from a second Gospel, the Gospel of the Kingdom.

The Gospel of Salvation vs. The Gospel of the Kingdom

Let's explore the differences between the Gospel of salvation and the Gospel of the Kingdom. *And Jesus said to him, "**Today salvation** has come to this house, because he also is a son of Abraham; "for the Son of Man has come to seek and to save that which was **lost**." Now as they heard these things, He spoke another parable, because He was near Jerusalem and because **they thought the Kingdom of God would appear immediately** (Luke 19:9-11).* After Jesus announced that salvation had come to the house of Zacchaeus, confusion arose because the people equated eternal salvation with the Kingdom of Heaven. The Kingdom of Heaven does not come immediately with salvation. The Kingdom is something more than seeking and saving the lost.

"*Not everyone who says to Me, 'Lord, Lord,' shall enter the Kingdom of Heaven, **but he who does the will of My Father in heaven**"* (Matthew 7:21). Understanding that eternal salvation is by faith and not works, to what other than salvation is Jesus referring? To enter the Kingdom of Heaven, it takes doing the **will of the Father**. There is nothing you can do to earn salvation. However, it takes a conscious effort, with help of the Holy Spirit, to be conformed into the image of Christ. The "good news" of the Kingdom is that sinlessness would some day be possible. The "bad news" is that it comes with a PRICE!

Sinlessness/perfection demands OBEDIENCE! This is in sharp contrast to salvation which is FREE! Read again the words of Paul from Ephesians 2. This time, do it carefully! With a keen sense, you will see that what emerge are two Gospels.

> ➤ *(Ephesians 2:8-10) For by grace you have been saved through faith, and that not of yourselves; **it is the gift of God, not of works,** lest anyone should boast. For we are His workmanship, **created in Christ Jesus for good works**, which God prepared beforehand **that we should walk in them.***

You have been saved by grace, not works, which was a FREE gift from God. **This is the Gospel of salvation.** Yet, you were also created in Christ Jesus for good works that you should walk in them. This is not free. You must do something. He saved you for free and the cost afterwards is that you should walk in good works. The Hebrew for "good works" is "mitzvoth," which is also translated as "commandments." According to both Jesus and Paul, those who are saved by faith should then walk in God's commandments. **This is the Gospel of the Kingdom.**

Judaism classically teaches that obedience brings salvation and blessings. Christianity classically teaches that faith brings salvation and blessings. The truth, however, is that it is faith-based obedience that brings salvation and blessings. The understanding of Faith-based obedience is encompassed by two Gospels, the Gospel of salvation and the Gospel of the Kingdom.

Again, notice the two Gospels demonstrated in the great commission in Matthew 28:19-20. *"Go therefore and make disciples of all the nations,* **baptizing them** *in the name of the Father and of the Son and of the Holy Spirit,* **"teaching them to observe all things that I have commanded you;** *and lo, I am with you always, even to the end of the age."* Amen. How do you make disciples? Baptize them (The Gospel of salvation) and teach them obedience to God's commandments (The Gospel of the Kingdom).

Observe the two messages preached by Paul in Rome in Acts 28:30-31. *Then Paul dwelt two whole years in his own rented house, and received all who came to him,* **preaching the Kingdom of God** *and* **teaching the things which concern the Lord Jesus Christ** *with all confidence, no one forbidding him.* He preached the Kingdom of God (The Gospel of the Kingdom) and things which concern Christ (The Gospel of Salvation).

In the book of Revelation, we see that in the very last days, there is a distinction between the two Gospels. They are revealed as two distinct characteristics.

➤ *(Revelation 12:17) And the dragon was enraged with the woman, and he went to make war with the rest of her offspring,* **who keep the commandments of God** *and* **have the testimony of Jesus Christ.**

➤ *(Revelation 14:12) Here is the patience of the saints; here are those who* **keep the commandments of God** *and* **the faith of Jesus.**

Sacrificial Obedience

Remember, Jesus came preaching about the Kingdom of Heaven and sent his disciples out to do the same. Salvation is free for you because Jesus paid the price. Becoming like Him requires your sacrificial obedience. You must take up your cross daily. It is going to take a Wilderness experience to reach the Promised Land. *"And you shall remember that the LORD your God led you all the way these forty years in the Wilderness,* **to humble you and test you, to know what was in your heart,** *whether you would keep His commandments or not" (Deuteronomy 8:2).* There is always a testing of our faith to bring about maturity. *My brethren, count it all joy when*

126

you fall into various trials, knowing that the testing of your faith produces patience. But let patience have its perfect work, that you may be perfect and complete, lacking nothing (James 1:2-4). After being persecuted and stoned Paul reminds us that, *"We must through many tribulations enter the Kingdom of God" (Acts 14:22).*

Faith unto salvation is absolutely FREE! But, the testing of the faith unto perfection is absolutely NOT! This book has emphasized the importance of Scriptural blueprints or patterns. The blueprints say that we must endure trials in the Wilderness to perfect our faith. However, spending 40 years in the Wilderness with a hard heart is a pattern we are admonished to break. Hebrews 3:7-9, 13 warns: *Therefore, as the Holy Spirit says: "Today, if you will hear His voice, do not harden your hearts as in the rebellion, in the day of trial in the Wilderness, where your fathers tested Me, tried Me, And saw My works forty years... but exhort one another daily, while it is called "Today," lest any of you be hardened through the deceitfulness of sin* (lawlessness)." It is going to cost you everything to enter the Kingdom of God, to become like Christ, just like it cost Him everything. Are you willing to make the sacrifice? Are you willing to take up the cross? Are you ready to confess?

To summarize, the Gospel of salvation teaches that salvation is by faith and it is free. The Gospel of the Kingdom teaches that perfection is by works and it costs you everything. (Note: The works only count after salvation). You must take up your cross daily. The good news is that the Kingdom has drawn near. Of course, without the power of the Holy Spirit, neither salvation nor perfection is even possible.

As we move ever closer to David's bold proclamation, you must cultivate your faith that you truly can become like Jesus. This is the secret to building the Spiritual Temple. This may not seem possible to you at the present time because, *"With men this is impossible, but with God all things are possible."* Remember, you have learned that when Elijah comes he will restore all things, including restoring the Kingdom of Heaven. And you will also learn in Chapter 9 that, presently, we have been given only a deposit of the Holy Spirit. Yet we are promised a double-portion outpouring in the future. Stay tuned.

The Government of God

Part of the restoration of the Kingdom of Heaven is the reinstitution of God's government on earth. Government requires laws and you should remember from Chapter 4 that when Elijah comes, he bears a message, **"Remember the Laws of Moses."** John and Jesus said, **"Repent, the Kingdom of Heaven is at hand."** Repent means to turn back to God's Laws. So, to paraphrase, John and Jesus were really saying, "Remember the Law, the Kingdom of Heaven is almost here." At the End of the Age, Elijah says, "Remember the Law, the Kingdom of Heaven is restored!"

At the end of Matthew 7, Jesus ends the Sermon on the Mount by teaching about the benefits or consequences of applying Kingdom principles. *"Therefore whoever hears these sayings of Mine, and does them, I will liken him to a wise man who built his house on the rock… But everyone who hears these sayings of Mine, and does not do them, will be like a foolish man who built his house on the sand" (Matthew 7:24, 26)*. Renew your mind and build upon the solid foundation of faith-based obedience. Let it transform you into the image and likeness of Christ. Be not conformed to this world. Its foundation is made of sand. When the wind and the rain come, everything built upon the world will collapse, and great will be its fall. It is time to unify in the faith and confess, "I can be like Jesus."

Unity of the Faith

By the grace of God, we have been given a gift of wisdom about the mystery of His plan for us. Ephesians 1:10 says, *that in the dispensation of the fullness of the times He might gather together in **one** all things in Christ, both which are in heaven and which are on earth — in Him*. Paul goes on to say in chapter 2 of Ephesians that God's plan is to remove the hatred of men towards one another. Jews and Gentiles alike will be one, *that He might reconcile them both to God in **one body** through the cross, thereby **putting to death the enmity** (Ephesians 2:16)*. What hatred is coming to an end? Answer: The hatred that prevents obedience and unity.

In Genesis, the ultimate picture of unity or oneness is that of marriage, *"the two shall become one flesh."* The Body of Christ must become *"one flesh"* built into one Spiritual House, the Spiritual Temple. *Having been built on the foundation of the apostles and prophets, Jesus Christ Himself being the chief cornerstone, in whom the whole building, being **joined together**, **grows into a holy Temple** in the Lord, in whom you also are being built together for a dwelling place of God in the Spirit (Ephesians 2:20-22).* Each one of us is an individual stone in the Spiritual Temple, Jesus being the Chief Cornerstone. We need to become ONE to build the Temple. We need unity of the faith to become like Christ.

There is one body and one Spirit, just as you were called in one hope of your calling; one Lord, one faith, one baptism; one God and Father of all, who is above all, and through all, and in you all (Ephesians 4:4-6). The understanding and acceptance of this oneness is paramount in establishing unity of the faith. In John 17:11, Jesus prayed for his disciples by saying, *"Holy Father, keep through Your Name those whom You have given Me, that they may be **one** as We are."* Jesus left us to complete the ministry He started. This is what He commissioned us to do and He sent the Holy Spirit to help us fulfill our mission. Paul teaches that the entire five-fold ministry of the Church exists to bring unity, which will make us Christ-like.

> ➤ *(Ephesians 4:11-15) And He Himself gave some to be apostles, some prophets, some evangelists, and some pastors and teachers, for the equipping of the saints for the work of ministry, for the edifying of the body of Christ, till we all come to the **unity of the faith** and of the **knowledge** of the Son of God, to a perfect man, **to the measure of the stature of the fullness of Christ;** that we should no longer be children, tossed to and fro and carried about with every wind of doctrine, by the trickery of men, in the cunning craftiness of deceitful plotting, but, speaking the truth in love, may **grow up** in all things into Him who is the head – Christ.*

Notice that the goal is unity in the faith and unity about the knowledge of the Son of God. It requires one unified people looking at the picture of one unified Savior before anyone grows up into the fullness and the stature of Christ. Good prophecy is like a detailed roadmap. The measure of the stature of the fullness of Christ is our destination. But with an inadequate prophetic roadmap we will not know where we are heading.

Instead of reaching our destination, bad prophecy leads us to poor theology which will inevitably get us lost in a maze of unstable doctrine. Unstable doctrine will always produce disunity; whereas good prophecy will cultivate unity. We must ultimately develop one unified faith inside of Christianity and reject the idea of thousands of denominations. The only way this will happen is with one common doctrine, God's doctrine; so members of the Body will no longer be children, tossed to and fro and carried about with every wind of doctrine, the false doctrines and the trickery of men.

Only through oneness in our faith and the knowledge of the Son of God will we join together and build the holy Temple in the LORD. It will take unified doctrines to fulfill our calling to become like Christ and to build the Spiritual Temple. Jesus is coming back to marry ONE bride and when He returns for His perfect bride, He will dedicate and inhabit ONE Spiritual Temple. And I tell you a great mystery, *"the two shall become one flesh."*

This idea of unity or oneness is not a new concept introduced to the Bible in the New Testament. It was presented right from the beginning. *Therefore a man shall leave his father and mother and be joined to his wife, and they shall become one flesh (Genesis 2:24).* Paul reveals the mystery of this union in Ephesians 5:31-32: *"For this reason a man shall leave his father and mother and be joined to his wife, and the two shall become one flesh." This is a great mystery,* **but I speak concerning Christ and the Church.** Jesus is returning for ONE spotless bride and together we will become "one flesh." To become "one flesh," He must return for only "one bride." It is vital that his segregated bride become unified into ONE body before He gets here. Unity is paramount! It is so fundamental to our faith, that when Jesus was asked about the greatest commandment, He responded first with a statement of unity.

The Greatest Commandment

In Mark 12:28-34, *one of the scribes came, and having heard them reasoning together, perceiving that He had answered them well, asked Him,* **"Which is the first commandment of all?"** *Jesus answered him, "The first of all the*

130

commandments is: *'Hear, O Israel, the* LORD *our God, the* LORD *is one.* *'And you shall love the* LORD *your God with all your heart, with all your soul, with all your mind, and with all your strength.' This is the first command- ment.* *"And the second, like it, is this: 'You shall love your neighbor as your- self.' There is no other commandment greater than these."* So **the scribe said to Him, "Well said, Teacher. You have spoken the truth, for there is one God, and there is no other but He.** *"And to love Him with all the heart, with all the understanding, with all the soul, and with all the strength, and to* **love one's neighbor** *as oneself, is more than all the whole burnt offerings and sacrifices." Now when Jesus saw that he answered wisely, He said to him,* **"You are not far from the Kingdom of God."** *But after that no one dared question Him.*

Many Christians do not recognize that when Jesus answered this question posed by the learned scribe, He first recited the "Shemah" from Deuteronomy 6:4. *"Hear, O Israel: The* LORD *our God, the* LORD *is one!* Shemah means *"to hear, to listen, to obey."* This verse is the watchword of the people of Israel. The Shemah was left out of Matthew's version of the event. Nevertheless, I believe it is the most important part of the answer. Only after proclaiming that the LORD is ONE, did He then con- tinue with the commandments of loving your God and loving your neighbor in verse 5. *"You shall love the* LORD *your God with all your heart, with all your soul, and with all your strength."*

The scribe was satisfied that what Jesus had spoken was truth. Jesus taught exactly what Moses taught in Deuteronomy, which is that there is no other God but He. The LORD is one! Once again, "Shemah" is Hebrew for "hear and obey." Jesus, in His great wisdom, stated that the greatest commandment is to hear and obey the commandment of unity. There is one body, one Spirit, one Lord, one faith, one baptism, and one God and Father of us all. We are to become ONE with God and ONE with our neighbor. Only then will we have perfect love. Jesus under- stood the importance of unity in our quest to be conformed into His image. *"Holy Father, keep through Your Name those whom You have given Me, that they may be* **one** *as We are."* When you truly understand this, as He revealed to the scribe, **"You are not far from the Kingdom of God."**

The Mystery of Unity

Paul teaches us about the unity that will inevitably pervade the Church when God's time has come. He claimed that his understanding about this mystery came to him by revelation; revelation that was not made known to generations before him.

> ➢ *(Ephesians 3:1-6) For this reason I, Paul, the prisoner of Christ Jesus for you Gentiles — if indeed you have heard of the dispensation of the grace of God which was given to me for you, **how that by revelation He made known to me the mystery** (as I have briefly written already, by which, when you read, you may understand my knowledge in the mystery of Christ), which in other ages was not made known to the sons of men, as **it has now been revealed by the Spirit to His holy apostles and prophets: that the Gentiles should be fellow heirs, of the same body, and partakers of His promise in Christ through the Gospel.***

Is the mystery of unity to which Paul is referring that Jews and Gentiles will take part in the same promise from God? The Gentiles are going to receive the same Savior and the same inheritance as the Jews. Is this the mystery to which Paul is referring? The answer is revealed by exploring a few Old Testament passages.

> ➢ *(Leviticus 19:34) The stranger who dwells among you **shall be to you as one born among you**, and you shall love him as yourself; for you were strangers in the land of Egypt: I am the LORD your God.*

> ➢ *(Ezekiel 47:23) "And it shall be that in whatever tribe the stranger dwells, there you shall **give him his inheritance**," says the Lord GOD.*

> ➢ *(Isaiah 52:10) The LORD has made bare His holy arm in the eyes of all the nations; **and all the ends of the earth shall see the salvation of our God.***

The prophets of old were aware that the Messiah was for the Gentiles and that Jews and Gentiles shared a common inheritance. This was not a mystery. But what they did not know was HOW this plan would come to pass. This is the mystery of unity to which Paul is referring. Paul was the first entrusted with the gift of making this mystery clear to the world. *Although I am less than the least of all God's people, this grace was given me: to preach to the Gentiles the unsearchable riches of Christ, **and to make plain to everyone the administration of this mystery,** which for ages past was kept hidden in God, who created all things (Ephesians 3:8-9 NIV).*

Making this mystery clear to the world requires two things:

No. 1: We must define what unity of the faith means.
Paul simply defines the mystery of unity by saying, *to them God willed to make known what are the riches of the glory of this mystery among the Gentiles: **which is Christ in you, the hope of glory** (Colossians 1:27).* Unity of the faith will occur when Believers congeal into one Body, and are prepared to then become one with Christ. How we achieve this unity of the faith is one of the great mysteries of the Kingdom. Nevertheless, we must become one flesh with each other before we can become one flesh with Him; **Christ in you, the hope of glory.**

No. 2: We must define how to make this message of unity clear to the world.
To make the mystery of unity clear to the world, it must first be solved. However, solving God's great mysteries was not left to Paul alone. In Chapter 1, you learned from Matthew 13 that it has been given to **YOU** to know the mysteries of the Kingdom of Heaven. This is why Jesus speaks to us in parables. We have the keys to unlock the mysteries; whereas in ages past they did not.

> ➤ *(Romans 16:25-26) Now to Him who is able to establish you according to my Gospel and the preaching of Jesus Christ, according to the **revelation** of the mystery kept secret since the world began but now has been **made manifest,** and **by the prophetic Scriptures** has been made known to all nations, **according to the commandment** of the everlasting God, **for obedience to the faith.***

In addition to informing us that the knowledge about God's mysteries is now available through the prophetic Scriptures, Paul also teaches us that revelation of these mysteries will produce obedience to the faith. Is Paul teaching a new doctrine? Again, like the Bereans, we can rely on the words of Moses to see if what Paul is saying is true.

> *(Deuteronomy 29:29) The secret things belong to the LORD our God, but those things which are revealed belong to us and to our children forever,* **that we may do all the words of this Law.**

Revelation of God's hidden treasures encourages obedience to the faith. This is why we must diligently strive to uncover the mysteries of the Kingdom of Heaven. The more we discover, the more radical our obedience to God will become. The more obedient we become, the more we will become unified; we'll become like one another and then become like Christ. This is unity of the faith and it is administered through radical, faith-based obedience. This will happen! Jesus is faithful to complete what He started; He is *"the author and finisher of our faith"* (Hebrews 12:2).

> *(Habakkuk 2:2-3) Then the LORD answered me and said: "Write the vision and make it plain on tablets, that he may run who reads it. For the vision is yet for an appointed time; but at the end it will speak, and it will not lie. Though it tarries, wait for it;* **because it will surely come, it will not tarry."**

The Good Steward

It is imperative, however, that we be found trustworthy with these deep secrets of God. *Let a man so consider us, as servants of Christ and stewards of the mysteries of God. Moreover it is required in stewards that one be found faithful (1 Corinthians 4:1-2).* In the parable of the poor steward in Luke 16, Jesus teaches of the fate of the unfaithful manager. A certain rich man had a steward, and an accusation was brought to him that this manager was wasting his goods. He required an account of his management, because under the circumstances, the rich man could no longer trust this man's stewardship. The steward thought to himself, *"What shall I do? For my master is taking the stewardship away from me."* Poor stewardship of God's hidden treasures will cause Him to take what He had given to you and give it to someone who is more faithful. The profound impact of this principle will be most apparent when applied to those in the leadership of the modern-day Church. In the end, pastors and teachers who are not found as faithful stewards will be removed from office and replaced with those who will be more trustworthy with God's treasures.

> KJV *(Jeremiah 23:1-4) Woe be unto the pastors that destroy and scatter the sheep of my pasture! saith the LORD. Therefore thus saith the LORD God of Israel against the pastors that feed my people; Ye have scattered my flock, and driven them away, and have not visited them: behold, I will visit upon you the evil of your doings, saith the LORD. And I will gather the remnant of my flock out of all countries whither I have driven them, and will bring them again to their folds; and they shall be fruitful and increase. And I will set up shepherds over them which shall feed them: and they shall fear no more, nor be dismayed, neither shall they be lacking, saith the LORD.*

When you have absolute obedience to the faith, you will be one with God and one with your brothers; Christ will be fully formed in you. You will be perfect. *The mystery which has been hidden from ages and from generations, but now has been revealed to His saints. To them God willed to make known what are the riches of the glory of this mystery among the Gentiles:* **which is Christ in you,** *the hope of glory. Him we preach,* **warning every man** *and* **teaching every man** *in all wisdom, that we may* **present every man perfect** *in Christ Jesus. To this end I also labor, striving according to His working which works in me mightily (Colossians 1:26-29).* The message that must go forth to all the world, warning them and teaching them, is that Christ must be fully manifest in you, so that you may be perfect at His coming. To be the bride who becomes one flesh with Christ at His second coming, we must become one flesh with our neighbor before He comes. This is the mystery of unity. This is the Gospel of the Kingdom. *And this Gospel of the Kingdom will be preached in all the world as a witness to all the nations, and then the end will come.*

Make the Message Clear

We have been given the role to make this message clear to the world. How do we achieve unity? We must confess with our mouths unto salvation and also believe in our hearts unto righteousness (perfection). This type of confession can only be made with a heart like David's when he made his daring declaration. When we all believe that unity is both possible and an absolute prerequisite before we WILL become like Him, it will transform the Body of Christ. It is your high calling. *Not that I have already attained, or am already* **perfected**; *but I press on, that I may lay hold of that for which Christ Jesus has also laid hold of me (Philippians 3:12).* If you don't believe it now, you will! *Therefore let us, as many as are mature, have this mind; and if in anything you think otherwise, God will reveal even this to you (v. 15).*

Just as Paul said about himself in Ephesians 6:19, *and for me, that utterance may be given to me, that I may open my mouth boldly to make known the mystery of the Gospel.* It has also been given to you to know the mysteries of the Kingdom of Heaven, and to teach them to the world. *But we* (must) *speak the wisdom of God in a mystery, the hidden wisdom which God ordained before the ages for our glory (1 Corinthians 2:7).*

In Matthew 16:19, Jesus said to Peter: *"And I will give you the keys of the Kingdom of Heaven."* We also have the keys to solve the mysteries of the Kingdom of Heaven *which in other ages was not made known to the sons of men, as it has now been revealed by the Spirit to His holy apostles and prophets (Ephesians 3:5).* One thing is for certain, God will eventually reveal His mysteries.

> ➤ *(Amos 3:7) Surely the* LORD GOD *does nothing, unless He reveals His secret to His servants the prophets.*

There are still mysteries to be revealed now and in the future. These mysteries will be uncovered all the way up to the very last days. It appears that the mystery of God is ended at the sound of the last trumpet, the second coming of Jesus Christ. *Behold, I tell you a mystery: We shall not all sleep, but we shall all be changed — in a moment, in the twinkling of an eye, at* **the last trumpet.** *For the trumpet will sound, and the dead will be raised incorruptible, and we shall be changed (1 Corinthians 15:51-52).* The last trumpet is the seventh trumpet blown by the seventh angel of Revelation 10:7. *But in the days of the sounding of* **the seventh angel** (the seventh trumpet), *when he is about to sound, the* **mystery of God would be finished,** *as He declared to His servants the prophets.* But until then, take joy in discovering the mysteries of the Kingdom of Heaven.

Paul's Progressive Message

In 1 Corinthians 2, Paul makes the stark contrast between his ministry to the lost soul or newborn Believer, and his ministry to the mature Believer. This is Paul's progressive message throughout his ministry. In verse 2, to the lost or weaker Believer he says, *"For I determined not to know anything among you except Jesus Christ and Him crucified."* He wants the demonstration of the Holy Spirit to cultivate faith in the power of God, not faith in the wisdom of men. On the other hand, the message to the mature Believer is much different.

> ➤ **(1 Corinthians 2:6, 7, 9-10)** *"However, we speak wisdom among those who are mature- -the wisdom of God in a mystery, the hidden wisdom which God ordained before the ages for **our glory**- -Eye has not seen, nor ear heard, Nor have entered into the heart of man the things which God has prepared for those who love Him. **But God has revealed them to us through His Spirit. For the Spirit searches all things, yes, the deep things of God."***

To the mature in the faith, the Spirit makes the deep things of God knowable. We can hardly imagine what God has in store for us. Before Christ, He had hidden His secrets from past generations. But now He has made the deep things of God available, revealing them by His Spirit to those who are mature enough to appreciate them. *When He, the Spirit of truth, has come, He will guide you into all truth! (John 16:13).* And He does it all for our glory. Our Glory! Are you, who are already saved, content with every sermon you hear ending with the call to salvation? Or are you hungry for the deeper things of God?

The Prophet Isaiah inquires about those who will receive the deeper things of God. Isaiah 28:9 asks, *"Whom will he teach knowledge? And whom will he make to understand the message? Those just weaned from milk? Those just drawn from the breasts?"* No! Those just weaned from milk are not mature enough for meat. They cannot discern the deeper things of God, and so would get spiritual indigestion if fed "meat." The writer of Hebrews describes those not prepared to digest the "meat" of God's Word this way. *For everyone who partakes only of milk is unskilled in the word of righteousness, for he is a babe. But solid food belongs to those who are of full age, that is, those who by reason of use have their senses exercised to discern both good and evil (Hebrews 5:13-14).* Are you prepared to receive revelation about the deeper things of God? Are you ready to digest the "meat" of God's Word? If so, listen to the parables of Jesus Christ.

The Parables of Jesus & the Mysteries of the Kingdom of Heaven

Jesus taught His disciples about the Kingdom of Heaven using many parables so He could relate heavenly concepts with earthly words. Those who did not believe could not comprehend the parables. *And He said, "To you it has been given to know the mysteries of the Kingdom of God, but to the rest it is given in parables, that 'Seeing they may not see, and hearing they may not understand (Luke 8:10).'"* As His disciples, we should be able to perceive and understand the secret treasures hidden in His parables. *All these things Jesus spoke to the multitude in parables; and without a parable He did not speak to them, that it might be fulfilled which was spoken by the prophet, saying: "I will open My mouth in parables; I will utter things kept secret from the foundation of the world (Matthew 13:34-35)."*

LORD, hear our prayers. As we seek your face and search your deepest mysteries, guide us into all truth and protect us from deception. You say "seek and we shall find." LORD, we are seeking the mysteries of the Kingdom of Heaven. Amen.

We are progressing to an age of maturity (solid food) in Christianity and much will be available to us. But Jesus warned in Luke 12:48, *"For everyone to whom much is given, from him much will be required; and to whom much has been committed, of him they will ask the more."* It has been given to you to know the mysteries of, and you have been given the keys to, the Kingdom of Heaven (Matthew 13:11, 16:19). Because you have been given so much, much is now required from you. But just as Jesus warned in the first century, guard yourself from those who wish to steal away your key. *"Woe to you Lawyers! For you have taken away the key of knowledge. You did not enter in yourselves, and those who were entering in you hindered"* (Luke 11:52). In Luke, lawyers are the teachers of doctrine. Just as in the first century, if you get enamored with the doctrines and commandments of men, you will lose the **key.**

What to do with the Talents?

Instead of squandering the gift of this key, let us, as faithful stewards, put the key in the door to the Kingdom of Heaven. Let us unlock one of its mysteries using the parable of the Talents. In Matthew 25:14-15 Jesus explains, *"For the Kingdom of Heaven is like a man traveling to a far country, who called his own servants and delivered his goods to them. And to one he gave five talents, to another two, and to another one, to each according to his own ability; and immediately he went on a journey."* Jesus teaches in parables to reveal things kept secret from the foundation of the world. Now using the key, let's solve the mystery.

The man traveling to a far country represents the Lord who has ascended into heaven where He waits for the restoration of all things. The servants are Believers who are given talents, entrusted as stewards of a certain treasure. We need to be found faithful with this treasure. A Greek "talent" is equivalent to either 82 ¼ pounds of silver or 164 ½ pounds of gold; and the Hebrew talent is equivalent to approximately 94 ½ and 189 pounds, respectively. So we are talking about a significant amount of wealth. In yet another parable, Jesus said that the Kingdom of Heaven is like a treasure hidden in a field. The mysteries of the Kingdom of Heaven are like hidden treasures.

> ➤ **(Isaiah 45:3)** *I will give you the treasures of darkness and hidden riches of secret places, that you may know that I, the* LORD, *Who call you by your name, Am the God of Israel.*

What will you do with these hidden treasures, these mysteries, when you find them? Will you be a good steward? *Let a man so consider us, as servants of Christ and stewards of the mysteries of God. Moreover it is required in stewards that one be found faithful* (1 Corinthians 4:1-2).

The talents represent a portion of the man's Kingdom (treasure) and he is testing his servants to see if they will be good stewards of his fortune. The Lord has done the same for us. The talents represent the hidden mysteries of the Kingdom. He left us with some pieces to the puzzle and when He returns, we should have completed the picture. *"Then he who had received the five talents went and traded with them, and made another five talents. And likewise he who had received two gained two more also. But he who had received one went and dug in the ground, and hid his lord's money"* (Matthew 25:16-18). There is sharp contrast between those who seek and those who hide under a rock. When the Lord returns, we will have to give an account for what we have done with what He has given us. And to whom much is given, much is required. If He told us that it has been given for us to know the mysteries of the Kingdom of Heaven, and He has; we ought to solve His mysteries before He returns. In verses 19-23 of Matthew 25 Jesus, represented by the lord of the servants, came to settle accounts with them. He rewarded his faithful servants who have solved the mysteries (doubled their fortunes). *"Well done, good and faithful servant; you were faithful over a few things, I will make you ruler over many things. Enter into the joy of your lord."* In verse 26, He said of the servant who hid from the Lord's revelation (buried the money in the ground), *"You wicked and lazy servant, you knew that I reap where I have not sown, and gather where I have not scattered seed."* In verse 29, he took even what little he gave to this wicked servant and passed it to the faithful servant who created the most wealth (solved the most mysteries). *"For to everyone who has, more will be given, and he will have abundance; but from him who does not have, even what he has will be taken away."*

The wicked servant did nothing with his master's deposit because he was afraid; *I knew you to be a hard man, reaping where you have not sown, and gathering where you have not scattered seed* (v. 24). Remember this Kingdom mystery about reaping and sowing. We will apply its secrets in Chapter 9, "Passing the Mantle." The lesson behind "reaping where you have not sown" emphasizes the importance of building precept upon precept in our understanding of God's mysteries. Over the past 2000 years, the Lord has given us the opportunity to build our understanding of the Kingdom of Heaven from generation to generation. If we receive a treasure, mystery, or revelation about the Kingdom from a past generation, it should be "invested in" and expanded upon in the next generation. *"But he who received seed (word of the Kingdom) on the good ground is he who hears the word and understands it, who indeed bears fruit and produces: some a hundredfold, some sixty, some thirty" (Matthew 13:23).* If it is not "multiplied," then we are not being good stewards.

Precept upon Precept

The LORD, speaking about the End of the Age in Isaiah 28:9-10 says, *"Whom will he teach knowledge? And whom will he make to understand the message? Those just weaned from milk? Those just drawn from the breasts? For precept must be upon precept, precept upon precept, line upon line, line upon line, here a little, there a little."* Has the Body of Christ been weaned off milk? Can the Church Body decipher the deep things of God or are they still in need of the basic elements. *For though by this time you ought to be teachers, you need someone to teach you again the first principles of the oracles of God; and you have come to need milk and not solid food. For everyone who partakes only of milk is unskilled in the word of righteousness, for he is a babe. But solid food belongs to those who are of full age, that is, those who by reason of use have their senses exercised to discern both good and evil (Hebrews 5:12-14).* Has the Body of Christ been "good and faithful" or "wicked and lazy"? Has it come to need milk again (and again) and not solid food? Unfortunately, similar to the condition of the religious leadership in the first century, over the past 2000 years, many who have claimed to be pastoring the Church have actually been leading members away from the Kingdom of Heaven. They are doing this by feeding their sheep a steady diet of milk, which does not allow the saints to distinguish the doctrines of men from the commandments of God. *But woe to you, scribes and Pharisees, hypocrites! For you shut up the Kingdom of Heaven against men; for you neither go in yourselves, nor do you allow those who are entering to go in (Matthew 23:13).* Now is the time for **YOU** to digest the "meat" of God, and uncover the mysteries of the Kingdom of Heaven. I pray *The Heart of David* is helping build your understanding of God's Kingdom, precept upon precept.

Now let's review a similar parable in the Gospel of Luke. You will notice striking similarities to the parable of the talents. Luke's account contains precious details not elaborated in Matthew. Also notice an interesting detail about the unfaithful servant. Matthew tells of only two groups of people, both of them servants (Believers). One is faithful, the other wicked. In Matthew 25:30, the lord takes away the talent from the wicked and lazy servant, gives it to the most profitable, and says, *"Cast the unprofitable servant into the outer darkness. There will be weeping and gnashing of teeth."* In Luke, he simply takes the *"mina"* from the wicked servant and rebukes him. He is not cast into outer darkness. However, Luke also speaks of a third party, the unbeliever and his fate.

*And Jesus said to him, "**Today salvation** has come to this house, because he also is a son of Abraham; "for the Son of Man has come to seek and to save that which was **lost**."* Now as they heard these things, He spoke another parable, because He was near Jerusalem and because **they thought the Kingdom of God would appear immediately** *(Luke 19:9-11).* In the First Century Church they were as confused as they are today, thinking that salvation would impart the Kingdom of Heaven. To correct this misunderstanding, Jesus gave us, in the form of a parable, a blueprint of His plan. Before He left to take His place at the right hand of the Father, He told us that the Kingdom was at hand; but that it would not appear immediately. He left us with a **deposit of treasure**, enough to do business for Him, and instructs us to get to work. When He returns, He will take account of how we handled His business. When the Kingdom comes, Jesus will have one question for you: "What did you do with My treasure while I was away?"

The Nobleman

*Therefore He said: "A certain nobleman went into a far country **to receive for himself a Kingdom and to return.** So he called ten of his servants* (Believers), *delivered to them ten minas* (approximately ten pounds of silver), *and said to them, '**Do business till I come**.'"* *(Luke 19:12-13)* The Lord has gone to heaven and is waiting for Elijah to complete the restoration before His return. He has left us with a treasure and commanded us to **"Do business till He comes."** He intends for us to take what He has left with us and expand His ministry while He is gone. We must solve the mysteries. Make no excuses; He has made His business known to us and He will hold us accountable. *"No longer do I call you servants, for a servant does not know what his master is doing; but I have called you friends, for all things that I heard from My Father I have made known to you"* (John 15:15). To be found as faithful stewards, just like Jesus, we must be about our Father's business. *And He said to them, "Why did you seek Me? Did you not know that I must be about My Father's business?" (Luke 2:49).*

"But his citizens (unbelievers) *hated him, and sent a delegation after him, saying, 'We will not have this man to reign over us.' "And so it was that when he returned, having received the Kingdom, he then commanded these servants, to whom he had given the money, to be called to him, that he might know how much every man had gained by trading. "Then came the first, saying, 'Master, your mina has earned ten minas.' "And he said to him, 'Well done, good servant; because you were faithful in a very little, have authority over ten cities.' "And the second came, saying, 'Master, your mina has earned five minas.' "Likewise he said to him, 'You also be over five cities'"* (Luke 19:14-19). You can see that this is an identical Kingdom principle as in the parable of the talents. When you have proven faithful with little, He will give you charge over many things.

"Then another came, saying, 'Master, here is your mina, which I have kept put away in a handkerchief. 'For I feared you, because you are an austere man. You collect what you did not deposit, and reap what you did not sow.' "And he said to him, 'Out of your own mouth I will judge you, you wicked servant. You knew that I was an austere man, collecting what I did not deposit and reaping what I did not sow. 'Why then did you not put my money in the bank, that at my coming I might have collected it with interest?' "And he said to those who stood by, 'Take the mina from him, and give it to him who has ten minas.' (But they said to him, 'Master, he has ten minas.') For I say to you, that to everyone who has will be given; and from him who does not have, even what he has will be taken away from him. 'But bring here those enemies of mine (unbelievers), *who did not want me to reign over them, and slay them before me'"* (Luke 19:20-27). Again we see the same principles applied. The wicked servant does nothing with what he has been entrusted. He is a poor steward.

Even what little he had is taken away and given to the one with the most. In His Kingdom economy, the Lord takes from the unfaithful servant and gives to the faithful servant. Also, notice again the Kingdom mystery of reaping where he had not sown. The wicked servant who does nothing to improve his master's business is judged by his very own knowledge that his master "reaps where he has not sown." *"Out of your own mouth I will judge you, you wicked servant."* We must acknowledge what our Lord expects from us and build His Kingdom precept upon precept. Your heart will leap with joy when you apply the Kingdom principle of "reaping where you have not sown" to your true calling revealed in the prayer of David's heart. By doing this, you will get a glimpse at the magnitude of your ministry.

Servants of the Master (Believers) will always fall into two categories, depending on the choices they make. The servant found faithful will inherit a ruler's reward. *"Well done, good servant; because you were faithful in a very little, have authority over more."* The servant, who does nothing to build his Master's business because he is afraid, inherits citizenship. *"From him who does not have, even what he has will be taken away."* However, Luke also mentions the unbeliever who the Master characterizes as, *"enemies of mine."* The fate of this third group is eternal separation; *"slay them before me."*

Summary

Throughout this chapter, we have investigated a number of the "mysteries of the Kingdom of Heaven." We started by defining the Kingdom of Heaven/Kingdom of God and the Gospel of the Kingdom. We have explored secrets such as sinlessness (perfection) and the power of conversion. We entertained the possibility of being corporately conformed into the image of Christ, and now understand that we must cultivate our faith so that this can happen. We identified faith-based obedience and distinguished it from works of Law. We learned that it is through trials that we enter the Kingdom of God. We differentiated the Gospel of the Kingdom from the Gospel of salvation, and identified the government of God. We also discovered the importance of oneness and unity of the faith. We saw how unity is represented by the "one flesh" of marriage, and also how it is obtained by good prophecy and faith-based obedience. We confirmed that there are mysteries of God waiting to be solved up until the very end of days. We also examined the consequences of the unfaithful steward. We learned that Paul had a progressive ministry; he presented a simple message to the lost and deep revelation to the mature. We learned that the Spirit of God reveals His deep mysteries for our glory.

As we progressed on our expedition, we added a few other discoveries in our quest for knowledge about the Kingdom. The Kingdom does not come as an immediate consequence of our eternal security. We recognized the Lord's treasures (talents) as mysteries of the Kingdom and acknowledged that we have the keys (authority) to unlock their secrets. We accepted that we have been given this authority and the responsibility to uncover these mysteries. We learned that we have been equipped to "do the Lord's business" until He returns, and that we must be fruitful and multiply what He has left with us. If we are faithful with little, He will give us much more. We should know our Master's business because He calls us friend. We are charged with building His Kingdom precept upon precept, line upon line; reaping even where we have not sown. And because we acknowledge that the Lord reaps where He has not sown, it will be to our judgment if we are not faithful stewards of the Master's business (ministry).

In the next chapter, we make the final turn. It begins the home stretch on this journey we have taken together. It represents one of the last few steps before we reach the Promised Land. In it, we will build upon the precepts laid down thus far, and prepare ourselves for a life-changing declaration. *For indeed, the Kingdom of God is within you.* After the Prayer of David, we have only to describe the global impact it will create and the role it plays on God's prophetic calendar. This final stretch, however, is the critical link between where you are today and where you are going. It is about your personal transformation as God's plans for humanity unfold. It is also about your personal responsibility for the metamorphosis of the body of Christ into the spotless bride. Will you voluntarily conform or be forced? Remember, either way, God will finish what He started. Whether willingly or kicking and screaming, you will conform! *Stand therefore, having girded your waist with truth, having put on the breastplate of righteousness, and having shod your feet with the preparation of the Gospel of peace. (Ephesians 6:14-15).*

Let's prepare to pray the Prayer of David.

Chapter Six

Preparing to Pray the Prayer of David

"The Kingdom of God does not come with observation;
For indeed, the Kingdom of God is within you."
Luke 17:20, 21

I n this chapter, we will explore some of the Lord's parables in search of the qualities needed to be cultivated in every disciple of Jesus Christ who is serious about pursuing the Kingdom. Jesus would say, *"The Kingdom of Heaven is like…"* The critical character traits that must be attained to become like Christ are found in these lessons. If you are born again, you **can** become like Christ, *for indeed, the Kingdom of God is within you!* At the end, we will join these crucial character traits with key principles about the Kingdom from Chapter 5. *Therefore gird up the loins of your mind, be sober, and rest your hope fully upon the grace that is to be brought to you at the revelation of Jesus Christ (1 Peter 1:13).*

New & Old

Jesus taught many parables in Matthew 13 and, afterwards, He said to his disciples, *"Have you understood all these things?" They said to Him, "Yes, Lord." Then He said to them, "Therefore every scribe instructed concerning the Kingdom of Heaven is like a householder who brings out of his **treasure*** *things new and old" (vs. 51-52).* A scribe in the first century would be comparable to a Biblical theologian of today. The first thing you need to acknowledge is that if a scribe (or theologian who knows the Law, letter for letter) needs to be instructed concerning the Kingdom of Heaven, then so do you. The householder's **"treasure"** contains the mysteries of the Kingdom. If we are to build His Kingdom, we must uncover its mysteries one after the other. Jesus taught in parables to help us uncover these mysteries. Once instructed *"concerning the Kingdom of Heaven,"* you will become equipped to connect the significance of what is revealed when you uncover both His *new and old* mysteries. You will be a valuable asset, capable of making significant contributions, helping to build the Kingdom of Heaven — line upon line, and precept upon precept. The entire Kingdom must be *built on the foundation of the apostles and prophets, Jesus Christ Himself being the chief cornerstone (Ephesians 2:20).*

The revelation of the mystery of building the Kingdom was kept secret since the world began until it became *manifest by the prophetic Scriptures (Romans 16:26).* As the master of the house, you must bring out of your treasure things new and old. It is through new revelation about the Scriptures of old that we unearth secrets of the Kingdom of Heaven. Nevertheless, all new revelation remains subject to what has come before. It cannot stand alone because *the spirits of the prophets are subject to the prophets. For God is not the author of confusion but of peace (1 Corinthians 14:32-33).* **New revelation must be built upon the old**, line upon line, precept upon precept. We must be **instructed** concerning the Kingdom of Heaven.

The Forceful Lay Hold of it

We must build the Kingdom line upon line, precept upon precept. What kind of person does it take to build the Kingdom of Heaven? *From the days of John the Baptist until now, the Kingdom of Heaven has been forcefully advancing, and **forceful men** lay hold of it (Matthew 11:12 NIV).* The Kingdom is advancing like a tsunami. It cannot be held back. Only those who aggressively seek the Kingdom will lay hold of it. *But seek first the Kingdom of God and His righteousness, and all these things shall be added to* you *(Matthew 6:33)*. It is like a mustard seed which is the smallest of seeds, but once planted it is like a pervasive weed. It takes over everything in its path and provides the sustenance of life. It spreads like yeast through dough, leavening every morsel. However, like the mustard seed and the yeast, the Kingdom is imperceptible at the onset. This stealthy characteristic may be what makes it so difficult to discern in whom the Kingdom is advancing. Nevertheless, after it has taken root, whether visible or not, it can't be stopped. We must be **forceful** to **advance** the Kingdom which will eventually overtake everything else.

Stewardship

"The Law and the prophets were until John. Since that time the Kingdom of God has been preached, and everyone is pressing into it (Luke 16:16). Before this powerful statement in Luke 16, Jesus tells a story of a man who has charge over his masters business. The master finds out that this man is a poor steward of his treasure and makes arrangements to release him. When the poor steward discovers he is losing his position, he arranges to find favor with those who owe his master. He changes their bill of debt to his master, making it appear that these debtors owe the master much less, hoping in return that they will take care of him after he gets fired. The master discovers his evil plot and comments, in verse 8, about how shrewd the evildoers of this age are. *"For the sons of this world are more shrewd in their generation than the sons of light."* They will receive their just reward in the world to come. No one can serve two masters. You either serve God or you serve money. We are expected to be good stewards with what God has entrusted to us. *Let a man so consider us, as servants of Christ and stewards of the mysteries of God. Moreover it is required in stewards that one be found faithful (1 Corinthians 4:1-2).* If we are ensnared with the attractions of the world, we will not have enough time or energy remaining to become skilled at cultivating the mysteries of the Kingdom. No one can serve two masters. If we wish to unlock the secrets of the Kingdom of Heaven, we must shun the lures of the world and be **good stewards** of God's mysteries.

Jesus taught the parable about stewardship in the presence of the religious leaders who had a love of money and hypocrisy towards God. They were not faithful in feeding the people the Word of God. The Lord characterized this type of leader in Mark 7:6-7 by saying, *"Well did Isaiah prophesy of you hypocrites, as it is written: 'This people honors Me with their lips, but their heart is far from Me. And in vain they worship Me, teaching as doctrines the commandments of men.'"* In Matthew 23:13, Jesus warned about the hypocritical religious leadership of the day, *"But woe to you, scribes and Pharisees, hypocrites! For you shut up the Kingdom of Heaven against men; for you neither go in yourselves, nor do you allow those who are entering to go in.* In the last days before the Lord's return, leaders of the very same persuasion will be removed from office for unfaithful service to God's people. The people will have been **"scattered"** into thousands of denominations (at present, there are approximately 33,830 Christian denominations). Denominational religions, boasting varying doctrines, are the greatest enemy to unity of the faith.

> ➤ KJV *(Jeremiah 23:1-4) Woe be unto the pastors that destroy and scatter the sheep of my pasture! saith the LORD. Therefore thus saith the LORD God of Israel **against the pastors that feed my people**; Ye have **scattered my flock**, and driven them away, and have not visited them: behold, I will visit upon you the evil of your doings, saith the LORD. And I will gather the remnant of my flock out of all countries whither I have driven them, and will bring them again to their folds; and they shall be fruitful and increase. And I will **set up shepherds over them which shall feed them**: and they shall fear no more, nor be dismayed, neither shall they be lacking, saith the LORD.*

If, as a pastor or leader, you are not feeding the people with the full counsel of God's Word, you will be removed from office. *My brethren, let not many of you become teachers, knowing that we shall receive a stricter judgment (James 3:1).* Leaders must be **faithful servants** who **avoid hypocrisy** to lay hold of the Kingdom of Heaven.

If you won't hear Moses and the prophets...

Later in Luke 16, Jesus compared the lives of a rich man and a poor man. After death, the rich man is burning in Hades while the poor man sits with Abraham. The rich man, although he refused to help the poor while alive, begs for the poor man to reach into Hades and wet the tip of his tongue with a drop of water. But it is too late for him; his condition is permanent. The rich man begs one other thing; "Please resurrect the poor man and send him to my father's house, where I have five brothers. His testimony may save them from the same torment as I." Abraham's reply may astound you.

> ➤ *(Luke 16:29-31)* '*They have Moses and the prophets; let them hear them.*' "*And he said, 'No, father Abraham; but if one goes to them from the dead, they will repent.*' "*But he said to him,* '**If they do not hear Moses and the prophets, neither will they be persuaded though one rise from the dead.**'"

Jesus said the same thing when talking with the Pharisees. He said if you don't believe Moses, you won't believe me because Moses wrote about me. Moses said, "*The secret things belong to the LORD our God, but those things which are revealed belong to us and to our children forever, that we may do all the words of this Law*" (Deuteronomy 29:29). Without the foundation of Moses and the prophets, even sending a resurrected dead man will not convince stubborn men of the truth. (Isn't that the truth?)

As for you the Believer, without building on the foundations of Moses and the prophets, you cannot uncover the deep and hidden treasures of the Kingdom. Kingdom business is founded on the secrets hidden in the Law and the prophets. Are you ready to be a wise and faithful steward? Open your mind to the words of Moses and the prophets and cast away the treasures of the Kingdom no longer. It has been given to you to know the mysteries of the Kingdom of Heaven. If you will not be a good steward, the treasure will be taken from you and given to another. "*Therefore I say to you, the Kingdom of God will be taken from you and given to a nation bearing the fruits of it*" (Matthew 21:43). If you want to discover the secrets of the Kingdom, **build your foundation on Moses and the Prophets.**

True Treasure: Kingdom of Heaven or earthly riches?

If you are concerned about the riches of this world, you will NEVER be able to uncover the mysteries. *"Children, how hard it is for those who trust in riches to enter the Kingdom of God! It is easier for a camel to go through the eye of a needle than for a rich man to enter the Kingdom of God"* (Mark 10:24-25). If you want the riches of the Kingdom of Heaven, you must be willing to sacrifice everything and search for them. *"Again, the Kingdom of Heaven is like treasure hidden in a field, which a man found and hid; and for joy over it he goes and sells all that he has and buys that field"* (Matthew 13:44). You have the keys to the Kingdom; *"Seek, and you will find; knock, and it will be opened to you. For everyone who asks receives, and he who seeks finds, and to him who knocks it will be opened"* (Luke 11:9-10). If you don't ask you will not receive. Jesus said in 1 John 2:15, *"Do not love the world or the things in the world. If anyone loves the world, the love of the Father is not in him."* If you are *asking, seeking, and knocking,* you must **be ready to sacrifice all earthly riches** to *receive, find, and open* the Kingdom of Heaven.

Become like a Child

Unless your righteousness exceeds the righteousness of the scribes and Pharisees, you will by no means enter the Kingdom of Heaven" (Matthew 5:20). Like a child, you must be pure, innocent, humble, and genuine in your search for the mysteries of the Kingdom. You cannot be in search of riches and personal gain or you will be shut out. *"Assuredly, I say to you, unless you are converted and become as little children, you will by no means enter the Kingdom of Heaven"* (Matthew 18:3). As **innocent** as a child, we must be **genuine** in pursuit of the Kingdom.

Holiness: A Peculiar People.
Can you tell the difference?

One of the mysteries of the Kingdom reveals the essential component of holiness or separation. You simply cannot look like everyone else. You should be radical! Jesus surrendered His life that we might be different from all other people. *Who gave himself for us, that he might redeem us from all iniquity, and purify unto himself a* **peculiar people, zealous of good works** *(Titus 2:14* KVJ*)*. It is a "peculiar people" who believe that Jesus is Messiah, and who are also zealous for good works. This is especially true when they understand that "good works" refers to God's commandments. As you learned earlier, Hebrew for good works is "Mitzvoth," God's commandments. However, in the first century, it was quite common for Believers to follow the Law of Moses. As a matter of fact, it was the norm. They looked and acted like each other, but were very different from the world. *And when they heard it, they glorified the Lord. And they said to him, "You see, brother, how many myriads* (thousands upon thousands) *of Jews there are who have* **believed***, and they are all* **zealous for the Law"** *(Acts 21:20)*. It is **"a peculiar people"** (who look different or set-apart) from the world and who chase after the Kingdom of Heaven.

It is also a peculiar mystery that it is possible to be no different than the world, and yet appear holy. Paul speaking of Israel in Romans 10:2 displayed this sad deception. *For I bear them witness that they have a zeal for God, but not according to knowledge.* Yet, the imposters will be found right along side His saints till the very end. *"Again, the Kingdom of Heaven is like a dragnet that was cast into the sea and gathered some of every kind, which, when it was full, they drew to shore; and they sat down and gathered the good into vessels, but threw the bad away. So it will be at the end of the age. The angels will come forth, separate the wicked from among the just"* *(Matthew 13:47-49)*. The righteous may be growing alongside the unrighteous, and you may never even know it. When you are sitting in Church this week, look to the left and to the right. Some of those so-called brothers may be the ones betraying you in the end. They are fervent for God, but not according to knowledge. They appear to be seeking after God with all their hearts, but inside they are lovers of iniquity. *"And because Lawlessness will abound, the love of many will grow cold"* *(Matthew 24:12)*. *"Now brother will betray brother to death, and a father his child; and children will rise up against parents and cause them to be put to death"* *(Mark 13:12)*. I am not telling you this so that you will become paranoid; but rather, so that you will be watchful and use discernment in your decisions about with whom you associate. We must use **great discernment** in pursuit of the Kingdom of Heaven.

Remember your high calling. You were chosen to do even greater works than Christ, and the world hates that. You must come out of the world and be holy. Separate yourself unto the Lord. In John 15:18-20, Jesus said, *"If the world hates you, you know that it hated Me before it hated you.* *"If you were of the world, the world would love its own. Yet because you are not of the world, but I chose you out of the world, therefore the world hates you.* *"Remember the word that I said to you, 'A servant is not greater than his master.' If they persecuted Me, they will also persecute you. If they kept My word, they will keep yours also."* Be prepared to be **persecuted** in pursuit of the Kingdom.

You will know Mine by their fruit

*"You did not choose Me, but I chose you and appointed you that you should go and **bear fruit**, and that your fruit should remain, that whatever you ask the Father in My name He may give you.* *"These things I command you, that you love one another"* (John 15:16-17). Jesus taught us the parable about the wheat and the tares in order to reveal this valuable secret about the Kingdom. Some may appear holy; but you will only truly know them by their fruit.

Another parable He put forth to them, saying: "The Kingdom of Heaven is like a man who sowed good seed in his field; *"but while men slept, his enemy came and sowed tares among the wheat and went his way.* *"But when the grain had sprouted and produced a crop, then the tares also appeared.* *"So the servants of the owner came and said to him, 'Sir, did you not sow good seed in your field? How then does it have tares?'* *"He said to them, 'An enemy has done this.'* *The servants said to him, 'Do you want us then to go and gather them up?'* *"But he said, 'No, lest while you gather up the tares you also uproot the wheat with them.* *'Let both grow together until the harvest, and at the time of harvest I will say to the reapers, "First gather together the tares and bind them in bundles to burn them, but gather the wheat into my barn"* (Matthew 13:24-30).

Wheat and tares appear almost identical while they are growing alongside one another. They are most distinguishable when the wheat sprouts its berry (fruit), and the tare remains a fruitless weed. Jesus explained this to us in His own words. Those who have eyes to see let them see.

He answered and said to them: "He who sows the good seed is the Son of Man. "The field is the world, the good seeds are the sons of the Kingdom, but the tares are the sons of the wicked one. "The enemy who sowed them is the devil, the harvest is the end of the age, and the reapers are the angels. "Therefore as the tares are gathered and burned in the fire, so it will be at the end of this age" (Matthew 13:37-40).

Again, the interesting thing about tares is that they look similar to wheat until the time comes that they should be putting forth fruit. The tares bear no fruit; they are worthless. Jesus says that you will know Mine (His true followers) by their fruit, and that the tares (the imitators) are to be thrown into the fire. Those truly seeking the Kingdom will **bear much good fruit.**

The Cost

The Kingdom of Heaven comes with a price. *"We must through many tribulations enter the Kingdom of God"* (Acts 14:22). For the Body of Christ to be transformed into His image, we must be mistreated by the outside world and, also in many cases, by our own brothers. *Blessed are those who are persecuted for righteousness' sake, for theirs is the Kingdom of Heaven (Matthew 5:10).* As Paul says, we must offer our lives as "living sacrifices," and sacrifices are 100% committed. For instance, you can't half sacrifice an animal. *"He who loves father or mother more than Me is not worthy of Me. And he who loves son or daughter more than Me is not worthy of Me. And he who does not take his cross and follow after Me is not worthy of Me"* (Matthew 10:37-38). However, when you do make the sacrifice, the rewards are great in this life, and in the life to come. *So He said to them, "Assuredly, I say to you, there is no one who has left house or parents or brothers or wife or children, for the sake of the Kingdom of God, "who shall not receive many times more* **in this present time,** *and in the* **age to come** *eternal life"* (Luke 18:29-30). While you are counting the cost, be assured that it is impossible for the mysteries of God to fall on fertile soil (that which is properly prepared to receive it) and not bear fruit. *"But he who received seed on the good ground is he who hears the word and understands it, who indeed bears fruit and produces: some a hundredfold, some sixty, some thirty"* (Matthew 13:23). We must offer our lives as **living sacrifices** in pursuit the Kingdom of Heaven.

Trust what is ahead, don't ever look back

In Philippians 3:13, Paul said, *but one thing I do, forgetting those things which are behind and reaching forward to those things which are ahead.* This is something Lot's wife did not do.

> ➢ *(Genesis 19:26) But his wife looked back behind him, and she became a pillar of salt.*

Lot's wife could not keep from looking back at her old life. Because of this, she was incinerated into a pile of mineral salts by the fire of the LORD. Israel grumbled and complained because they thought that life was better in Egypt. At least Egypt provided food and water they complained. Their unwillingness to trust in God's provision in the Wilderness, and His promised inheritance, cost them 40 years of fruitless wandering. And everyone over 20 years of age, except Joshua and Caleb, lost their lives before reaching the Promised Land.

But it has happened to them according to the true proverb: "A dog returns to his own vomit," and, "a sow, having washed, to her wallowing in the mire" (2 Peter 2:22). It would be better to have never known the call of God, than to have heard His call and turned your back. *For it is impossible for those who were once enlightened, and have tasted the heavenly gift, and have become partakers of the Holy Spirit, and have tasted the good word of God and the powers of the age to come, if they fall away, to renew them again to repentance, since they crucify again for themselves the Son of God, and put Him to an open shame (Hebrews 6:4-6).*

It has been given to you to know the mysteries of the Kingdom of Heaven. However, you will be persecuted as you press on to lay hold of them. No matter how difficult it gets, don't ever stop advancing. Jesus said in Luke 9:62, *"No one, having put his hand to the plow, and looking back, is fit for the Kingdom of God."* In complete humility, Paul said, *Brethren, I do not count myself to have apprehended; but one thing I do, **forgetting those things which are behind** and reaching forward to those things which are ahead, I press toward the goal for the prize of the upward call of God in Christ Jesus (Philippians 3:13-14).* While we are chasing after the Kingdom, we must **never look back!**

Forgiveness

"Therefore the Kingdom of Heaven is like a certain king who wanted to settle accounts with his servants (Matthew 18:23). One servant owed such large debt (ten thousand talents) that he could never in 100 lifetimes repay his master. For you to understand the magnitude of this debt, we are talking about the modern-day equivalent of somewhere between 100 million and billions of dollars. (The total depends on whether we calculate talents of silver or gold.)

Moved to compassion for this servant, **the king forgives his entire debt.** This is the exact perspective you should have when you consider what debt the blood of Jesus has paid personally for you. You have been forgiven an unfathomable amount and the more you are forgiven, the more you should love. In the LORD'S Prayer, we ask the LORD to *forgive us our debts* **as we forgive the debts of others.** However, in spite of the great mercy bestowed upon him by the king, this ungrateful servant sends a debtor of his own to prison. The debtor owed him just a trivial amount; but because he too was incapable of paying the debt, (in this case 100 *denarii,* the equivalent of about 14 ounces of silver or approximately $102.90.) the ungrateful servant is compassionless and throws his debtor in prison. Can you imagine God forgiving you so much, yet you being unwilling to forgive another so little? This greedy and ungrateful servant was delivered by the king for torture; his just reward. *"So My heavenly Father also will do to you if each of you, from his heart, does not forgive his brother his trespasses"* (Matthew 18:35). We must have the **heart to forgive** any trespass if we want to apprehend the Kingdom of Heaven.

God's Economic Principles

The Kingdom of Heaven has its own economy. We have already witnessed from previous parables that the Kingdom economy seams a bit unfair, at least from a worldly perspective. When you are faithful with the little treasures that He gives to you, He will take additional treasures from those who have been unfaithful, and give them to you so you have an even greater abundance. *"Those who have the most will be given even more."* You can also **reap where you have not sown.** Now witness how **even the latecomers** can receive His full reward.

Many are Called, few are Chosen

In the parable about the vineyard in Matthew 20, the owner goes out and hires laborers at many different hours throughout the day. At the end of the day he pays every worker a day's wages, exactly what he had promised each of them. The hired hands who worked the most hours were angry with the owner of the vineyard because they were not paid more; or perhaps their anger grew from their desire that those who worked fewer hours should be paid less. Either way, the owner explained to the angry workers that he paid them exactly what he had promised. What right do they have to be angry if he desires to give his own money to the others? He paid all of them as promised. The Kingdom of Heaven and its full treasure are available to all who seek, no matter when you join the search. *"So the last will be first, and the first last. For many are called, but few chosen" (Matthew 20:16).* There is, however, a difference between the called (the saved) to whom He keeps His promises, and the chosen (the elect) who seek first the Kingdom. We must be willing to **seek the Kingdom, above everything else,** if we wish to find it.

The Rich Young Man

In Matthew 19:16, a wealthy young man inquired of Jesus, *"What good thing shall I do that I may have eternal life?"* The answer is interesting, considering that the Lord then instructed this inquisitive young man, in verses 17-18, to *"keep the commandments,"* and then went on to name six of them. Why would the Lord say such a thing? He knows that eternal life is a FREE gift, attained only by faith. Yes, but witness the Divine insight displayed by Jesus as the interaction continues. The man replied in verse 20, *"All these things I have kept from my youth. What do I still lack?"* Jesus is the *Living Word* of God and *the word of God is living and powerful, and sharper than any two-edged sword, piercing even to the division of soul and spirit, and of joints and marrow, and is a discerner of the thoughts and intents of the heart. (Hebrews 4:12)* Discerning the thoughts and intents of this young man's heart, in verse 21, Jesus said to him, **"If you want to be perfect,** *go, sell what you have and give to the poor, and you will have treasure in heaven; and come, follow Me."* The man inquired about obtaining eternal life, which is a free gift, but Jesus knew he was interested in more than just salvation. He was seeking the Kingdom of Heaven; he was after perfection. The young man was really asking: "What must I do to be like You Lord?" And Jesus answered, *"If you want to be **perfect**, go, sell what you have and give to the poor."* But in verse 22, *when the young man heard that saying, he went away sorrowful, for he had great possessions.* We must **not be tied to earthly riches** to pursue the Kingdom of Heaven.

The Wedding Invitation

In the parable about the king who arranged a marriage for his son in Matthew 22, we can see the entire blueprint of God's Kingdom. *"The Kingdom of Heaven is like a certain king who arranged a marriage for his son"* (Matthew 22:2). He sends out invitations only to be rejected. *And the rest seized his servants, treated them spitefully, and killed them* (Matthew 22:6). Likewise, our heavenly Father sent forth His invitation by way of His servants the prophets, only to be rejected by Israel.

> ➤ **(Acts 7:52)** *"Which of the prophets did your fathers not persecute? And they killed those who foretold the coming of the Just One, of whom you now have become the betrayers and murderers…"*

Using the parable as a blueprint, we see that after the invitation was turned down, God then extended His invitation to others. *Then he said to his servants, 'The wedding is ready, but those who were invited were not worthy. 'Therefore go into the highways, and as many as you find, invite to the wedding'* (Matthew 22:8-9).

It says in Romans 11:25 that *"Blindness in part has happened to Israel until the fullness of the Gentiles has come in."* Even though almost all Believers up to nearly 15 years after the resurrection were "Jewish," Israel, as a nation, rejected God's invitation. He then reached out to the gentiles. We can trust that this was God's sovereign plan, and that after the lost world is grafted into Israel's inheritance, natural Israel will come back to the fold. *"So those servants went out into the highways and gathered together all whom they found, **both bad and good**. And the wedding hall was filled* *with guests" (Matthew 22:10)*. This is the great commission. They went out preaching the Kingdom of Heaven. They filled the dragnet, drawing in both good and bad, only to be separated later. *"But when the king came in to see the guests, he saw a man there who did not have on a wedding garment" (Matthew 22:11)*. The "bad" (unsaved) cannot account for why they have been invited to the wedding supper. As a consequence, they are cast into outer darkness where there is weeping and gnashing of teeth. You must be prepared, in season and out of season; be ready to give a defense to everyone who asks you a reason for the hope that is in you. If you are not clothed with the righteousness of Christ, you cannot share in the wedding supper.

Jesus ends this parable with a phrase He had used before; *"For many are called, but few are chosen" (Matthew 22:14)*. We experience the division of mankind into three groups. Two groups stay at the feast. Both groups are Believers, the "called" and the "chosen." The third group is the unbeliever who is cast into outer darkness. Every place in the New Testament that we see the words "called" {klay-tos'} and "chosen/elect" {ek-lek-tos'}, a combined 34 times in Greek, it is undoubtedly referring to Believers. So we have two groups of Believers and one group of non-believers. This makes for an interesting question: We know the plight of the unbeliever, but how can we explain the distinction between the **called** and **chosen?** *"These shall make war with the Lamb, and the Lamb shall overcome them: for he is Lord of lords, and King of kings: and they that are with him are **called, and chosen,** and faithful" (Revelation 17:14)*. Normally, in eternity, we consider only two groups, the Believer and the unbeliever. In modern theological circles, the eternal division of Believers into two subgroups is really never addressed. However, it does seem to be found in Scripture.

Scripture makes reference to those who will reign with Christ for one thousand years. *Blessed and holy is he who has part in the first resurrection. Over such the second death has no power, but they shall be priests of God and of Christ, and shall **reign** with Him a thousand years (Revelation 20:6)*. Who are they reigning over? Not everyone called to the wedding supper will rule and reign with Christ in His Kingdom. Instead of ruling, some will be subjects or citizens of the Kingdom. In addition, this ruling position does not end in the "new heaven and new earth" either, but goes on eternally.

There shall be no night there: They need no lamp nor light of the sun, for the Lord God gives them light. And they shall **reign** *forever and ever (Revelation 22:5).* The difference between the "called" (all who are saved), and the "chosen" (all who are saved plus), is certainly a topic worthy of deep exploration; one we will investigate thoroughly in future books. *This is a faithful saying: For* **if we died with Him,** *We shall also live with Him* (the called). *If* **we endure, we shall also reign with Him** (the chosen) *(2 Timothy 2:11-12).* Being called is a narrow road; being chosen is even narrower! Seekers of the Kingdom must **press beyond their call to salvation** and reach towards the goal of **ruling with Christ.**

Will you be prepared?

"Then the Kingdom of Heaven shall be likened to ten virgins who took their lamps and went out to meet the bridegroom. Now five of them were wise, and five were foolish" (Matthew 25:1-2). The wise were prepared and the foolish were unprepared. If you are unprepared, you will not know when He is coming.

> ➤ *(Thessalonians 5:1-4) But concerning the times and the seasons, brethren, you have no need that I should write to you. For you your-selves know perfectly that the Day of the LORD so comes as a thief in the night. For when they say, "Peace and safety!" then sudden destruction comes upon them, as labor pains upon a pregnant woman. And they shall not escape. But you, brethren, are not in darkness, so that this Day should overtake you as a thief.*

The times and seasons are the Feasts of the LORD; this is what the term "times and seasons" means in the Bible. Paul knew that the Believers in Thessalonica were very knowledgeable about the Feasts, as they should be. As a Believer, if your lamp is not trimmed with oil at the right time, you will be in darkness at His coming. You cannot be fully prepared for His coming without keeping the Feasts. You should acknowledge the importance of the commandments of God to keep the Feasts, so you too will know the times and seasons. We must be **prepared** to pursue the Kingdom of Heaven.

Greatest or Least in the Kingdom

The Kingdom of Heaven has a hierarchy. There are "greatest" and "least" in the Kingdom. *"Therefore whoever humbles himself as this little child is the greatest in the Kingdom of Heaven"* (Matthew 18:4). Little children don't mind if God has more than ten commands.

*"Assuredly, I say to you, among those **born of women** there has not risen one greater than John the Baptist; but he who is **least in the Kingdom of Heaven** is greater than he"* (Matthew 11:11). Why? Because *flesh and blood cannot inherit the Kingdom of God; nor does corruption inherit incorruption* (1 Corinthians 15:50). Jesus taught us in John 3:3 and 3:5, *"Most assuredly, I say to you, unless one is **born again**, he cannot see the Kingdom of God."* Because, *unless one is **born of water and the Spirit**, he cannot enter the Kingdom of God.* Without the transforming power of the Spirit, even the greatest of men born of woman, is less than the least in the Kingdom of God. Now, of course, John will be with us in eternity; however, this reference is using John's greatness as a prophet and being born of the flesh, and compares it to what is available to us if we are born of the Spirit. Without the Spirit, there is NO CHANCE of being conformed to the image of Christ.

In addition, Jesus also taught that faith-based obedience will make us great in the Kingdom.

> ➤ NIV **(Matthew 5:17-19)** *"Do not think that I have come to abolish the Law or the Prophets; I have not come to abolish them but to fulfill them. I tell you the truth, until heaven and earth disappear, not the smallest letter, not the least stroke of a pen, will by any means disappear from the Law until everything is accomplished. Anyone who breaks one of the least of these commandments and teaches others to do the same will be called least in the Kingdom of Heaven, but whoever practices and teaches these commands will be called great in the Kingdom of Heaven."*

Stop and consider what you have been taught about God's commandments. Have you truly been taught that not the smallest letter, not the least stroke of a pen, will by any means disappear from the Law until

162

heaven and earth pass away? Have you been taught to keep ALL of God's commandments and not to break even the least of them? Or, have you been taught that we can't possibly keep them all, so why even try? Or worse yet, that trying would lead you into bondage? Haven't you been taught that we have freedom in Christ, so we don't need to keep all of God's commandments because Jesus did them for us? This is a nice teaching that is very easy on the ears. The problem is that it just doesn't line up at all with what Jesus taught. Jesus, in his very first sermon, told us that those who keep and teach the commandments will be called "great" in the Kingdom of Heaven; while those who break even one command, and teach others to break them also, will be called "least." Why are almost all Christian leaders teaching such a different gospel, and condemning their flocks to be "least" in the Kingdom?

In Matthew 5:18, Jesus makes it perfectly clear that every bit of the Law will stand until *"all be fulfilled."* We will know everything has been fulfilled when "heaven and earth have passed away." As a good friend of mine likes to say, "Even to the casual observer, it is clear that heaven and earth are still here." So, why does Christianity teach that the Law has been done away with, even though heaven and earth have not passed away? It is a good question for which I have yet to receive a satisfactory answer.

The Bible states that heaven and earth do not pass away until after Jesus returns and reigns for one thousand years. *Now I saw a new heaven and a new earth, for the first heaven and the first earth had passed away. Also there was no more sea (Revelation 21:1).* Therefore, we still live at a time in history when not the smallest letter, not even the least stroke of a pen, has disappeared from the Law. Ask yourself, has what you been taught concerning the commandments of God been consistent with the teaching of Moses, Paul, John the Baptist and, most importantly, Jesus Himself? Are you willing to let your beliefs be dictated by the doctrines and commandments of men, instead of the Word of God? God's Word teaches that the first road will make you *least* in the Kingdom, while the other will make you *great?* **Faith-based obedience** to God will make you greatest in the Kingdom.

Summary

We are ready to wind up this chapter and continue on with the most exciting prayer of your life. In Chapter 5, we explored some of the **mysteries** of the Kingdom of Heaven. Now, at the end of Chapter 6, let us recap a few **characteristics** required in those who wish to pursue the Kingdom. We will conclude this chapter by merging the two and develop an even clearer picture.

Qualities of the Kingdom Seeker

All who wish to pursue the Kingdom of Heaven must be *instructed*, even as the wisest scholar. We must have at our disposal a thorough grasp of Moses and the prophets, if we are to build the Kingdom precept upon precept. For all who seek the Kingdom, it is critical to understand their words and to *build on their foundation*. Applying the Spirit, to the words of Moses and the prophets, is your only chance to uncover the deep things of God. You now know that along with many other aspects, the Kingdom of Heaven has an *aggressive characteristic*, and that it is advancing by the work *forceful* men, even though it has an almost imperceptible beginning. We must take Kingdom business seriously because *poor stewardship* of the mysteries carries with it a steep penalty. We *cannot serve two masters*. Better than the business of the world, we should know our Father's business, and do it well. This is because the LORD stands ready to remove the unfaithful steward. Especially dangerous is when unfaithful stewards act in leadership, *knowing that they shall receive a stricter judgment*.

Have Kingdom questions? *Ask and you shall receive, seek and you will find, knock and the door will be opened.* I hope you recognize that the *riches of this world* can easily distract you from becoming like Christ, and that it takes *childlike innocence* to establish Kingdom living. We must be different from the rest of the world, a holy and *peculiar people*. Living this way will surely bring *persecution*. However, as we grow into the perfect image of Christ, we will not easily distinguish the true children of the Kingdom from imposters, for even Satan disguises himself as an angel of light. To expose imposters, we must examine the *"fruit"* carefully.

It will cost everything to enter the Kingdom of God so we must offer our lives as *living sacrifices*. Once you set your eyes on the prize, you *can never look back!* Acknowledge that you were forgiven so much, that it should be *impossible to hold an offense* against others. This you must do to become like Christ.

We are building the government of God. The Kingdom of Heaven has its own economy which seams a bit unfair, at least from a worldly perspective. We must be *faithful with His little treasures*, because the Lord will *take from* those who have been *unfaithful* and *give to* us who are *faithful*, so we have an even greater abundance. Also, in God's economy, you can *reap where you have not sown. Even the latecomers* can receive His full reward. However, to pursue the Kingdom of Heaven, we *cannot be tied to earthly riches.* Seekers of the Kingdom must *press beyond their call to salvation* and reach towards the goal of *ruling with Christ.* Many have this high calling, but few will ever achieve it. You can rest safely, however, knowing that the Body of Christ **will** come to perfection and we **will** receive our full inheritance. Nothing can stop the Kingdom from advancing; you must, however, *be ready!* Have your lamps trimmed.

Finally, we discovered that *faith-based obedience* to God will make you *greatest* in the Kingdom of Heaven. The good news for all who are born again, by faith, is that you can be great in the Kingdom of God. *Add to your faith virtue, to virtue knowledge, to knowledge self-control, to self-control perseverance, to perseverance godliness, to godliness brotherly kindness, and to brotherly kindness love... Therefore, brethren, **be even more diligent to make your call and election sure,** for if you do these things you will never stumble; for so an entrance will be supplied to you abundantly into the everlasting Kingdom of our Lord and Savior Jesus Christ (2 Peter 1:5-7, 10-11).* Through His promises, you can escape the corruption that is in the world and become partakers of His divine nature. On the other hand, if you *strive to be first, you will certainly be last.*

Chapter Conclusion

By no means have we done an exhaustive study about the Kingdom of Heaven. It would take many volumes to explore this topic. Hopefully we will soon add to this body of work. The Kingdom of Heaven is at hand and it is forcefully advancing. The Body of Christ is being transformed into

His perfect sinless image, precept upon precept, line upon line, and from glory to glory. As we look back at all the essential qualities from this chapter and attributes of the Kingdom from Chapter 5, we shall attempt to synthesize them into one statement.

The Kingdom of Heaven is being exactly like Christ Jesus, who built the foundation of His ministry upon Moses and the Prophets, line upon line and precept upon precept, ministering to every person at their point of need. Revealing the Kingdom in His perfection (sinlessness), Jesus showed us: Love and forgiveness in every thought and action; faith-based obedience; preparation and sacrifice; willingness to be unjustly persecuted; endurance and faithfulness through tribulation; rulership and servanthood; all power and authority; fruitfulness, patience and perseverance; holiness and peculiarity; great discernment and priorities not bound to a world whose riches are passing away; humility and childlike innocence; responsibility and foresight; good stewardship, a man well instructed in His Father's business, ready to reap a harvest for which He has not sown, able to forcefully advance the Kingdom while never looking back; doing so while demonstrating what unity of man with God, and complete harmony with his neighbor looks like. This is done all in support of His Father's government for which there will be no end, and to the glory of God His Father. Amen.

Seek the Kingdom of Heaven first and everything you need in life will be given to you on your journey. To prepare to pray the Prayer of David you must search to understand the attributes of the Kingdom of Heaven and cultivate essential Kingdom qualities within yourself. Let me remind you, *"The Kingdom of Heaven is within you."* Mark the attributes that you have come to understand, and the characteristics you currently demonstrate. The ones left blank represent your homework.

Attributes of the Kingdom			
The Kingdom of Heaven	The Government of God	Unity of the Faith	Line upon line, precept upon precept
The Kingdom of Heaven in you	Works of Law vs. Faith-based Obedience	Faithful with little given much more	Reap a harvest where you have not sown
Gospel of Salvation	The Keys to the Kingdom	The first will be last & last will be first	Progressive ministry
Gospel of the Kingdom	There are mysteries of the Kingdom	Foundation built on Moses & the Prophets	Corporate perfection (Sinlessness)

The Character & Qualities of a Kingdom Seeker			
Love	Rulership	Holiness	Good Stewardship
Forgiveness	Servanthood	Peculiarity	Well instructed in his Father's business
Kingdom invades all thought & action	Endurance through tribulation	Great discernment	Able to forcefully advance the Kingdom
Faith-Based Obedience	All power & authority	Perfection (Sinlessness)	Never looks back
Preparation	Fruitfulness	Humility	Unity with God
Sacrifice	Patience	Childlike innocence	Complete harmony with his neighbor
Willingness to be unjustly persecuted	Perseverance	Responsibility	Entire life supports his Father's government
Faithfulness	Priorities not bound to the world	Foresight	

Wow! We did it. I hope you are as inspired and motivated as I am. We must take on each and every one of these characteristics to succeed. I know it may seem impossible, but you should feel confident that you can do it, because the Kingdom is already within you. As the Body of Christ, we have it in us. We have the potential to become the manifestation of the Son of God. We could look like He, act like He, and do even greater works than He, as He promised. We have been entrusted with His Divine plan to build the Spiritual Temple and for the establishment of His government.

The Temple must be erected in the Promised Land, so first you must leave the Wilderness. The Jordan surges before you. How can you cross over? Again, it is by faith; faith to be and do everything for which you were made. For such a time as this, God placed you here. David prayed with boldness and spiritual foresight. He knew the heart of God and he knew His business. As a forerunner, you have the same calling. Join me now as we arrive at the shore of the Jordan. Prepare for the Prayer of David; prepare to pass over on dry ground!

Chapter Seven

A Man After God

*The LORD has sought for Himself a man after His own heart, and the
LORD has commanded him to be commander over His people.*
1 Samuel 13:14

I n this final chapter before the Prayer of David, we will focus our
attention on the character of the man. We will look at his life and
examine the history of which he is a part. All he was, everything he knew
and did, and all of his successes and failures, positioned and prepared him
for one prophetic moment!

Who was David and why was he so uniquely qualified to paint this
mysterious picture on God's prophetic tapestry? *"He raised up for them
David as King, to whom also He gave testimony and said, 'I have found David
the son of Jesse, a man after My own Heart, who will do all My will'"*
(Acts 13:22b). David was a man after the heart of God. He believed God
and lived his life trusting that the LORD would fulfill His promises. When
faced with the giant Philistine, David said in 1 Samuel 17:26: *"For who is
this uncircumcised Philistine, that he should defy the armies of the living God?"*
In the hour of his greatest need, David recalled how God was with him.
*"The LORD, who delivered me from the paw of the lion and from the paw of the
bear, He will deliver me from the hand of this Philistine"* (v. 37). He had
unyielding faith when he stood against the enemy. *"This day the LORD will
deliver you into my hand, and I will strike you and take your head from you"*
(v. 46). He was a man after the Heart of God.

After David was anointed by Samuel to replace Saul as King, he had
the opportunity to slaughter King Saul. He could have insured his own

life by protecting himself from the man who continually hunted him. Instead, David chose to trust the LORD's plan for provision. He honored the institutions of God, respecting even God's anointed who had gone astray. We have in David, an example of a man who knows the Heart of God and understands His institutions.

> ➤ *(1 Samuel 24:10) "Look, this day your eyes have seen that the LORD delivered you today into my hand in the cave, and someone urged me to kill you. But my eye spared you, and I said, 'I will not stretch out my hand against my lord, for he is the LORD's anointed.'"*

First, we will explore David's life and observe his extraordinary relationship with his heavenly Father. Then, in Chapter 8, when you read the words of his prayer, you will wonder why he would have proposed something so shocking, so extreme, and so daring. He proposed what appears to be a challenge to God's institution. But was it? Would a man with a heart like David's want to alter God's institution? We might want to consider the alternative. Perhaps what David proposed was actually meant to advance God's institution, not change it. Quite simply, it was a risk few other men in history would dare to take. Maybe we can find clues about how and why a man would take such a risk by examining the life of David.

The Extraordinary Life of David

David's life was extraordinary, but it was not without failure. In addition to his historic fame for slaying Goliath, writing many of the Psalms, and being the kingly line from which Messiah was born, David also fashioned an insidious plan for a man to be slaughtered so he could take his wife. How can this be the same man of whom God says is "a man after My own Heart"? The answer emerges from David's heart of true repentance when mixed with forgiveness from an infinitely merciful God. Witness the beauty and simplicity of David's confession and the LORD's mercy after his sin is exposed. *So David said to Nathan, "I have sinned against the LORD." And Nathan said to David, "The LORD also has put away your sin; you shall not die" (2 Samuel 12:13).*

Later on, David's sorrowful reaction to his sin with Bathsheba inspired Psalm 51. In my opinion, this is the most beautiful display of genuine repentance in Scripture.

> ➤ *(Psalm 51:2-3) Wash me thoroughly from my iniquity, and cleanse me from my sin. For I acknowledge my transgressions, and my sin is always before me... (vs. 9-13) Hide Your face from my sins, and blot out all my iniquities. Create in me a clean heart, O God, and renew a steadfast spirit within me. Do not cast me away from Your presence, and do not take Your Holy Spirit from me. Restore to me the joy of Your salvation, and uphold me by Your generous Spirit. Then I will teach transgressors Your ways, and sinners shall be converted to You!*

In addition to cleansing you from your iniquities and allowing you to do great things for God, true repentance stands as a powerful testimony to the lost. Those who are forgiven much, love much; and to those who are given much, much is required. The Apostle Paul persecuted followers of Jesus and consented to murder. Forgiven, he later composed over 25% of the New Testament, the book by which the world has come to know Christ. I encourage you to read all of Psalm 51 during your next time of devotion. It inspires repentance and exposes David's inner parts.

The LORD chose David as King for one reason only. He said to Samuel: *"Fill your horn with oil, and go; I am sending you to Jesse the Bethlehemite. For I have provided Myself a King among his sons." "Do not look at his appearance or at the height of his stature, because I have refused him. For the Lord does not see as man sees; for man looks at the outward appearance, but the LORD looks at the heart"* (1 Samuel 16:1, 7). David was chosen because of what was in his heart. So, to find out what the man was made of, let's open the chambers and peer deeply into the heart of David.

David's Heart

These are just a few of the traits God knew he could use in a man like David. They explain why he was able to be so bold. These confessions come to us from a few of David's Psalms.

➤ *(9:1) I will praise You, O LORD, with my whole heart; I will tell of all Your marvelous works. (19:8) The statutes of the LORD are right, rejoicing the heart; The commandment of the LORD is pure, enlightening the eyes. (27:8) When You said, "Seek My face," My heart said to You, "Your face, LORD, I will seek." (40:7-8) Then I said, "Behold, I come; in the scroll of the book it is written of me. I delight to do Your will, O my God, and Your Law is within my heart." (40:10) I have not hidden Your righteousness within my heart; I have declared Your faithfulness and Your salvation; I have not concealed Your lovingkindness and Your truth from the great assembly. (51:10) Create in me a clean heart, O God, and renew a steadfast spirit within me. (57:7) My heart is steadfast, O God, my heart is steadfast; I will sing and give praise. (101:2) I will behave wisely in a perfect way. Oh, when will You come to me? I will walk within my house with a perfect heart. (119:10-11) With my whole heart I have sought You; Oh, let me not wander from Your commandments! Your word I have hidden in my heart, that I might not sin against You! (119:111-112) Your testimonies I have taken as a heritage forever, for they are the rejoicing of my heart. I have inclined my heart to perform Your statutes forever, to the very end. (33:11) The counsel of the LORD stands forever, the plans of His heart to all generations. (15:1-2) Who may abide in Your Tabernacle? Who may dwell in Your holy hill? He who walks uprightly, and works righteousness, and speaks the truth in his heart.*

David had a heart of praise. He rejoiced in God's ways, sought after the LORD in all things, delighted to do God's will, and obey His Laws. David's heart was evangelical in spirit; it was not afraid to tell of His wonders. The heart that beat within David was repentant, faithful, and always striving for perfection. It was filled with commitment, obedience, passion, and a never-ending joy that sprung forth from knowing God. His heart was steadfast until the very end, a heart that will abide in the Tabernacle of the LORD forever. God knew that David would ultimately yield his own will for his heavenly Father's.

Throughout the Psalms, we share in David's life and experiences. We see his authentic repentance, his spirit of praise and worship, his childlike faith that God would protect him, and his belief that God would avenge him and set him on high in the midst of all his enemies. In David's worship, we witness his profound love for God's Laws. From his heart, David wrote the longest chapter in the Bible. All 176 verses of Psalm 119 give honor to the LORD in all His ways and pay tribute to the beauty of His Law. On this subject, I am compelled to borrow notes from Matthew Henry, an 18th century Biblical scholar and author of the voluminous commentary which bears his name.

"The general scope and design of it is to magnify the Law, and make it honourable; to set forth the excellency and usefulness of divine revelation, and to recommend it to us, not only for the entertainment, but for the government, of ourselves, by the psalmist's own example, who speaks by experience of the benefit of it, and of the good impressions made upon him by it, for which he praises God, and earnestly prays, from first to last, for the continuance of God's grace with him, to direct and quicken him in the way of his duty."

Matthew Henry -circa 1710

Mr. Henry understood the immense advantage of using God's Laws as the fibers to weave together the moral, economic, and political fabric of our individual lives and our society. As the Body of Christ, it is our duty to establish these agendas using God's Law, if we hope to reap the immeasurable benefits of living under God's government.

Throughout Psalm 119, in all but one of its 176 verses, David confesses to the goodness and value of God's Laws. Keep in mind, David is a man whose heart exemplifies the heart of God. We would be wise to emulate his example. To capture the diverse essence of God's instructions (the Torah), David uses ten different words with identical meaning to characterize the expression of God's will. The Law is called His: way, testimonies, commandments, precepts, word, judgments, righteousness, statutes, truth, and in verse 132, he even calls it His name! The Apostle Paul confirms that it is through the Law that God reveals His will. *Indeed you are called a Jew, and rest on the Law, and make your boast in God, and know His will, and approve the things that are excellent, being instructed out of the Law (Romans 2:17-18).*

Again, let us turn to Matthew Henry who expresses it so well: *"There are **ten different words** by which **divine revelation** is called in this psalm, and they are synonymous, each of them expressive of the whole compass of it (both that which tells us what God expects from us and that which tells us that we may expect from Him) and of the system of religion which is founded upon it and guided by it."* Matthew Henry refers to God's Laws as divine revelation; in other words, His will for our lives, "both what He expects from us and what we can expect from Him."

He continues, *"The great esteem and affection David had for the word of God is the more admirable considering how little he had of it, in comparison with what we have, no more perhaps in writing than the first books of Moses, which were but the dawning of this day, which may shame us who enjoy the full discoveries of divine revelation and yet are **so cold towards it**."* Matthew Henry wrote this in the early 1700's. What excuse can we possibly fabricate today, the Information Age, to defend ourselves from ignorance of the Law?

David's Two-edged Sword

Other than Samuel (who lived before David), all the Major and Minor Prophets came years after David. Elijah's ministry, the closest to David's reign, started approximately 95 years after David's death. Elisha's ministry spanned 110-170 years after David. All other prophets lived hundreds of years after David. He would only have had access to the writings of Moses, the history of Joshua and the Judges, perhaps the story of Job, and probably some version of Ruth, as this was his direct family history. These would have been his only written sources of, what we call today, Scripture. He would not have considered his own writings as Scripture and, of course, having lived one thousand years before Christ, he did not have the advantage of Jesus' teachings either. David, however, did have one advantage. This advantage bears the razor-sharp blade of a two-edged sword. One side explains his profound understanding of the LORD'S commandments. The other, his willingness and foresight to risk moving beyond them. This exposes a great mystery. God's full revelation is always unveiled on both sides of the same coin. One side appears to negate the other, but, in reality, they are the same message from different perspectives. In many cases, one message simply enhances the other. Contemplate how similar this is to our Savior's earthly ministry. He never changed a single Law of His Father. He did however advance them. *"You have heard that it was said to those of old, 'You shall not commit adultery.' But I say to you that whoever looks at a woman to lust for her has already committed adultery with her in his heart"* (Matthew 5:27-28). Advancing His Father's commandments was at the heart of Jesus' ministry. Jesus was the seed of David and He had the heart of David. When we share David's same heart, we can proceed to explore his extraordinary revelation.

As the king, David had many responsibilities, the greatest of which was to guide the nation of Israel to act in obedience to God. When Israel had no king; *"everyone did what was right in his own eyes"* (Judges 21:25b). Because of this kingly responsibility, David had to develop a superior understanding of the power of God's commandments. How is it that David developed such a profound understanding of God's Laws? Contained in the Scriptures is a unique and vital commandment for every King of Israel to obey. As part of the king's duties, he had to write for himself a Torah scroll, a copy of the five books of Moses. *"You shall surely set a king over you whom the LORD your God chooses…"* *"Also it shall be, when he sits on the throne of his Kingdom, that **he shall write for himself a copy of this Law in a book,** from the one before the priests, the Levites. And it shall be with him, and **he shall read it all the days of his life, that he may learn to fear the LORD his God and be careful to observe all the words of this Law and these statutes,** that his heart may not be lifted above his brethren, that he may not turn aside from the commandment to the right hand or to the left, and that he may prolong his days in his Kingdom , he and his children in the midst of Israel"* (Deuteronomy 17:15, 18-20).

David wrote for himself a personal copy of the Torah, just as a scribe would copy all the words of the Law. He was commanded to read it all the days of his life so that he would maintain a holy fear of the LORD his God. Through this constant reading, he would be careful to observe all the words contained in the Law of Moses. Remember, David was selected to be king because God knew that he was a man after His own Heart, and that he would do God's will. Why do I emphasize this particular requirement, that the King of Israel must write for himself a complete book of the Law? Because I want you to be certain, beyond any doubt, that King David knew and understood exactly what was expected of him. God is merciful and definitely tolerates some level of ignorance. However, ignorance of the Law would have been no excuse for David. It is apparent that David knew each of God's commandments, and the Psalms testify that he loved them all. **This is one edge of the sword!**

Illustrating a few excerpts of these commandments should add to the drama surrounding David's prayer by confirming just how risky it was for David to make such a bold request. It was in his heart to advance the LORD'S commandments. In so doing, he exercised a level of faith and foresight that changed the course of history, and laid the foundation for the future ministry of God's chosen people, the children of God. **This is the other edge of the sword!**

The Pattern on the Mountain

The following words reflect various selections of the LORD'S divine plan to assemble His Tabernacle and its furnishings, as well as His altar in the Wilderness. He paints this picture for three entire chapters in the book of Exodus. God has gone through pain-staking details to recreate the pattern of the Tabernacle in heaven, and then relate it to Moses. In four places throughout these detailed instructions, God admonishes Moses in similar fashion; *"Be sure you make everything according to the patterns I showed you on the mountain."* We have been emphasizing the importance of patterns throughout this book. In Hebrews 8:5, the writer confirms the significance of these patterns which *serve the copy and shadow of the heavenly things, as Moses was divinely instructed when he was about to make the Tabernacle. For He said, "See that you make all things according to the pattern shown you on the mountain."*

Do you remember in Chapter 5, how we emphasized the importance of discovering God's mysteries? We went to great efforts to explore the mysteries of the Kingdom of Heaven. Jesus' most magnificent discourse about the Kingdom of Heaven, which begins in Matthew 5:1, is His Sermon on the Mount. *And seeing the multitudes, He went up on a moun-*

tain, and when He was seated His disciples came to Him. Yes, the Sermon on the Mount is done on the mountain. Jesus reveals the specific pattern for the Kingdom of Heaven while **on the mountain.** Both the Kingdom of God and the Tabernacle of God are built using blueprints given on the mountain. *"Be sure you make everything according to the patterns I showed you on the mountain."* There are deep spiritual connections between His Kingdom and His Tabernacle. If you continue searching for these types of Scriptural patterns, a whole new world of revelation and depth of understanding is available for you. It's the prophetic way.

I have selected a few as examples to show you just how specific God was when relaying His blueprint for building the Tabernacle in the Wilderness. The LORD tells Moses to collect an offering of materials from the children of Israel to build the Tabernacle and create all of its furnishings. *"And this is the offering which you shall take from them: gold, silver, and bronze; blue, purple, and scarlet thread, fine linen, and goats' hair; ram skins dyed red, badger skins, and acacia wood; oil for the light, and spices for the anointing oil and for the sweet incense; onyx stones, and stones to be set in the ephod and in the breastplate. And let them make Me a sanctuary, that I may dwell among them."* Then for the first of four times, God makes it very clear in verse 9; **"According to all that I show you, that is, the pattern of the Tabernacle and the pattern of all its furnishings, just so you shall make it"** *(Exodus 25:3-8).*

Can it be more apparent that God is commanding that the Tabernacle, and all that is in it, be made exactly according to His plan? It is beautiful and perfect, precisely how God designs it. Through three entire chapters in Exodus, God describes in exhaustive detail, every aspect of the Tabernacle; its contents and furnishings; the Ark and Mercy Seat; the Lid of Atonement; Altar and utensils; and the courtyard. He specifies the size and shape of every part; the measurements in length, width, and height of every pole, panel and curtain; and the material for every table, dish, pan, pitcher, bowl, shovel, fork and firepan. He confers the description of every ring, fastener, and knob. He assigns every material used to construct each item, whether from wood, brass, gold, silver or bronze, or whether from animal skins or hair, including precious stones and fine linen. He describes the oil for the light; spices for the anointing oil and for the sweet incense; and the blue, purple and scarlet thread used in every curtain or tapestry. He defines the placement, number and artistic design of each item right down to the hammered work of the Lampstand and its oil. And then again, in Exodus 25:40, God commands, *"And see to it that you make them according to the pattern which was shown you on the mountain."*

In other areas of the Torah, Moses is instructed in vivid detail about the role of priesthood. God designs all their garments and duties. In addition to every detail about raising the tent, God specifies the exact method for disassembling and moving the Tabernacle to another location. He specifically describes who could take down the Tabernacle and how to move it. Israel is even instructed exactly when to move and where to settle. *Whenever the cloud was taken up from above the Tabernacle, after that the children of Israel would journey; and in the place where the cloud settled, there the children of Israel would pitch their tents (Numbers 9:17).* God was also very explicit about who could carry the Ark of the Covenant and how to hold it. The Tabernacle in the Wilderness was obviously designed for mobility and displays the characteristics of being temporary. But who would dare to even suggest its replacement?

Recognizing that David was extremely familiar with all of these instructions, it increases, ever more, the dilemma of his apparent decision **to place the Ark in a tent of his own making after He brought it to Jerusalem.** On one side of the razor-sharp two-edged sword, David knew every detail of these commandments to build the Tabernacle according to exact specifications and place the Ark in it in an exact manner. On the other side, David was able to see something different; it was something beyond, yet somehow not in conflict with the commandments of God. To the untrained eye, he committed what appeared to be sin. But was it? In Exodus 26:30, the LORD said, *"And you shall raise up the Tabernacle according to its pattern which you were shown on the mountain."* What could David see? What Tabernacle on what mountain was in his sights? And more importantly, how does David's foresight relate to you as a follower of Christ?

A Review of History

Want to be shocked? Let's do a quick review of history about the Tabernacle in the Wilderness and the Ark of the Covenant. I simply cannot wrap my rational intellect around some of the decisions made by God's chosen people. Nevertheless, in spite of the apparent insanity, God's plan for humanity advances unscathed.

We'll start with the detailed instructions for building the tabernacle in Exodus 25, 26, and 27. But don't forget to include all the details of the Tabernacle services and the duties performed by the priests, which were daily, on each Sabbath, and for every Feast of the Lord. They all centered on the function of the Tabernacle. As stated, there were very precise instructions for moving the Ark and the Tabernacle. Israel's entire government and social structure were based on God's Laws (as ours should be). The Tabernacle, His commandments, Feasts and Sabbaths were the center of Hebrew life.

Ready for this? Before Israel had its first king, and soon after Samuel became the prophet and judge over Israel, the unthinkable happened. Israel lost a battle with Philistines. Instead of seeking the LORD and trusting for His provision, the elders of Israel panicked and decided to **take the Ark out of the Holy of Holies in the Tabernacle, which was located in the city of Shiloh, and parade it before their army.** Hoping to use the presence and power of God in the Ark as a tool to defeat their enemies, these foolish Israelites lost the battle again. And this time they lost the Ark itself to a pagan army. Oy vey!

Why was moving the Ark and parading it before their enemy a bad idea? In the past the Ark had been used to display the power of the living God. What was different this time? The answer: In the past, it was always the LORD who instructed them how, when, and why to move the Ark. For example, when Israel crossed the Jordan into the Promised Land, they did so, on dry ground. *And the LORD said to Joshua, "This day I will begin to exalt you in the sight of all Israel, that they may know that, as I was with Moses, so I will be with you. You shall command the priests who bear the Ark of the Covenant, saying, 'When you have come to the edge of the water of the Jordan, you shall stand in the Jordan.'"... So it was, when the people set out from their camp to cross over the Jordan, with the priests bearing the Ark of the covenant before the people, and as those who bore the Ark came to the Jordan, and the feet of the priests who bore the Ark dipped in the edge of the water (for the Jordan overflows all its banks during the whole time of harvest), that the waters which came down from upstream stood still, and rose in a heap very far away at Adam, the city that is beside Zaretan. So the waters that went down into the Sea of the Arabah, the Salt Sea, failed, and were cut off; and the people crossed over opposite Jericho.* **Then the priests who bore the Ark of the Covenant of the LORD stood firm on dry ground in the midst of the Jordan;** *and all Israel crossed over on dry ground, until all the people had crossed completely over the Jordan... (Joshua 3:7-8, 14-17). And it came to pass, when the priests who bore the Ark of the covenant of the LORD had come from the midst of the Jordan, and the soles of the priests' feet touched the dry land, that the waters of the Jordan returned to their place and overflowed all its banks as before (Joshua 4:18).* Wow! What a display of power. Who wouldn't want to use this kind of power against their enemies? It is very tempting. But we must wait on the LORD for His instructions. Doing His will, in His timing, whatever it happens to be, is the best way to defeat our enemies.

In another account, when Israel took the city of Jericho, it was the LORD who commanded them to take the Ark before them. *And the LORD said to Joshua: "See! I have given Jericho into your hand, its king, and the mighty men of valor. You shall march around the city, all you men of war; you shall go all around the city once. This you shall do six days.* **And seven priests shall bear seven trumpets of rams' horns before the Ark.** *But the seventh day you shall march around the city seven times, and the priests shall blow the trumpets" (Joshua 6:2-4).* The power of the LORD caused the walls of Jericho to crumble. I'm sure that the elders of Israel thought to do the same to the Philistines.

In this case, however, a pagan army captured the Ark, so it seems obvious that the elders of Israel used the Ark against all proper protocol. There is no evidence that the LORD directed them to do so, and as far as I can tell, they did not enroll the best of characters to complete their conquest. At that time, Eli was priest attending to the Tabernacle in Shiloh. He had two sons, Hophni and Phinehas. *Now the sons of Eli were corrupt; they did not know the LORD (1 Samuel 2:12).* (Can you imagine? They worked as "servants of God," yet they did not know God.) While serving under their father, the priest, they corrupted the sacrifices of the people to the point that the people despised bringing offerings before the LORD.

They also committed fornication with women who assembled at the door of the Tabernacle of meeting. When Eli approached them concerning their sins they ignored him. *"No, my sons! **For it is not a good report that I hear**. You make the LORD's people transgress. If one man sins against another, God will judge him. But if a man sins against the LORD, who will intercede for him? Nevertheless they did not heed the voice of their father, because **the LORD desired to kill them"** (1 Samuel 2:24-25).* After they ignored their father's warning, Eli did not press the issue with his sons, and the LORD pronounced judgment against Eli's whole house.

> ➢ *(1 Samuel 2:29, 31-34) "Why do you kick at My sacrifice and My offering which I have commanded in My dwelling place, and honor your sons more than Me, to make yourselves fat with the best of all the offerings of Israel My people? Behold, the days are coming that I will cut off your arm and the arm of your father's House, so that there will not be an old man in your House. **And you will see an enemy in My dwelling place,** despite all the good which God does for Israel. And there shall not be an old man in your House forever. But any of your men whom I do not cut off from My altar shall consume your eyes and grieve your heart. And all the descendants of your House shall die in the flower of their age. **Now this shall be a sign to you that will come upon your two sons, on Hophni and Phinehas: in one day they shall die, both of them."***

Meanwhile, Samuel was growing in favor with the LORD and God also revealed to him the fate of Eli's house. *Then the LORD said to Samuel: **"Behold, I will do something in Israel at which both ears of everyone who hears it will tingle.** In that day I will perform against Eli all that I have spoken concerning his House, from beginning to end. For I have told him that I will judge his House forever for the iniquity which he knows, **because his sons made themselves vile,** and he did not restrain them. And therefore I have sworn to the House of Eli that the iniquity of Eli's House shall not be atoned for by sacrifice or offering forever"* (1 Samuel 3:11-14).

God replaced Eli as His spokesman; and the word of Samuel came to all Israel. The LORD revealed Himself to Samuel in Shiloh and all Israel knew that Samuel had been established as a prophet of the LORD. They also were very well aware of the character of Eli's two sons. Nevertheless, in a mind numbing act, after losing a battle against the Philistines, Israel did not choose to seek the advice of Samuel, God's anointed. Instead, they choose to seek the aid of Eli's corrupt progeny. *"Why has the LORD defeated us today before the Philistines?* **Let us bring the Ark of the covenant of the LORD from Shiloh to us, that when it comes among us it may save us from the hand of our enemies"** *(1 Samuel 4:3).* Imagine the insolence! God did not tell them to take the Ark and use it as such. Nevertheless, in their arrogance and rebellion, they take it upon themselves to parade the Ark in front of the Philistines hoping to invoke its power. And to add fuel to the fire, look who they enroll to assist them in their quest. *So the people sent to Shiloh, that they might bring from there the Ark of the Covenant of the LORD of hosts, who dwells between the cherubim. And the two sons of Eli,* **Hophni** *and* **Phinehas,** *were there with the Ark of the Covenant of God (1 Samuel 4:4).*

The elders of Israel enroll the help of two men with vile reputations. They were men carrying a prophetic death sentence for committing blatant sins for which they had not repented. They essentially invite the enemy into the dwelling place of God, just as the LORD warned Eli would happen; *"and you will see an enemy in My dwelling place"* (1 Samuel 2:32). The people had Samuel, the anointed man of God, to guide them. But instead, they placed their trust in two men who clearly did not know the LORD, and who had a death sentence from the Almighty hanging over their heads. This is surely a recipe for disaster. The result... *So the Philistines fought, and Israel was defeated, and every man fled to his tent. There was a very great slaughter, and there fell of Israel thirty thousand foot soldiers.* **Also the Ark of God was captured; and the two sons of Eli, Hophni and Phinehas, died (1 Samuel 4:10-11).** The LORD warned, *"Behold, I will do something in Israel at which both ears of everyone who hears it will tingle."* Prophecy fulfilled! The LORD is true to His word. Nevertheless, man's rebellion does not alter the plans of Almighty God. As you will see, man's colossal mistake actually invites God to advance His plan for humanity. This monumental blunder ultimately sets the stage for David's mighty proclamation many years later.

A bizarre string of events advances God's plan

After the Ark was captured, the Philistines were only able to retain it for seven months because keeping the Ark was bringing curses and destruction upon them. The pagans were happy to return the Ark so its rightful owners could put it back where it belonged. Right? Not completely. The Philistines returned it, but Israel DID NOT put it back in the Tabernacle which had camped at Shiloh for approximately 350 years. Instead, it first went to Beth Shemesh. Although they rejoiced over its return, God struck down fifty thousand and seventy Israelite men because *"they had looked into the Ark of the LORD."* The Ark should not be handled with such informality, but with reverence and a holy fear. It was ultimately carried to Kiriath Jearim, where it remained for 20 years in the house of Abinadab.

At some point during those 20 years, the people demanded a king, and Saul was chosen to rule Israel. The Tabernacle was moved from Shiloh to Gibeon, while the Ark remained in Kiriath Jearim. And the city of Shiloh was met with severe judgment because sacrifice to pagan gods was tolerated in the midst of the Tabernacle. *So they set up for themselves Micah's carved image which he made, all the time that the House of God was in Shiloh (Judges 18:31).* That's right; another blatant mistake allowed by Eli and his sons during their administration.

> ➤ *(Psalm 78:58-60) For they provoked Him to anger with their high places, and moved Him to jealousy with their carved images. When God heard this, He was furious, and greatly abhorred Israel, so that He for-sook the Tabernacle of Shiloh, the tent He had placed among men...*

The Tabernacle in Shiloh

Shiloh bears the distinction of being chosen as the first place where God would establish His Name. God promised Moses that Israel would find rest from all their enemies, after they crossed over the Jordan into the Promised Land. The LORD would then select a location to place the seal of His Name.

> ➤ *(Deuteronomy 12:10-11)* *"But when you cross over the Jordan and dwell in the land which the* LORD *your God is giving you to inherit,* **and He gives you rest from all your enemies round about,** *so that you dwell in safety,* **then there will be the place where the** LORD **your God chooses to make His Name abide."**

In order to find rest however, Joshua must subdue His enemies from before him. After Israel crossed the Jordan it took seven years to conquer the Land, but at last, *Joshua took the whole Land, according to all that the* LORD *had said to Moses; and Joshua gave it as an inheritance to Israel according to their divisions by their tribes.* **Then the Land rested from war (Joshua 11:23).** However, even after Israel conquered the Land, it took many more years to divide it amongst the tribes and possess it. Jewish scholars say it took seven additional years to divide the Land. *Now Joshua was old, advanced in years. And the* LORD *said to him: "You are old, advanced in years, and there remains very much Land yet to be possessed" (Joshua 13:1).*

After Israel's conquest of the Promised Land around 1401 BCE, God fulfilled His promise of choosing a place where His Name would abide. *Now the whole congregation of the children of Israel assembled together* **at Shiloh, and set up the Tabernacle of meeting there.** *And the Land was subdued before them. But there remained among the children of Israel seven tribes which had not yet received their inheritance. Then Joshua said to the children of Israel: "How long will you neglect to go and possess the Land which the* LORD *God of your fathers has given you?" (Joshua 18:1-3).* Even though it would be seven years before all the tribes of Israel settled into the land of their inheritance, Shiloh was the first city where God would establish His Name. And it would be in that place that His Name would dwell for 350 years.

Shiloh is in the midst of Israel, in the land given as an inheritance to the tribe of Ephraim. However, is Shiloh the city of God that will be the permanent resting site of the Tabernacle? Is Shiloh the dwelling place of His Name forever, a place that shall not be moved? The Tabernacle was not moved from Shiloh for approximately 350 years. However, it did not remain there forever. In a stunning foreshadow of Jesus overturning the tables of the money changers in the Temple, Jeremiah writes of Shiloh's destiny and her eventual judgment. How sad a testimony for the city that bears the distinction of being the first location where God established His Name.

> ➤ NIV *(Jeremiah 7:11-12) "Has this house, which bears my Name, become a den of robbers to you? But I have been watching! declares the LORD. Go now to the place in Shiloh where **I first made a dwelling for my Name**, and see what I did to it because of the wickedness of my people Israel."*

In search of a permanent home, the Tabernacle was eventually moved from the city of Shiloh. *There is a river whose streams shall make glad the* **city of God, The holy place of the Tabernacle of the Most High** *(Psalm 46:4-5). God is in the midst of her, **she shall not be moved**; God shall help her, just at the break of dawn.* Where is the city of God that will not be moved? And where is the Tabernacle of the Most High in which His name will dwell forever?

> ➤ *(Psalm 87:2-3) The* LORD *loves the gates of Zion more than all the dwellings of Jacob. Glorious things are spoken of you, O city of God!*

Shiloh- A Prophetic View

In search of a city that shall not be moved, let us consider for a moment the prophetic significance and Scriptural blueprint of Shiloh. *Judah is a lion's whelp; from the prey, my son, you have gone up. He bows down, he lies down as a lion; And as a lion, who shall rouse him? The scepter shall not depart from Judah, nor a Lawgiver from between his feet, **until Shiloh comes**; and to Him shall be the obedience of the people (Genesis 49:9-10).* On his death bed, Jacob spoke prophecy over his twelve sons. He calls Judah a lion, and hints that it is through his line that the Messiah would come as a Lawgiver, a Lion from the tribe of Judah. We can confirm this title in Revelation 5:5. *"But one of the elders said to me, "Do not weep. Behold, the **Lion of the tribe of Judah**, the Root of David, has prevailed to open the scroll and to loose its seven seals."* Remember, we are looking for the Tabernacle of the Most High in a city that shall not be moved.

Jacob said to Judah that the scepter shall not depart from Judah, nor a Lawgiver from between his feet, **until Shiloh comes.** Was this prophecy fulfilled in the city of Shiloh with the reassembling of the Tabernacle of Moses after Israel's conquest of the Promised Land? The Tabernacle of Moses was temporary. The Tabernacle moved around many times in the Wilderness and it did come to rest in the Promised Land in Shiloh. However, this was only a temporary version of the Tabernacle established in a temporary place. David somehow understood this in his spirit 350 years later. This was evidenced by his inspiration to replace the Tabernacle of curtains with a Temple made of stone. However, did David believe that a Temple of stone could ultimately contain God Almighty? I believe, in a critical moment in history, David saw much more than this and passed on his prophetic vision to Solomon. *"And now I pray, O God of Israel, let Your word come true, which You have spoken to Your servant David my father. But will God indeed dwell on the earth? Behold, heaven and the heaven of heavens cannot contain You.* **How much less this Temple which I have built!"** *(1 Kings 8:26-27).* Where is the city of God that will not be moved and where is the Tabernacle of the Most High in which His Name will dwell forever?

The city of God that shall not be moved is a reference to Jerusalem, however, not the earthly Jerusalem. *But you have come to Mount Zion and to the city of the living God, the heavenly Jerusalem, to an innumerable company of angels (Hebrews 12:22).* The heavenly city is the New Jerusalem. *"He who overcomes, I will make him a pillar in the Temple of My God, and he shall go out no more. And I will write on him the Name of My God and the name of* **the city of My God, the New Jerusalem,** *which comes down out of heaven from My God. And I will write on him My new Name"* *(Revelation 3:12).*

Let's review the events leading up to David's most profound prophetic moment, and set the stage for the prayer you have been waiting for. Notice how God uses all things to advance His Kingdom.

Man's apparent blunder means God's advance

Remember, it was the elders of Israel who committed the great blunder of removing the Ark from the Tabernacle, which had been established at

Shiloh after Israel's conquest of the Promised Land. The people thought to use the Ark as a great weapon against the Philistines, only to have their master plan backfire in their faces. They lose the battle; Eli's sons are killed; and the Philistines capture the Ark.

Daily life for Israel (the children of God) was built around God's institution. Extreme reverence for prayer, the Tabernacle and its services, and the Ark of the Covenant (and all that it represented), was the center of Hebrew life. What inspired the people to remove that which symbolized the presence, power, and Spirit of God from the Tabernacle, and use it apart from the institution for which it was created? Answer: Hard hearts and pure disobedience. *In those days there was no king in Israel; everyone did what was right in his own eyes (Judges 21:25).*

When Eli discovered his sons were dead, he fell over backwards and broke his neck. Eli's family was cut off for their role in separating the Spirit of God from the institution of God. Separating *"the LORD'S Spirit and power"* from His *"institution"* would be a continuing problem that would plague God's people for generations to come. Today in the Church, we suffer from the long-term effects of this separation. The division of His Spirit from His institution remains the single greatest opponent of unity and is the primary cause of diversity among God's chosen people. Of course, individually, when we receive the Lord into our hearts, the Spirit of the Lord dwells in us. Corporately, the Church certainly contains the Spirit of God. But, the institution of God is divided among thousands of denominations. We don't look or act like one organization, representing one God who has one set of rules (a unified institution). Therefore, His Spirit is dispersed among a disjointed institution. To fix this problem, we need to recognize that we are all individual living stones who need to come together to build the Spiritual Temple. We need to restore the government, rules, and institution of God. Without coming together in unity, we will remain as isolated stones endeavoring to build personal temples out of our own little bricks. However, what the people do in their foolishness, God uses to advance His plan and establish His Kingdom. *Of the increase of His government and peace there will be no end (Isaiah 9:7).* There will be more on this topic in Chapter 10, *Building the Spiritual Temple.*

If ever there was a story where nobody wins, it is this one. Actually, God's plan advances in spite of man, so He wins. The Philistines win the battle and hold the Ark for seven long months. However, they find themselves transporting it from one city to another trying to hide from the judgment of Almighty God. When the Ark was placed in the Temple of Dagon, the people find their pagan god fallen over and smashed to pieces in the morning. *But the hand of the LORD was heavy on the people of Ashdod, and He ravaged them and struck them with tumors, both Ashdod and its territory. And when the men of Ashdod saw how it was, they said, "The Ark of the God of Israel must not remain with us, for His hand is harsh toward us and Dagon our god"* (1 Samuel 5:6-7). In response, the Philistines willingly return the Ark to Israel and it finds its way to Kiriath Jearim where it remained until David moved it to Jerusalem 20 years later. You would think after such a monumental blunder that the Ark would be returned to the Tabernacle, which had been relocated to Gibeon. But the Ark would never again rest in the Holy of Holies in the Tabernacle erected by Moses.

God warned what would happen if man followed after the dictates of his own heart:

> ➤ *(Deuteronomy 29:19-21) "And so it may not happen, when he hears the words of this curse, that he blesses himself in his heart, saying, 'I* **shall have peace, even though I follow the dictates of my heart'** *— as though the drunkard could be included with the sober. The LORD would not spare him; for then the anger of the LORD and His jealousy would burn against that man, and every curse that is written in this Book would settle on him, and the LORD would blot out his name from under heaven. And the LORD would separate him from all the tribes of Israel for adversity, according to all the curses of the covenant that are written in this Book of the Law."*

Another Act of Rebellion

In addition to the "Ark" fiasco, in another act of disobedience, the people demanded that Samuel give them a king. Samuel was old, and his two sons did not walk in his ways, so the people demanded that they needed someone to rule over them and judge them.

➤ *(1 Samuel 8:5b, 6b, 7)* *"Now make us a king to judge us like all the nations." But the thing displeased Samuel when they said, "Give us a king to judge us." So Samuel prayed to the* LORD. *And the* LORD *said to Samuel, "Heed the voice of the people in all that they say to you; for they have not rejected you,* **but they have rejected Me, that I should not reign over them."**

God warned them of what evil would come upon them with a king, but the people demanded one anyway. "We want a king!" So instead of allowing God to rule over them, they settled for Saul who proved unrighteous in all his ways. The people preferred an unrighteous king to a holy and righteous God. What a nightmare! **However, what the people do in their foolishness, God uses to advance His plan and establish His Kingdom.**

As you well know, it was David that succeeded Saul as king of Israel. And it was in God's plan for David's life that he would change the course of history. David, a man after God's own Heart would advance the Temple and be the ancestor of Messiah. What the people do in their foolishness, God uses to advance His plan and establish His Kingdom.

David is anointed as king, is chased around by Saul for a few years, is lifted up in the Wilderness, and protected by the LORD. He then ascends the throne of Judah and next all of Israel. He declares Jerusalem as capital of the united Kingdom, builds his own beautiful palace in the city, and subdues the remaining enemies of Israel. Finally he proclaims, **"The Ark should immediately be moved from Kiriath Jearim back to its proper place in the Holy of Holies in the Tabernacle of Moses in Gibeon!"** Correct? Not Correct! David DOES NOT actually move the Ark of the Covenant to God's Tabernacle, the Tabernacle that was constructed according to every detail of His divine plan which He gave to Moses on the mountain, and told him; *"And see to it that you make them according to the pattern which was shown you on the mountain."* He DOES NOT return the Ark to the Tabernacle that was perfect and beautifully designed by Almighty God Himself. Instead, he decided to move the Ark, which had been kept safely in Kiriath Jearim for 20 years, to Jerusalem, where he had built himself a royal palace. By that time, the entire

Tabernacle had been moved from Shiloh to Gibeon because Shiloh had gone the way of the heathen, and the LORD had removed its anointing. Clearly then, Shiloh was not the permanent place for His Tabernacle.

But the journey of the Ark to Jerusalem was not without trials. God warned Israel precisely how to handle and move His holy things. *"And when Aaron and his sons have finished covering the sanctuary and all the furnishings of the sanctuary, when the camp is set to go, then the sons of Kohath shall come to carry them;* **but they shall not touch any holy thing, lest they die"** *(Numbers 4:15).* This was perfectly clear, but they didn't heed the warning. During David's first attempt to bring the Ark to Jerusalem, he had it placed on an ox cart, and the result was disastrous. *And when they came to Nachon's threshing floor,* **Uzzah put out his hand to the Ark** *of God and took hold of it, for the oxen stumbled. Then the anger of the LORD was aroused against Uzzah, and God struck him there for his error; and he died there by the Ark of God (2 Samuel 6:6-7).* David became so distraught over Uzzah's death that he moved the Ark to the house of Obed-Edom where it rested for three months. Later, he continued its procession to Jerusalem with gladness. With reverence and holiness, he moved the Ark only six paces each time, stopping to make sacrifices to the LORD before every move. When the Ark arrived in Jerusalem, they *set it in its place in the midst of the Tabernacle* **that David had erected for it** *(2 Samuel 6:17b).*

David chose to bring the Ark to Jerusalem and place it in a tent of his **OWN MAKING,** as opposed to the one designed by Almighty God Himself, which was still in Gibeon just a few miles away. It sounds absolutely outrageous, doesn't it? However, shortly afterwards, he becomes increasingly dissatisfied with the Ark dwelling in his tent. It's the moment of truth. What will David do with the Ark? Will he now return it to the original Tabernacle? The answer lies ahead in David's noble assertion. And as you will learn, it was not his sin, but his foresight, that was guiding him.

The time has come to hear his words, and pray the prayer, of a man after God's own Heart!

Chapter Eight

The Prayer of David

"Now it was in the heart of my father David to build a Temple
for the name of the LORD God of Israel."
2 Chronicles 6:7

Here we are standing at the shore of the Jordan. What will it take for us
to cross over on dry ground? It's going to take the heart of David, the
innocence of a shepherd boy, the tenacity of a lion slayer, the authentic
repentance of a forgiven sinner, the unbridled passion of a true worshiper,
and the leadership of a mighty King. It will require boldness to proclaim
the unthinkable with the faith of a man after God's own heart, faith to see
the un-seeable and to know the unknowable. David was capable of something few other men in history would dare to do. He was able to anticipate God's desire before being told, and then he was bold enough to
declare it aloud! What can a man accomplish who loves God so deeply
and wants to honor Him so completely that he can foresee the divine plan
of his Creator before being told? He can achieve what God has not yet
asked! Sound risky? Potentially blasphemous? These will almost certainly be your initial feelings when you realize just how daring David was. Add
the prophetic to a man with David's heart and we have the formula for one
very bold prayer!

My hope for you is that, like David, you have formed such a bond of
uninhibited intimacy with God, that your love for Him will inspire you to
adopt David's vision and join me in his daring prayer. David prayed what
can be considered to be the Believer's equivalent to the Sinner's Prayer.
Now it is your turn! It is time to step into the Jordan. Sin has been
crouching at your door, holding you back from claiming your **FULL** inher-

itance as sons of God. The time has come for you to master it. Across the Jordan, giants lay waiting. Like sin, they represent everything that holds you back from your full inheritance. When you cross over, you must conquer them. If you believe that sin cannot be conquered, you stand guilty of the same lack of faith displayed by those who believed the bad report from the faithless men who originally spied out the Promised Land for Moses. However, I come to bring a good report. "Have no fear. God has already delivered 'the giants' into your hands. The victory is yours!" Now you are ready. Mix unshakable faith, a giant slayer with the heart of David, and the awesome power of the Holy Spirit, and what we have is the sure recipe to part the waters. The time has come for you to step into the river and pass over on dry ground!

Finally...The Prayer of David

You have endured seven chapters waiting to discover what took place in David's life, the cry of his heart during a prophetic moment in time, which would change the course of history forever. Read these words, not with eyes that observe the past. nor with eyes that perceive the present, but with prophetic eyes that envision the future of man's high calling. Remember, after David brought the Ark of God to Jerusalem, he placed it in a tent that he had erected himself. Shortly thereafter, David became increasingly discontent with his decision. He became unsettled about his choice for the new home of the Ark of the Covenant, and he was moved to find a solution. Let's say his uneasiness was inspired determination. Now, try to perceive David's thoughts and words, through his eyes and with his heart.

"Lord, I will build You a House!"

This is David's bold declaration in which I am inviting you to participate! Will you announce that you are willing to build a House for the LORD, a Spiritual Temple? To pray this prayer you must, in faith, confess that you believe you CAN and WILL become like Christ. During your prayer of repentance (Sinner's Prayer), you confessed with your mouth unto salvation. Declare, "LORD, I will build You a House," and you will have believed in your heart unto PERFECTION! If you share David's heart, your children will become "Sons of David." They will be the new Solomon Generation!

It is in David's heart to build a House for the LORD. It is a bold and magnificent proclamation. Prophetically, he is thinking, "Almighty God, I know that you want me to advance your Kingdom. I am willing to step out in faith and boldly proclaim what has never been attempted before; *'LORD, I will build You a House!'"*

Like David, the act of faith, evidenced by your willingness to declare to God and to the world that you will build the Spiritual Temple for the LORD, is enormous. The impact of praying this prayer, while acknowledging its true meaning and prophetic implications, is what will propel the Church to attain its high calling; *till we all come to the unity of the faith and of the knowledge of the Son of God, to a perfect man, to the measure of the stature of the fullness of Christ (Ephesians 4:13).* It will take an army of men and woman with hearts like David (a man after God's own heart) to attain this high calling. This Prayer of David is your step of faith in that direction. Pray it with me, in faith, believing that with God all things are possible; "*LORD, I will build You a House.*" Then experience the transforming power of the Holy Spirit to conform you into the image and likeness of Christ!

The effect of God's people praying this prayer, with hearts like David's, will be the establishment of complete worldwide UNITY throughout the Body of Christ. We will become one faith, one body moving in one direction, together being transformed into the perfect image of Christ and fulfilling His ministry, doing even greater works than He.

Now if the prospect of truly becoming like Jesus and fulfilling the work of His perfect ministry doesn't excite you, then nothing will. If this is the case, you would probably be bored witnessing the dead being raised. On the other hand, if being transformed into the image of Christ is your high calling, if it is the will of our heavenly Father for your life, then you are likely feeling a burst of energy and exhilaration. You should feel inspired to press on to this upward call in Christ Jesus.

Keep in mind how extraordinary this revelation is. Christ's ministry has ONE overriding goal:

> ➤ *(Ephesians 4:13) Till we all come to the unity of the faith and of the knowledge of the Son of God, to a perfect man, to the measure of the stature of the fullness of Christ.*

In this book, we have been exploring and uncovering the mysteries of how this will happen. How will God's Kingdom be established and what role do you play? Remember, if you think you have nothing to do with it, you won't. On the other hand, if you think you play an important part, you will. Utilizing this exciting proposition as motivation, let's continue on. We'll use David, and others like him, to guide us toward our goal.

Why was it so extraordinary that David would pray such a prayer?

Let's explore the account of when this event took place. It was a magnificent moment in time in David's life, when with a heart after God, he was able to peer into the future and see what his LORD wanted.

2 Samuel 7:1-3

*Now it came to pass when the King (David) was dwelling in his house, and the LORD had given him rest from all his enemies all around, that the King said to Nathan the prophet, "See now, I dwell in a house of cedar, **but the Ark of God dwells inside tent curtains."** Then Nathan said to the King, "Go, **do all that is in your heart**, for the LORD is with you."*

What was in David's heart? **"LORD, I will build you a House!"** The LORD will make His name dwell among you <u>after</u> He has given you rest. It was after David had rest from all his enemies that he could truly focus on his higher calling. To hear from God, the LORD advises us all to *be still, and know that I am God (Psalm 46:10).*

After all the risk and effort it took to bring the Ark to Jerusalem, and place it in a tent of curtains that David had erected himself, suddenly David asserts that it is not good enough! The original Tabernacle, designed by YAHWEH Himself, and erected by Moses, was still functioning in Gibeon. What prompted David to bypass returning the Ark to its lawful location in the first place? Why did he instead put it in his own tent of curtains? And if that was not risky enough, he now asserts that a tent made of curtains is not fit for the Ark of God. Why wouldn't it be, when Almighty God Himself designed it that way? And we know that David understood all the details that went into the planning and building of

God's Tabernacle (the one made of curtains). And we know God says in Deuteronomy 12:32: *"Whatever I command you, be careful to observe it; you shall not add to it nor take away from it."* Yet still, David is dissatisfied and wants to build God a new Temple, one made of wood and stone; *"See now, I dwell in a house of cedar,* **but the Ark of God dwells inside tent curtains."** The desire of David's heart is, "LORD, I will build you a *new* House." A house that, in essence, replaces the "perfect" Tabernacle made of curtains, designed by God Himself. David wants to create a new dwelling place for God, **not made of curtains!** Is David committing sin? Are his thoughts and words blasphemous? He knows what the books of Moses say about the holiness of this institution. What is he proposing? You would think that such an assertion would earn David a lightning bolt from heaven! And initially, it doesn't look good for the man after God's own heart.

2 Samuel 7:4-7

But it happened that night that the word of the LORD came to Nathan, saying, "Go and tell My servant David, 'Thus says the LORD: **"Would you build a House for Me to dwell in?** *For I have not dwelt in a House since the time that I brought the children of Israel up from Egypt, even to this day, but have moved about in a tent and in a Tabernacle. Wherever I have moved about with all the children of Israel,* **have I ever spoken a word to anyone** *from the tribes of Israel, whom I commanded to shepherd My people Israel, saying, 'Why have you not built Me a House of cedar?"*

Watch out! At first it appears that God is not happy. He has never dwelt among His people in a House of cedar. **Has God ever asked anyone to build Him a House other than His perfectly designed Tabernacle?** Has YAHWEH Almighty, Creator of the universe, ever proposed such a thing? This kind of proposal from David could surely mean his demise.

The LORD's response could have been, "Who do you think you are, David, proposing something that I have not asked for? Didn't I say, *"Whatever I command you, be careful to observe it; you shall not add to it nor take away from it."* And you know My Law David. You have no excuse! You are blasphemous and evil. I showed Moses many times that he must build the Tabernacle of the LORD precisely how I instructed. Build everything according to the pattern shown you on the Mountain! Do not vary even one thing. David, are you proposing something different? I will bring curses upon you and your entire house throughout your generations forever!"

Or perhaps, David can see something that God wants, something that God is waiting for. Maybe God chose David because he knew the heart of God, and that David would recognize what God wanted of His servant without even asking. Perhaps, David was proposing exactly what God was waiting for.

2 Samuel 7:8

"Now therefore, thus shall you say to My servant David, 'Thus says the LORD of hosts: The LORD goes on to bless David and promises that, through him, Israel would find permanent rest. He would establish the house of David forever. And that it would be through Solomon, David's natural son, that a Temple of stone and cedar would actually rise. *"When your days are fulfilled and you rest with your fathers, I will set up your seed after you, who will come from your body, and I will establish his Kingdom. He shall build a House for My Name, and I will establish the throne of his Kingdom forever"* (2 Samuel 7:12-13). We know God's promise about the natural son of David (Solomon), and how he would build a House for the Name of the LORD. And we should know that the prophecy about how the throne of <u>his</u> Kingdom would be established forever was, in fact, a foreshadow of the work of Christ Jesus (also the son of David). Christ would be born through the kingly line of David. The Messiah is the ultimate "Son of David," and it is through His ministry that we shall build a House for the Name of the LORD. The throne of <u>His</u> Kingdom will be established forever.

Wow! What prophetic foresight by David. His bold declaration opened the floodgates of heaven. The line of David would be established forever, and through his line a Temple would be erected. However, David understood (and, therefore, we should know) that his prayer was not ful-filled in the establishment of a Temple of stone. But rather in the con-struction of the Spiritual Temple — and that is where you come in! *You also, as living stones, are being built up a Spiritual House (1 Peter 2:5).*

Afterwards, David then does the only thing a man after God's own heart would do. He gives God all the credit. *"Now what more can David say to You? For You, Lord GOD, know Your servant. For Your word's sake, and according to Your own heart,* **You have done all these great things, to make Your servant know them"** *(2 Samuel 7:20-21).* And then David prays, *"Now, O LORD God, the word which You have spoken concerning Your servant and concerning his House, establish it forever and do as You have said. So let Your Name be magnified forever, saying, 'The LORD of hosts is the God over Israel. And let the House of Your servant David be established before You. For You, O LORD of hosts, God of Israel, have revealed this to Your servant, saying, 'I will build You a House.' Therefore Your servant has found it in his heart to pray this prayer to You'"* *(2 Samuel 7:25-27).*

> *If you prayed, "LORD, I will build You a House,"*
> *tell us about it. Visit TheHeartofDavid.com*

David acknowledged that it was God who birthed this prophetic moment. **You have done all these great things, to make Your servant know them.** This is what God breathed into David's heart and I pray that He is doing the same for you. Will you build Him a House? Will you pray like David? David's words have both a temporal (Solomon's Temple) and a spiritual (the Spiritual Temple) fulfillment.

The Prayer of David's Heart (Summarized)

No. 1: *"See now, I dwell in a House of cedar, but the Ark of God dwells inside tent curtains."*

> **God has placed a higher calling in your heart. If you are not pur-suing it, you will feel like something is missing.**

I want to build You a House of inanimate stones – Solomon's Temple
I want to build You a House of living stones – The Spiritual Temple

No. 2: *"Would you build a House for Me to dwell in?"*

God is asking if you are willing to become like Christ (the Spiritual Temple), a perfect man, the fullness of the measure of the stature of Messiah.

Would you build Me a House of inanimate stones? – Solomon's Temple
Would you build Me a House of living stones? – The Spiritual Temple

No. 3: *"L*ORD*, I will build You a House!"*

Your answer should be… Yes Lord I will become perfect (sinless)!

Yes, I will build You a House of inanimate stones – Solomon's Temple
Yes, I will build You a House of living stones – The Spiritual Temple

No. 4: *The L*ORD *answers, "He shall build a House for My name, and I will establish the throne of his Kingdom forever."*

It is in David's heart to pray, but it is actually the "Sons of David" who are transformed into the image of Christ.

Solomon (son of David) built the House of inanimate stones – Solomon's Temple
The Solomon generation (Sons of David) will build the House of living stones – The Spiritual Temple

The Prophetic Moment

Taking into account everything you now know about David, it is easier to recognize that he was not ultimately praying about the Temple that Solomon would build. He had the foresight to proclaim that God's anointed could build Him a House, a Spiritual House. More than a millennium after David, his prophetic understanding of God's ultimate plan is firmly established.

> ➤ *(Hebrews 9:11) But Christ came as High Priest of the good things to come, with the greater and more perfect Tabernacle **not made with hands, that is, not of this creation.***

The permanent Tabernacle will be one that will not be moved or taken down. It will not be a tent of curtains or a house of stone. David prophetically knew that he was not merely praying to build a Temple of inanimate stones, but a Temple of living stones built into a Spiritual House.

> ➤ *(1 Peter 2:5) You also, **as living stones, are being built up a spiritual House**, a holy priesthood, to offer up spiritual sacrifices acceptable to God through Jesus Christ.*

> ➤ *(Hebrews 3:6) But Christ as a Son over His own House, **whose House we are** if we hold fast the confidence and the rejoicing of the hope firm to the end.*

Furthermore, three hundred years after David, Isaiah confirmed what I believe to be David's prophetic intention: *Look upon Zion, the city of our appointed feasts; Your eyes will see Jerusalem, a quiet home, **a Tabernacle that will not be taken down; not one of its stakes will ever be removed, nor will any of its cords be broken.** But there the majestic LORD will be for us a place of broad rivers and streams, in which no galley with oars will sail, nor majestic ships pass by (for the LORD is our Judge, the LORD is our Lawgiver, the LORD is our King; He will save us) (Isaiah 33:20-22).* A Tabernacle will be constructed that will not be taken down. It will not be moved; it will be a Spiritual Temple in the New Jerusalem, the City of our God.

> ➤ *(Acts 7:44-50) "Our fathers had the Tabernacle of witness in the Wilderness, as He appointed, instructing Moses to make it according to the pattern that he had seen, "Which our fathers, having received it in turn, also brought with Joshua into the land possessed by the Gentiles, whom God drove out before the face of our fathers until the days of David, "who found favor before God and asked to find a dwelling for the God of Jacob. **"But Solomon built Him a house.** "However, the Most High does not dwell in Temples made with hands, as the prophet (Isaiah) says: 'Heaven is My throne, And earth is My footstool. **What house will you build for Me?** says the LORD, Or what is the place of My rest? Has My hand not made all these things?'*

Passing the Mantle

"Now it was in the heart of my father David to build a Temple for the Name of the LORD God of Israel. But the LORD said to my father David, 'Whereas it was in your heart to build a Temple for My Name, you did well in that it was in your heart. **Nevertheless you shall not build the Temple, but your son who will come from your body, he shall build the Temple for My Name'"** *(2 Chronicles 6:7-9).*

Inasmuch as we have been studying Biblical blueprints, you may well recognize yet another important pattern. It takes one generation to prepare the soil and plant the seed. The next generation reaps the harvest. Moses passed to Joshua, David passed to Solomon, Elijah passed to Elisha, John the Baptist (spirit of Elijah) passed to Jesus (Y'shua), and Y'shua passed His mantle to us (His Body). Because our focus has been on David, for the sake of continuity, I will call the generation who reaps the harvest "The Solomon Generation." The Kingdom and all of its components are built precept upon precept, line upon line. Do you remember the Kingdom mystery of reaping where you had not sown? It is the generation that follows those bold enough to proclaim David's prayer who will reap the harvest of building the Spiritual Temple. Of those receiving the mantle, Jesus said, greater things you will do! So, if we pray with faith that "we will build Him a House," it will be our children, "The Solomon Generation," who will build it. My encouragement to you is, "Take up the mantle and pave the way as forerunners!"

David was king over Israel for 40 years, just as Moses was the leader in the Wilderness for 40 years. Both had to hear and obey God's plan. Both had to hand God's plan to the next generation. Both would pass the mantle to another who would lead in the "Promised Land."

> ➤ **(1 Chronicles 28:10-12, 19-20)** *"Consider now, for the LORD has chosen you to build a House for the sanctuary; be strong, and do it." Then David gave his son Solomon the* **plans...** *and the plans for all that he had* **by the Spirit...** **"All this,"** *said David,* **"the LORD made me understand in writing, by His hand upon me, all the works of these plans."** *And David said to his son Solomon, "Be strong and of*

good courage, and do it; do not fear nor be dismayed, for the LORD *God — my God — will be with you.* **He will not leave you nor forsake you,** *until you have finished all the work for the service of the House of the* LORD."

Just as God gave Moses the plans for the Tabernacle in the Wilderness, and David the plans for Solomon's Temple, He will give us (the last David generation) the plans for the Spiritual Temple and the Kingdom of Heaven. Have no fear; God's plan will come to completion. He will not leave us or forsake us. He is the author **and finisher** of our faith. Like David, we will pass the plans to our "sons," who will complete God's work. And our encouragement to them must be: **"Be strong and of good courage, and do it!"**

David Prepared

With a pure heart, David made provision for Solomon to successfully complete the mission.

> ➢ *(1 Chronicles 29:1-2a, 3) Furthermore King David said to all the assembly: "My son Solomon, whom alone God has chosen, is young and inexperienced; and **the work is great, because the Temple is not for man but for the** LORD **God.** Now for the House of my God I have prepared with all my might... Moreover, because I have set my affection on the House of my God, I have given to the House of my God, over and above all that I have prepared for the holy House, my own special treasure of gold and silver."*

David offered his own personal treasures to build the LORD'S House. Moreover, he gave above and beyond what was needed. Jesus advised we do the same. *"Do not lay up for yourselves treasures on earth, where moth and rust destroy and where thieves break in and steal; "but lay up for yourselves treasures in heaven, where neither moth nor rust destroys and where thieves do not break in and steal" (Matthew 6:19-20)*. David received the plans to build the Temple and collected what was needed to build it. There was no shortage of supplies to complete the task because the LORD provided what was needed with great abundance.

> ➤ *(1 Chronicles 29:16) "O* LORD *our God,* **all this abundance** *that we have prepared to build You a House for Your holy Name is from Your Hand, and is all Your own.*

God has provided the plans to build the Spiritual Temple. They are hidden in the mysteries of the Kingdom of Heaven. We must be good stewards to solve the mysteries and then make the message clear to the next generation. What will you pass on to your children? I believe that we <u>are</u> the David generation who corporately declares, "LORD, I will build you a Spiritual House!" And when we do, we will usher in the Solomon Generation. Be ready to pass the mantle!

In this book, you have gone from Captivity in Section One, to the Wilderness in Section Two. At this moment, you are standing on the shore of the Jordan ready to cross into the Promised Land that is described in Section Three. It is on the Wilderness side of the river that God will release the later-rain outpouring of the Holy Spirit. You will appreciate this more fully in Chapter 9 when we explore, in detail, the double-portion outpouring of the Spirit. The outpouring of the Spirit occurs on this side of the Jordan; but the fruit manifests in the Promised Land.

To demonstrate this pattern, we have the wonderful relationships between Elijah and Elisha, and between Moses and Joshua. Elijah and Moses are Wilderness prophets, the prophets of preparation. David, like Elijah and Moses, also stood at the shore of *his* Jordan, ready to pass on his plans and provision to Solomon. It is at the shoreline that the mantle passes to the next generation. Recall now that both Elisha and Joshua passed over on dry ground, and so must the Solomon generation.

David prayed for and encouraged Solomon

David prayed for his son; *"and give my son Solomon a loyal heart to keep Your commandments and Your testimonies and Your statutes, to do all these things, and to build the Temple for which I have made provision (1 Chronicles 29:19)."* He also encouraged him; *and David said to his son Solomon,* **"Be strong and of good courage, and do it;** *do not fear nor be dismayed, for the* LORD *God, my God, will be with you.* **He will not leave you nor forsake you,** *until you have finished all the work for the service of the House of the* LORD *(1 Chronicles 28:20).*

Don't fear the Giants

On the other side of the Jordan there are giants in the Land. The question for you is: Whose report will you believe? Before Israel's first opportunity to cross into the Promised Land, twelve men spied out the Land and only Joshua and Caleb gave a good report. Those who gave a bad report inspired fear in the children of Israel. *"There we saw giants"* *(Numbers 13:13).* They complained against Moses and said to one another, *"Let us select a leader and return to Egypt"* *(Numbers 14:4).* Can you imagine? They had been in the Wilderness for more than a year, during which they witnessed countless miracles by the hand of God. Nevertheless, when they arrived at the moment of their inheritance, because of fear, they decided that going back to bondage in Egypt was easier and safer than trusting God to defeat their enemies. For this rebellion, God pronounced that all the people above 20 years of age, except Caleb and Joshua, would die in the Wilderness. He assigned them one year in the Wilderness for each of the 40 days the spies were in the Promised Land. The ten spies, who brought the evil report about the Land, died by the plague before the LORD. For this very same reason, David reassured Solomon; *"He will not leave you nor forsake you."* David did not want Solomon to make the same fearful mistake as the rebels in the Wilderness, or the fainthearted Israelites who believed them. *"Be strong and of good courage, and do it!"*

In our pursuit of Christ-like perfection, the giants in the land actually represent sin. *Sin is crouching at your door; it desires to have you, but you must master it (Genesis 4:7b NIV).* Remember, **He will not leave you nor forsake you.** If you believe that you cannot master sin, then you believe a bad report. You may be saying in your heart *"Let us select a leader and return to Egypt."* That is, "Let me find someone espousing an easier 'gospel' so I don't need to make the changes the Wilderness requires." Do not go back! Today, if you hear His voice, do not harden your hearts as in the rebellion, as in the day of trial in the Wilderness. Instead, pray the Prayer of David . Say, "Father, I will build You a House. I confess with my mouth and believe in my heart that I CAN become like Jesus! I will become a living stone in the walls of the Spiritual Temple." Believe this and pass over on dry ground!

A word of advice to the Solomon Generation

Now these are the last words of David. Thus says David the son of Jesse; thus says the man raised up on high, the anointed of the God of Jacob, and the sweet psalmist of Israel: **"The Spirit of the LORD spoke by me, and His word was on my tongue"** *(2 Samuel 23:1-2).*

In the first century, Jesus said to His disciples, *"The harvest truly is plentiful,* **but the laborers are few.** *Therefore pray the Lord of the harvest to send out laborers into His harvest."* As we make the message clear and gather an army of forerunners at the shore of the Jordan, we will learn to establish a system for how to equip enough laborers to preach the Gospel of the Kingdom to **all** the world. *"And this Gospel of the Kingdom will be preached in all the world as a witness to all the nations, and then the end will come"* *(Matthew 24:14).* Like David's advice to Solomon, hearken unto the Spirit of the LORD and have His word always on your tongue.

Elijah is coming back and his spirit will eventually call out to **all** the laborers. As forerunners or spies, we must make the prophetic journey across the Jordan first. We must return with a good report, living proof that the Land is good and that the giants can indeed be conquered. In order for the rest of the people to come to the shore of the Jordan, we must first free them from Captivity. We must go all the way back to Egypt to demand that the world "Let my people go!" We must instruct the people to, "Repent, for the Kingdom of Heaven is at hand." We must warn them to **NOT** harden their hearts while in the Wilderness, but rather be faithful to explore and uncover the mysteries of the Kingdom. Together, we will make this "Gospel of the Kingdom" clear to the world. To exit the Wilderness, we must acknowledge the ministry of Elijah and "Remember the Law of Moses." We must follow the example of David and proclaim today, "LORD, I will build You a house." In the words of Christ Jesus, the Son of God Himself, we must believe we can *"Be perfect, just as My Father in heaven is perfect."*

I consider that our present sufferings are not worth comparing with the glory that will be revealed in us. The creation waits in eager expectation for the sons of God to be revealed. NIV **Romans 8:18-19**

If you boldly proclaim the Prayer of David, and you dare to believe that you might build the Spiritual Temple, you have the faith to be transformed into the image of Christ. You will do even greater works than He. Step into the Jordan and watch the waters part before you. Pass over on dry ground. Ahead of you is the Land of milk and honey. Step with faith toward your inheritance. Your sandals will not only be perfectly dry, but not in the least bit worn out when you reach your destination. Behold! The manifestation of the sons of God!

Section Three:
The Solomon Generation

Chapter Nine

Passing the Mantle

*"Consider now, for the Lord has chosen you to build a
House for the sanctuary; be strong, and do it."*
1 Chronicles 28:10

W e have emerged from the dry river bed and find ourselves standing in the midst of the LORD'S promises. *According to the doings
of the land of Egypt, where you dwelt, you shall not do; and according to the
doings of the Land of Canaan, where I am bringing you, you shall not do; nor
shall you walk in their ordinances (Leviticus 18:3).* In the Land that we have
come to inherit, we must remain faithful to follow the LORD in all His
ways. We have believed sufficiently in His promises to cross over, yet there
is still another act of faith for us to complete. There are giants in the Land
and we need to conquer them before we can posses it. Remember, however, we have entered only as forerunners, spies you might say, a small rep-
resentation of the whole. We have entered only as a shadow of the future
crossing. At this time we cannot stay and possess the Land. It is not the
role of our generation. In the future, in God's grand scheme, the generation that births great men, as bold as Moses, David, and Elijah, will prepare the way of the LORD and make straight a path in the Wilderness. The
generation that follows these bold forerunners will cross the Jordan, conquer the Land, posses it, and build the Temple. However, after this final
prophetic crossing of the Jordan, it is SIN that is the giant that must be
conquered; it is AUTHORITY that is the land that will be possessed; and
it is the PERFECTION of the Body that is a Spiritual Temple of living
stones erected in place of a House of lifeless stones.

If you prayed the Prayer of David with the heart of David, you might just echo the words of the Prophet Isaiah who said, *"Here am I! Send me."* I will do whatever it takes. With a new heart we can receive the passing of the mantle, the passing of the authority, and the endowment of a double-portion of power. If we can trust in Biblical patterns, we will have "eyes to see" and "ears to hear" a new and higher calling.

The Wilderness Generation

In addition to declaring that he would build a House for the LORD, which we now recognize as the prophetic declaration inspiring us to build the Spiritual Temple, David's life also represents the prophetic overlay of the generation that **did not** enter into the Promised Land. As wonderful as was David's heart and all his fame, he still was not the man to build the Temple. David was so focused that he could sense God's will. He was so fervent in his faith that he would assertively declare his intentions. And David was so favored by the LORD that God blessed him with the plans, and chose him to gather the materials to build the Temple. However, David was not the man who would actually build God's House. In a sense, David did not enter the Promised Land. David had to pass his anointing to the next generation to complete the will of God.

Why? Why would the LORD not allow David to perform the actual building? I want you to consider that question very carefully and relate it to the work of our generation; for we also must prepare the way for the next generation: The Solomon Generation.

> ➤ *(1 Chronicles 28:2-3) King David rose to his feet and said: "Listen to me, my brothers and my people. I had it in my heart to build a House as a place of rest for the Ark of the Covenant of the LORD, for the footstool of our God, and I made plans to build it. But God said to me,* **'You are not to build a House for my Name, because you are a warrior and have shed blood.'**

David was a warrior and a man of force. What prophetic picture does this paint? We too are a generation of warriors, warriors who must advance the Kingdom of Heaven. Prophetically speaking, every generation since

John the Baptist has been the "Davidic Generation" of warriors. Concerning this generation, Jesus said in Matthew 11:11-12: *"Assuredly, I say to you, among those born of women there has not risen one greater than John the Baptist; but he who is least in the Kingdom of Heaven is greater than he. And from the days of John the Baptist until now the Kingdom of Heaven suffers violence, and the violent take it by force."* In Matthew 10:34, Jesus said of his first coming, *"Do not think that I came to bring peace on earth. I did not come to bring peace but a sword."* Really it is the work of the forerunners, like the Moses, David, and the Elijah generation, who will forcefully advance the Kingdom. The New International Version says it this way: *From the days of John the Baptist until now, the Kingdom of Heaven* **has been forcefully advancing, and forceful men lay hold of it** *(Matthew 11:12).*

Moses, David, and Elijah all had to pass on the work commissioned to them by the LORD for the next generation to complete. And greater works were done by that next generation. Moses led the people to the shore of the Jordan, but Joshua led them into the Promised Land and conquered the "giants" therein. David was inspired to build a "House for the LORD," but it was Solomon who built the Temple in all its majesty, and the Glory of the LORD dwelt inside it. Elijah passed on a double-portion of his anointing to Elisha; and even after Elisha died, his bones resurrected a man (2 Kings 13:21). Even though they were physically born in the same generation, John the Baptist made a path straight in the Wilderness for the Lord and then said in John 3:30, *"He must increase, but I must decrease,"* thereby passing the mantle. One generation proclaims, "The Kingdom of Heaven is at hand." While the next generation proclaims, "The Kingdom of Heaven has arrived." Of course these are all prophetic overlays. It is not until the final "Solomon Generation" that the Kingdom will have come. LORD, Thy Kingdom come, Thy will be done. So in a prophetic sense, we are all the Moses/David/Elijah Generation, and the next generation, if we will be so faithful as to "make the message clear," will be the Joshua/Solomon/Elisha Generation.

We can discover some of the characteristics and roles of our generation, and the next, by exploring God's plan for the passing of the mantle. I understand that it may appear that these are stories from the past. However, Jesus made it perfectly clear that these events would repeat in predictable patterns. *"Why then do the scribes say that Elijah must come first?" Jesus answered and said to them, "Indeed, Elijah is coming first and will restore all things. But I say to you that Elijah has come already"* (Matthew 17:10-12). Elijah has come and is coming. *"Behold, I will send you Elijah the prophet before the coming of the great and dreadful day of the LORD"* (Malachi 4:5). Indeed, Elijah is coming first and will restore all things. Learn to read the blueprint and you may become a master builder. It is very possible that we are **THE** generation of Elijah who is coming again before the great and dreadful day of the LORD.

If true, then our job as the Moses/David/Elijah Generation is to restore all things.

> ➤ **(Acts 3:19-21)** *"Repent therefore and be converted, that your sins may be blotted out, so that times of refreshing may come from the presence of the Lord, and that He may send Jesus Christ, who was preached to you before,* **"whom heaven must receive until the times of restoration of all things,** *which God has spoken by the mouth of all His holy prophets since the world began."*

Jesus is waiting in heaven until the restoration of all things. I understand that some teach that God will do the restoring. For instance, the NIV says it this way: *He must remain in heaven until the time comes* **for God to restore everything,** *as he promised long ago through his holy prophets.* However, the NIV is the only major translation that paraphrases this verse in such a way. All others say that Jesus is waiting in heaven **"until"** the times of restoration of all things; and Jesus taught us that *"Elijah is coming first and* **will restore all things."**

The restoration involves many things including, unity of our faith, as well as belief that we can defeat the Lord's enemies, becoming masters over sin. The Lord will not return until the restoration of all things. *But this Man, after He had offered one sacrifice for sins forever, sat down at the right hand of God, from that time* **waiting till His enemies are made His footstool** (Hebrews 10:12-13). Our role is to make the Gospel of the Kingdom clear to the next generation so they can make the message clear to the entire world. Like David, we can collect the building materials, but the Solomon Generation assembles the House of God.

How is David like Moses?

Whereas David could not build the permanent place for the name of the LORD to dwell, neither did Moses. Moses was promised that after Israel crossed over the Jordan and found rest from all their enemies, "*...then there will be the place where the LORD your God chooses to make His name abide*" (*Deuteronomy 12:11*). However, Moses never crossed the Jordan to find rest. Just like David passed the privilege on to Solomon, Moses had to choose a man to whom he could pass the anointing. (Please keep your prophetic glasses on.) I recognize that neither Joshua nor Solomon assembled a dwelling in which God's name would "abide forever." Nevertheless, the necessity to pass the mantle was prophetically established so we could recognize the LORD'S blueprint for history. There will be a generation that passes the mantle one final time after the restoration of all things.

Moses' Great Blunder

In the case of Moses, he could not enter the Promised Land because of one seemingly obscure mistake. Nevertheless, it made him, in a prophetic sense, "a man of blood" like David. Shortly after the exodus, Israel found itself without water in the Wilderness. Instead of choosing to trust the LORD, they complained. *And the LORD said to Moses, "Go on before the people, and take with you some of the elders of Israel. Also take in your hand your rod with which you struck the river, and go. Behold, I will stand before you there on the rock in Horeb; and you shall strike the rock, and water will come out of it, that the people may drink." And Moses did so in the sight of the elders of Israel* (*Exodus 17:5-6*). Water poured forth and Israel drank. The demonstration of the power of God through Moses was awesome. I dare say that any assembly of born again Christians today, or even pagans for that matter, would be equally as awed by this demonstration of power.

However, later on towards the end of their journey, the Israelites were faced with the same dilemma. Again they grumbled and complained and Moses and Aaron sought the LORD.

> *Then the LORD spoke to Moses, saying, "Take the rod; you and your brother Aaron gather the congregation together. **Speak to the rock** before their eyes, and it will yield its water; thus you shall bring water for them out of the rock, and give drink to the congregation and their animals." So Moses took the rod from before the LORD as He commanded him. And Moses and Aaron gathered the assembly together before the rock; and he said to them, "Hear now, you rebels! Must we bring water for you out of this rock?" Then Moses lifted his hand and **struck the rock twice** with his rod; and water came out abundantly, and the congregation and their animals drank. Then the LORD spoke to Moses and Aaron, "**Because you did not believe Me**, to hallow Me in the eyes of the children of Israel, therefore you shall not bring this assembly into the Land which I have given them" (Numbers 20:7-12).*

Let's examine this critical demonstration of a **lack of faith** displayed by Moses, the great Wilderness prophet of Israel. To the untrained eye, it may seem like Moses performed yet another great miracle in the sight of the people. Earlier, just a few months into their journey, Moses performed a similar miracle. Moses needed enough water to satisfy the thirst of two to three million sun-scorched Israelites; and the LORD told Moses to bring forth this much needed water from a rock. Moses struck the rock, and the people witnessed fresh water gushing forth. This miracle testified to the awesome power and supernatural provision of God. You know the satirical saying, "You can't get water from a rock!" Well, that's true of course, unless you are Moses.

When the same problem arose a second time, in what appears to be almost 40 years later, Moses again needed to intercede for the people, seeking the LORD'S favor for the people's provision. Moses had already witnessed God's faithfulness to make good on His promise in the exact same circumstance before, so this was easy. When God says to strike the rock and water will come forth, you can trust Him. However, notice on second occasion that the LORD did not say to "strike the rock." He told Moses to "speak to the rock!" But instead of speaking to the rock, Moses resorted to that in which he was already comfortable, and he struck the rock again. In fact, he struck it two times, giving us the sense that it may not have worked the first time. Ultimately, water did flow from the rock that God might provide for His people. But unlike the first episode of thirst, which proved the people, this test was for Moses. God then responded with what appears to be an overreaction.

> *"Because you did not believe Me,*
> *to hallow Me in the eyes of the children of Israel,*
> *therefore you shall not bring this assembly into the Land*
> *which I have given them."*

Moses is found guilty of a lack of faith. This is incredible, don't you think? Wouldn't you feel somewhat excited and proud of God's power working in you if you could strike a rock and bring forth water? However, Moses struck the rock instead of speaking to the rock. The LORD created an opportunity, through Moses, for the people to witness the power of God's WORD! In its place, Moses made a subtle expression of his own will, power, and authority. His disobedience is a demonstration of a "lack of faith." The "striking the rock" technique had worked before, so it was a tested method. However, he had never seen "speaking" work before, and so that would have been an action based on faith alone. And remember, God views disobedience as a sign of a lack of faith. Hebrews 3:18-19 describes it this way: To whom did the LORD swear that they would not enter the Promised Land, but to those who **did not obey Him?** So we see that they could not enter in because they **did not believe Him!**

Let's discover the prophetic consequence of Moses' poor example. Jesus is the Rock and He said in John 7:37b-38, *"If anyone thirsts, let him come to Me and drink. He **who believes in Me**, as the Scripture has said, out of his heart will flow rivers of living water."* Moses' lack of faith in the Word of God, in this one instance, was a shadow of the eternal consequences of a lack of faith for all future generations. In other words, a lack of faith brings death (in the wilderness). Just like David, this makes Moses a man who shed blood! Remember, God said to David, *'You are not to build a House for my Name, because you are a warrior and have shed blood.'* A lack of faith will forever keep you out of the Promised Land. *Now with whom was He angry forty years? Was it not with those who sinned, whose corpses fell* *in the Wilderness? And to whom did He swear that they would not enter His rest, but to those who did not obey? So we see that they could not enter in because of unbelief (Hebrews 3:17-19).*

Another possible explanation for why God dealt so harshly with Moses for "striking the rock" is because Jesus (the Rock) would only be struck once for all time for our sins. When Moses chose to strike the rock a second (and third) time, he was making a misrepresentation of the Messiah's ministry. Just some food for thought. Keep this in mind; in *The Heart of David* I am trying to illustrate to you that within the Scriptures exist the blueprints or patterns of God's plan for mankind. So today, and I mean this very day, if YOU hear His voice, do not harden your hearts as they did in the Wilderness!

Moses, like David, must pass the mantle & die in the Wilderness

Then Moses went and spoke these words to all Israel. And he said to them: "I am one hundred and twenty years old today. I can no longer go out and come in. Also the LORD has said to me, 'You shall not cross over this Jordan.' The LORD your God Himself crosses over before you; He will destroy these nations from before you, and you shall dispossess them. Joshua himself crosses over before you, just as the LORD has said…" Then *Moses called Joshua and said to him in the sight of all Israel, "Be strong and of good courage, for you must go with this people to the Land which the LORD has sworn to their fathers to give them, and you shall cause them to inherit it"* (Deuteronomy 31:1-3, 7). (Note the prophetic overlay. If you remember, David borrowed these same words of encouragement, "Be strong and of good courage," when he passed the mantle to Solomon.) *Then the LORD said to him, "This is the Land of which I swore to give Abraham, Isaac, and Jacob, saying, 'I will give it to your descendants.' I have caused you to see it with your eyes, but you shall not cross over there."* So Moses the servant of the LORD died there in the land of Moab, according to the word of the LORD (Deuteronomy 34:4-5).

Accepting the mantle from the Moses/David/Elijah Generation

Joshua accepted his position as the LORD'S anointed in Deuteronomy 34:9-10.

> ➤ *Now Joshua the son of Nun was full of the spirit of wisdom, for* **Moses had laid his hands on him;** *so the children of Israel heeded him, and did as the LORD had commanded Moses.* **But since then there has not arisen in Israel a prophet like Moses,** *whom the LORD knew face to face.*

We learned earlier from Deuteronomy 18 that in the future the LORD would raise up **another prophet like Moses** from among Israel, another prophet to carry on the ministry of Moses. All his words would be heeded by the people. This confirms our understanding of prophetic overlays. There is always a Joshua who follows Moses, a Solomon who follows David, and an Elisha who follows Elijah.

> ➤ *(Joshua 1:1-3) After the death of Moses the servant of the LORD, it came to pass that the LORD spoke to Joshua the son of Nun, Moses' assistant, saying:* **"Moses My servant is dead. Now therefore, arise, go over this Jordan,** *you and all this people, to the Land which I am giving to them — the children of Israel. Every place that the sole of your foot will tread upon I have given you, as I said to Moses."*

When you receive the call, like Joshua, you must without hesitation *arise and go over* **YOUR** *Jordan!* You must do so with power, confidence, and authority. When the call goes out to cross over, do not waver. A lack of faith will earn you thirty-nine extra years in the Wilderness. Remember, every place that the soles of your feet tread **WILL** be yours.

Bear in mind what we established from our earlier studies. It is Elijah who is the prophet like Moses who will be raised up in the Last Days before the second coming of our Lord. Jesus taught us that Elijah has come and is coming again to restore all things. The LORD warned that if you don't listen to him, *He would come and strike the earth with a curse!* Just like Moses passed his anointing to Joshua, David to Solomon, and Elijah to Elisha, Elijah, who will come again to restore all things, will pass on his mantle to the generation who will build the Spiritual Temple and usher in the Kingdom of God.

An excellent example of taking up the mantle

The 9th Century BCE Elisha serves as the perfect prototype of a servant who takes up the mantle of God's anointed, thus becoming God's anointed. He demonstrated the excellent faith needed to accept the power and authority passed on to him. Let's take a look at the passing of power and authority from Elijah to Elisha in 2 Kings. We'll trace the amazing blueprints of God's plan for those who love Him. Paul taught us in 1 Corinthians 2:9-10 that, *"Eye has not seen, nor ear heard, nor have entered into the heart of man the things which God has prepared for those who love Him. But God has revealed them to us through His Spirit."* I want you to notice Elisha's heart and his willingness to persevere. See his acknowledgement of Elijah's power and authority, and his bold request for it to pass to him. Observe the fulfillment of his request and how he readily accepts the power and authority passed on to him. Most importantly, watch how Elisha puts such authority to immediate use. Also witness the validation of his legitimate claim to authority by others. Notice the short "testing" period, even though there is no doubt that he is favored by God. And behold, in Christ-like fashion, the removal of death and bareness. Finally, there is judgment for those who come against him. See if you can recognize how these events shadow our relationship with Christ. All power and authority in heaven and earth was given to Jesus and He passed it on to us.

We will pick up the story in 2 Kings 2. This story takes place as Elijah makes his way from the Promised Land side of the Jordan back to the Wilderness side. The Wilderness is where the Wilderness prophet must complete his ministry. He is taken up by God in the Wilderness. Then Elisha (prophetically the same as Joshua, Solomon, and Jesus), with the double-portion anointing, must cross the Jordan on dry ground. Elisha, like Christ, becomes the Promised Land prophet with all truth, all power, and all authority. The Solomon Generation has the same calling! Again, how beautiful are the mysteries of Scriptural overlay.

Elisha's heart is prepared to seek the House of God

And it came to pass, when the LORD was about to take up Elijah into heaven by a whirlwind, that Elijah went with Elisha from Gilgal. Then Elijah said to Elisha, "Stay here, please, for the LORD has sent me on to Bethel" (Bethel means "the House of God"). *But Elisha said, "As the LORD lives, and as your soul lives, I will not leave you!" So they went down to Bethel* (2 Kings 2:1-2). Elijah is going on to the "House of God" and Elisha is going with him. Nothing will stop him.

Elisha pressed on to the high calling

Now the sons of the prophets who were at Bethel came out to Elisha, and said to him, "Do you know that the LORD will take away your master from over you today?" And he said, "Yes, I know; keep silent!" Then Elijah said to him, "Elisha, stay here, please, for the LORD has sent me on to Jericho." But he said, "As the LORD lives, and as your soul lives, I will not leave you!" So they came to Jericho. Now the sons of the prophets who were at Jericho came to Elisha and said to him, "Do you know that the LORD will take away your master from over you today?" So he answered, "Yes, I know; keep silent!" Then Elijah said to him, "Stay here, please, for the LORD has sent me on to the Jordan." But he said, "As the LORD lives, and as your soul lives, I will not leave you!" So the two of them went on (2 Kings 2:3-6). Elijah asked his servant to stay behind a second time, yet Elisha pursued his master with determination and grit. He demonstrated fortitude and perseverance. He proved he would run the race with certainty.

Elijah demonstrated his power and authority

And fifty men of the sons of the prophets went and stood facing them at a distance, while the two of them stood by the Jordan. Now Elijah took his mantle, rolled it up, and struck the water; and it was divided this way and that, so that the two of them crossed over on dry ground (2 Kings 2:7-8). Elisha witnessed Elijah's anointing.

219

Elisha requested a double-portion of Elijah's power and authority

*And so it was, when they had crossed over, that Elijah said to Elisha, "Ask! What may I do for you, before I am taken away from you?" Elisha said, "Please let a **double-portion** of your spirit be upon me." So he said, "You have asked a hard thing. Nevertheless, if you see me when I am taken from you, it shall be so for you; but if not, it shall not be so"* (2 Kings 2:9-10). Elisha was bold. He wanted a double-portion of the spirit of Elijah. He would need it to face the Jordan on his way back to the Promised Land and he wanted the faith to do it with confidence. There are always giants in the Land of promise that need to be faced with utter faith!

Elisha recognized that his request would be fulfilled

Then it happened, as they continued on and talked, that suddenly a chariot of fire appeared with horses of fire, and separated the two of them; and Elijah went up by a whirlwind into heaven. And Elisha saw it, and he cried out, "My father, my father, the chariot of Israel and its horsemen!" So he saw him no more. And he took hold of his own clothes and tore them into two pieces (2 Kings 2:11-12). Elijah was taken up alive and left behind his spirit. His spirit filled Elisha, later on John the Baptist, and today it dwells in the hearts of the forerunners. In addition to these, **"The Prophet"** Elijah is <u>coming again</u> to restore all things.

Elisha accepted the power and authority

*He also **took up the mantle** of Elijah that had fallen from him and went back and stood by the bank of the Jordan* (2 Kings 2:13). Elisha faced the Jordan and had to decide: Will I pass over on dry ground? Remember, it was at Israel's first opportunity to cross the Jordan into the Promised Land that they fell victim to a bad report and lost faith. There were giants in the

Land and the people became afraid. They complained: *"Would it not be better for us to return to Egypt?"* (Numbers 14:3). Elisha does not want to make the same mistake!

The LORD instructed Moses to send one leader from each of the tribes to spy out the land. All but two of them came back with a bad report. *"We are not able to go up against the people, for they are stronger than we"* (Numbers 13:31). But Joshua and Caleb had faith in the LORD'S promises. *"The Land we passed through to spy out is an exceedingly good land"* (Numbers 14:7). As a forerunner, when **YOU** test the Promised Land, will you give a good or bad report to the people when you come back? If you are someone waiting for the news, will you believe the report that the giants are too large and too strong, or will you enter boldly into the Jordan like Elisha did?

Elisha represents the model of how to respond when faced with giants on the other side of the river. Prophetically speaking, it represents how we should respond when faced with the prospect of becoming sinless. There are four groups and you must decide into which category you fall. The first two groups contain forerunners. One will spy out the Land and say that the giants (sin) can be conquered. *"Let us go up at once and take possession, for we are well able to overcome it"* (Numbers 13:30). The other will bail out and say. *"We are not able to go up against the people, for they are stronger than we"* (Numbers 13:31). I believe, if you have come thus far in *The Heart of David*, you are a forerunner and you must bring back the report. Which spy are you going to be?

The other two groups contain those who are waiting in the Wilderness for the report. If you are one of these people, your job is to decide whose report you believe? If you believe that sin cannot be mastered, you will die in the Wilderness. *Except for Caleb the son of Jephunneh and Joshua the son of Nun, you shall by no means enter the Land which I swore I would make you dwell in... But as for you, your carcasses shall fall in this Wilderness* (Numbers 14:31-32). If you believe that sin desires to have you, but that you should rule over it, you will enter the Promised Land with boldness like Joshua and Caleb. *"But My servant Caleb, because he has a **different spirit** in him and has followed Me fully, I will bring into the Land where he went, and his descendants **shall inherit it**"* (Numbers 14:24).

Elisha put his power & authority to immediate use

Then he took the mantle of Elijah that had fallen from him, and struck the water, and said, "Where is the LORD God of Elijah?" And when he also had struck the water, it was divided this way and that; and Elisha crossed over (2 Kings 2:14). **Elisha crossed over on dry ground!**

The mantle has passed- Elisha's legitimate claim is validated

Now when the sons of the prophets who were from Jericho saw him, they said, **"The spirit of Elijah rests on Elisha."** *And they came to meet him, and bowed to the ground before him (2 Kings 2:15).* The disciple has taken on a double-portion anointing of his master. It is clear that Elisha has become like his master and taken on his ministry. Isn't this precisely what Paul said **WE** should do in Ephesians 4:13? We must mature as Believers *till we all come to the unity of the faith and of the knowledge of the Son of God, to a perfect man, to the measure of the stature of the fullness of Christ.*

A moment of doubt even after the truth

Then they said to him, "Look now, there are fifty strong men with your servants. Please let them go and search for your master, lest perhaps the Spirit of the LORD has taken him up and cast him upon some mountain or into some valley." And he said, "You shall not send anyone." But when they urged him till he was ashamed, he said, "Send them!" Therefore they sent fifty men, and they searched for **three days** *but did not find him. And when they came back to him, for he had stayed in Jericho, he said to them, "Did I not say to you, 'Do not go'?" (2 Kings 2:16-18).*

Remember the crazy question John posed to Jesus from prison in Luke 7:20? *"John the Baptist has sent us to You, saying, 'Are You the Coming One, or do we look for another?"* Don't you scratch your head, wondering how he could ask such a bonehead question? Didn't John proclaim, "Behold, the Lamb of God"? Nevertheless, our humanity always seems to birth an element of doubt. Wow! What prophetic mastery the story of Elisha displays. The sons of the prophets are essentially asking Elisha, even after they announce that the spirit of Elijah rests on him, "Are you the one or do we look for another?" There seems to be a need for three days of doubt and three days of separation to confirm God's anointed. Moses requested three days' journey into the Wilderness three times. Israel wandered three days in the Wilderness and found no water. Israel prepared three days to cross over the Jordan. After three days, young Jesus' parents found Him teaching in the Temple. For three days, the crowds who followed Jesus had nothing to eat and then He fed them. It took three days for Jesus to rise again and three days to build another Temple made without hands. For three days the disciples hid themselves fearing for their lives, believing the Master was dead. Is the Master dead? *"For as Jonah was three days and three nights in the belly of the great fish, so will the Son of Man be three days and three nights in the heart of the earth (Matthew 12:40).* Elisha waited three days. His master was not dead. His spirit lived on in Elisha.

Signs & wonders are present when the Kingdom is at hand

Then the men of the city said to Elisha, "Please notice, the situation of this city is pleasant, as my lord sees; but the water is bad, and the ground barren." And he said, "Bring me a new bowl, and put salt in it." So they brought it to him. Then he went out to the source of the water, and cast in the salt there, and said, "Thus says the LORD: *'I have healed this water; from it there shall be no more death or barrenness.'" So the water remains healed to this day, according to the word of Elisha which he spoke* (2 Kings 2:19-22). The anointed of God have the power to speak forth life! *Then Jesus went about all the cities and villages, teaching in their synagogues, preaching the Gospel of the Kingdom, and healing every sickness and every disease among the people (Matthew 9:35).*

Judgment of the unbeliever

Then he went up from there to Bethel; and as he was going up the road, some youths came from the city and mocked him, and said to him, "Go up, you bald-

223

head! Go up, you baldhead!" *So he turned around and looked at them, and* **pronounced a curse on them** *in the Name of the LORD. And two female bears came out of the woods and mauled forty-two of the youths.* *Then he went from there to Mount Carmel, and from there he returned to Samaria (2 Kings 2:23-25).* Elisha pronounced judgment foreshadowing Christ's judgment in the end! *I charge you therefore before God and the Lord Jesus Christ,* **who will judge the living and the dead** *at His appearing and His Kingdom (2 Timothy 4:1).*

Elisha was brave enough to press on to the high calling, bold enough to ask for what he wanted, and confident enough to receive it. So, we can clearly see that passing and receiving the mantle of power and authority takes on this pattern:

1. Preparation of the heart.
2. Willingness to press on to the high calling.
3. Acknowledgement of the power and authority that is available.
4. Request for a double-portion of power and authority to be passed on.
5. Recognition that the request will be fulfilled.
6. Acceptance of the power and authority handed over.
7. Immediate application of the newly transferred power and authority.
8. Validation of the legitimate claim to authority.
9. A pause for confirmation of God's anointed.
10. Signs & wonders affirming Kingdom business is being accomplished.
11. Judgment of the unbeliever.

Let's put this in perspective with our relationship to Jesus, the passing of His mantle, and then bring together how this connects with David and his bold prayer. The bottom line is this: We have a high calling and the authority to complete our mission. Jesus said in John 17:17-18:

➤ *"Sanctify them by Your truth. Your word is truth. As You sent Me into the world,* **I also have sent them into the world."**

And in John 14:12 He said:

➤ *"Most assuredly, I say to you, he who believes in Me, the works that I do he will do also; and greater works than these he will do, because I go to My Father."*

Jesus sent us into the world to do even greater works than He, and if you apply the lesson in the parable about the nobleman, you will recall that He has equipped us to complete the mission. The master says, "Do business until I return!" Our Master has made His business known to us. Surely, we are obligated to be good stewards of our Master's business.

➤ *(John 15:14-15) "You are My friends if you do whatever I command you. No longer do I call you servants, for a servant does not know what his master is doing; but I have called you friends, for all things that I heard from My Father I have made known to you."*

And before He left to sit at the right hand of the father he passed the mantle.

➤ *(Matthew 28:18-20) And Jesus came and spoke to them, saying, "All authority has been given to Me in heaven and on earth. Go therefore and make disciples of all the nations, baptizing them in the Name of the Father and of the Son and of the Holy Spirit, teaching them to observe all things that I have commanded you; and lo, I am with you always, even to the end of the age." Amen.*

He has passed on His mantle to us and has sent His spirit to help us finish the work He started.

➤ *(John 16:12-15) "I still have many things to say to you, but you cannot bear them now. However, when He, the Spirit of truth, has come, He will guide you into all truth; for He will not speak on His own authority, but whatever He hears He will speak; and He will tell you things to come. He will glorify Me, for He will take of what is Mine and declare it to you. All things that the Father has are Mine. Therefore I said that He will take of Mine and declare it to you."*

ALL that the Father has given to Jesus, Jesus has passed on to us. EVERYTHING! His mantle has passed. And "All authority" ultimately reflects the Father's authority.

➤ *(John 17:22-23) "And the glory which You gave Me I have given them, that they may be one just as We are one: I in them, and You in Me; that they may be made perfect in one, and that the world may know that You have sent Me, and have loved them as You have loved Me."*

We are given all power and authority to become perfect, just like Jesus, the "manifestation of the Sons of God." This defines the high calling and the cry of David's heart! (In the next chapter we will discuss this call to perfection as we assemble the Spiritual Temple.)

> ➤ *(Matthew 5:48)* *"Therefore you shall be perfect, just as your Father in heaven is perfect.*

As a prophetic foreshadow alluding to what God has in store for us, Elisha asked for, and received, a double-portion outpouring of the Elijah's spirit. Ask and it shall be given unto you. We have been offered the power. Take it! The Father, through Christ Jesus, has given you wisdom and revelation. You have been given eyes to see and ears to hear. You should know the expectation of your calling and you should be able to recognize and receive the exceeding greatness of His power toward you. God has granted you the same power that He demonstrated when He raised Jesus from the dead *(Ephesians 1)*. The magnitude of this power may appear daunting at the present time. It will, however, make perfect sense when you develop a clear understanding of the **latter rain outpouring of the Holy Spirit**. At that moment you will comprehend the exceeding greatness of His power toward you.

The outpouring of the Holy Spirit

Just like the many patterns we have discovered throughout this book, the giving of the Holy Spirit follows a Scriptural blueprint. It was at Mt. Sinai on the Feast of Shavuot, what we as Christians call "Pentecost," that the LORD offered His Torah as a proposal of marriage to Israel. It was on the same Feast, almost one thousand five hundred years later, that the first outpouring of the Holy Spirit descended on Jerusalem and filled the hearts of faithful men. Why were they in Jerusalem? Because they were being obedient to God's commandment which says to be in Jerusalem for the Feast.

> ➤ *(Acts 2:1-5) When the Day of Pentecost had fully come, they were **all with one accord in one place** (unity). And suddenly there came a*

sound from heaven, as of a rushing mighty wind, and it filled the whole House where they were sitting. Then there appeared to them divided tongues, as of fire, and one sat upon each of them. And they were all filled with the Holy Spirit and began to speak with other tongues, as the Spirit gave them utterance. And there were dwelling in Jerusalem Jews, devout men, from every nation under heaven.

True to form, we can expect that the latter rain outpouring of the Holy Spirit will take place on the same Feast day. Doesn't this stimulate your excitement to learn more about keeping the Feasts of the LORD? Of course, we must practice the Feasts with primary emphasis on Christ. In the End, and into the Millennial Kingdom, we will see the same gatherings to keep the Feasts of the LORD.

> ➤ *(Zechariah 14:16) And it shall come to pass that everyone who is left of all the nations which came against Jerusalem shall go up from year to year to worship the King, the LORD of hosts, and* **to keep the Feast of Tabernacles.**

In that day, many will seek the Jews for advice on how to keep the Feasts.

> ➤ NIV *(Zechariah 8:22-23) And many peoples and powerful nations will come to Jerusalem to seek the LORD Almighty and to entreat Him. This is what the LORD Almighty says: "In those days ten men from all languages and nations will take firm hold of one Jew by the hem of his robe and say, 'Let us go with you, because we have* **heard that God is with you.'"**

Why will men of many nations seek to follow Jewish people in the Last Days? Men seeking the LORD in the Last Days will follow the example of Jews because they have "heard that God is with them." Paul, speaking of the final inheritance of the Jews in Romans 11:12 said, *now if their fall is riches for the world, and their failure riches for the Gentiles,* **how much more their fullness!** The Jews come into their fullness when they have finally added faith to the Word of God (faith in Y'shua the Messiah).

When a Jew adds faith to the Word, they have an advantage over non-Jews. *What advantage then has the Jew, or what is the profit of circumcision?*

Much in every way! Chiefly because to them were committed the oracles of God (Romans 3:1-2). The term "oracles of God," when used in the New Testament, refers to the contents of the Mosaic Law (Torah). In the End, adding faith to the contents of the Mosaic Law will cause *"many peoples and powerful nations"* to grab hold of the "tzitzit" (the fringes or hem of the garment) of a Jew (or other Believer knowledgeable in the Mosaic Law) and follow after him because his superior understanding of the Mosaic Law will help them discern the will of God.

> ➤ **(Romans 2:17-18)** *Indeed you are called a Jew, and rest on the Law, and make your boast in God,* **and know His will,** *and approve the things that are excellent, being instructed out of the Law.*

We must learn to understand the prophetic significance of the Law (Torah), including all the Feasts and the weekly Sabbath, to be prepared for the End. Be sober and watching!

How can we be sure that there is "more" Holy Spirit to come? The answer is simple. Read the blueprint! The apostle Paul said it best. *Now it is God who makes both us and you stand firm in Christ. He anointed us, set his seal of ownership on us, and put his Spirit in our hearts as a deposit, guaranteeing what is to come (2 Corinthians 1:21-22 NIV).* In the First Century, at the Feast of Shavuot (Pentecost), God placed a deposit of His Spirit with mankind. The Greek word for the English word translated as "deposit" is {ar-hrab-ohn'}. It means "a down payment for which the full amount will subsequently be paid." We have a down payment of the Holy Spirit and the full payment is coming! Interestingly enough, this Greek word is Hebrew in origin, {ar-aw-bone'}, meaning a "pledge or security," or as Paul described it, *"a deposit guaranteeing what is to come."* What is coming is the latter rain outpouring of the Holy Spirit; the full dose!

The Last Days

Think about it!

In the First Century, on the day of Pentecost, after the outpouring of the Spirit, Peter described what had taken place as an intermediate prophetic overlay of what will take place again before the second coming of the Lord. Using the exact technique that Jesus used when describing John the Baptist, *"He is Elijah who **has come and*** *is coming,*" Peter used Joel's prophesy to explain what **had happened** and what **will happen** again. Peter described what onlookers had witnessed as the pouring out of the Holy Spirit that was prophesized to happen in the Last Days. In Acts 2:15-21 Peter announced; "*For these are not drunk, as you suppose, since it is only the third hour of the day. But this is what was spoken by the prophet Joel: 'And it shall come to pass in the* **Last Days,** *says God, that* **I will pour out of My Spirit** *on all flesh; your sons and your daughters shall prophesy, your young men shall see visions, your old men shall dream dreams. And on My menservants and on My maidservants I will pour out My Spirit in those days; and they shall prophesy. I will show wonders in heaven above and signs in the earth beneath: Blood and fire and vapor of smoke.* **The sun shall be turned into darkness, and the moon into blood, before the coming of the great and awesome day of the LORD.** *And it shall come to pass that whoever calls on the Name of the LORD shall be saved.'*"

Peter referred to Joel's prophecy, about the pouring out of the Spirit, as occurring in the Last Days, immediately before the Day of the LORD. As Christians, we recognize that the great and awesome Day of the LORD **DID NOT** occur in the First Century. However, it is completely accurate to consider the First Century as part of the Last Days. Let me explain.

Again we must consider the blueprint. God's entire pattern for creation and rest fits into the model of one week. Biblically, a "week" consists of seven *somethings*. A week of years equals seven years. A week of weeks (49 years) leads us to a Jubilee (the 50th year). In the case of creation, a week equals seven days. However, to God, a day is not necessarily 24 hours. *But, beloved, do not forget this one thing, that with the LORD one day is as a thousand years, and a thousand years as one day (2 Peter 3:8).* In the seven day week, the last day (Saturday) is the Sabbath day. (Actually, it's sunset Friday to sunset Saturday, as the Biblical day is sunset to sunset. But for this illustration we'll just refer to the last day of the week as "Saturday.") By applying Peter's formula to the week of creation (*one day is as a thousand years*), there are six thousand years of work and one thousand years of rest (Sabbath); six thousand years for man and then the Millennial Kingdom. Why?

Because God's creation took place in six days and on the seventh day (the last day) He rested from all His work.

Using this blueprint, the Sabbath rest day (the seventh day) is the prophetic picture of the "Millennial Kingdom" (the seventh millennium) referred to in Revelation 20:4, in which we rule and reign (and rest) with Christ for one thousand years. Saturday is the day signifying that His Kingdom reigns (the Day of the LORD has come). Therefore, Thursday and a Friday are the Last Days (the last two days) before His coming. Using this blueprint, let's do the math. One day equals one thousand years, so Thursday and Friday represent the last two thousand years before his coming (the Last Days). Anything that has occurred within the two thousand years since Christ's first coming can accurately be considered to have taken place in the Last Days. The Last Days span from the beginning of Thursday till the end of Friday night, and then the Day of the Lord arrives.

Follow how the New Testament refers to both His first coming and His second coming as occurring in the "Last Days."

> ➤ *(Hebrews 1:1-2) God, who at various times and in various ways spoke in time past to the fathers by the prophets, has in these* **Last Days** *spoken to us by His Son...* The Son has already spoken in these Last Days (The First Coming).

> ➤ *(2 Peter 3:3-4) Knowing this first: that scoffers will come in the* **Last Days**, *walking according to their own lusts, and saying, "Where is the promise of His coming? For since the fathers fell asleep, all things continue as they were from the beginning of creation."*

When 2 Peter was written, Christ had already come the first time, so the question: *"Where is the promise of His coming?"* is referring to His Second Coming. Scoffers will come in those Last Days (The Second Coming).

The Latter Rain

When Peter referred to Joel's prophecy about God pouring out His Spirit on all flesh in the **Last Days**, *'And it shall come to pass in the Last Days, says God, that I will pour out of My Spirit on all flesh'* (Acts 2:17

quoting Joel 2:28), he was referring to the days of both Christ's first and second comings. Peter understood the prophetic overlay of the former and latter rains so masterfully displayed by Joel. The former rain is the first outpouring of the Spirit and the latter rain is the second outpouring of the Spirit, both taking place in the Last Days, separated by two thousand years. Paul also understood this prophetic pattern as reflected in 2 Corinthians 5:5. *Now it is God who has made us for this very purpose and has given us the Spirit as a **deposit** (the former reign), guaranteeing what is to come (the latter reign).*

In order to further understand these former and latter rains, we will review the section of Joel's prophecy that immediately precedes the section quoted by Peter in Acts 2. It hints to the nature of the double fulfillment of this prophecy. Those who have eyes to see let them see.

> ➤ *(Joel 2:23) Be glad then, you children of Zion, and rejoice in the LORD your God; for He has given you the former rain faithfully, and He will cause the rain to come down for you — **The former rain, and the latter rain in the first month** (the NIV says both autumn and spring rains, as before). "And it shall come to pass afterward that I will pour out My Spirit on all flesh" (v. 28).*

Joel says in verse 28, "afterward" God will pour out his Spirit. In Acts, Peter refers to this "afterward" as the Last Days *(in **the Last Days**, says God, that **I will pour out of My Spirit on all flesh**).*

[Note: When considering a portion of Joel 2:23 *(He will cause the rain to come down for you — The former rain, and the latter rain in the first month)*, did you ever wonder how both the former and latter rains can come in "the first month"? A pretty bright and studied Jewish Believer in Israel explained to me that this is possible because there are actually two "New Years." There is one in the first month of the Biblical calendar (when we celebrate Passover), and the other in the seventh month (when we celebrate the Feast of Trumpets), which is also celebrated as the Jewish civil holiday of Rosh Hashanah (New Year). One is the *first month* of the first half of the Biblical calendar year, highlighting the Spring Feasts. The other is the *first month* of the second half of the Biblical calendar year, highlighting the Fall

231

Feasts. Essentially, both the first and seventh months are "the first month." They are set sixth months apart, one in the spring and one in the autumn, as cleverly depicted in the NIV translation of Joel 2:23.]

What Joel goes on to reveal in verses 24-27 is that God's full abundance shall eventually be restored and the people will know that "*He is the LORD their God and there is no other.*" Joel's prophecy says that this understanding of God's unity will happen after the **former** and **latter** rains have poured down. Do you recognize this concept of unity? *He is the LORD their God and there is no other.* We studied it extensively in Chapter 5. That's right; it is the Shemah. The LORD is One. Unity is paramount!

Unity of the faith prepared the people for the first outpouring of the Spirit.

> ➢ *(Acts 2:1) When the Day of Pentecost had fully come, they were all with* **ONE accord in ONE place.** The people had come together in one place to keep the Feast in unity. *(Psalm 133:1) How good and how pleasant it is for brethren to dwell together in unity!*

And unity of the faith will be essential for the sons of God to be revealed before Jesus comes again.

> ➢ *(Ephesians 4:11-13) And He Himself gave some to be apostles, some prophets, some evangelists, and some pastors and teachers, for the equipping of the saints for the work of ministry, for the edifying of the body of Christ,* **till we all come to the unity of the faith** *and of the knowledge of the Son of God, to a perfect man, to the measure of the stature of the fullness of Christ.* Unity will prepare the way for a greater outpouring of His Spirit prior to His second coming.

For each season, He gives us the rain faithfully, the former rains and latter rains as promised. The LORD says: *I will pour out My Spirit in those days before the coming of the great and awesome Day of the LORD.* He has poured out His former rains faithfully and He will pour out his latter rains faithfully. We are entering the rainy season again. The latter rains are coming. *He shall come down like rain upon the grass before mowing, like showers that water the earth (Psalm 72:6).*

The Third Day

Come, and let us return to the LORD; *for He has torn, but He will heal us; He has stricken, but He will bind us up. After* **two days** *He will revive us;* **on the third day** *He will raise us up, that we may live in His sight. Let us know, let us pursue the knowledge of the* LORD. *His going forth is established as the morning;* **He will come to us like the rain, like the latter and former rain to the earth** *(Hosea 6:1-3).* The LORD poured out the former rain two days ago (two thousand years) and two thousand years later (after two days) He will revive us with the latter rain outpouring of the Holy Spirit. On the third day (at the beginning of the Millennial Kingdom, the start of the seventh millennium) He will raise us up so we may live in His sight, the light of His face forever. *In the light of the King's face is life, and his favor is like a cloud of the latter rain (Proverbs 16:15).*

Now do you agree that there are two outpourings of the Spirit? The Lord's ministry is like the early rain AND the latter rain. *Therefore be patient, brethren, until the coming of the Lord. See how the farmer waits for the precious fruit of the earth, waiting patiently for it until it receives the early and latter rain. You also be patient. Establish your hearts, for the coming of the Lord is at hand (James 5:7-8).* We already had the early rain and His first coming. Now we wait patiently for the latter rain and His second coming. *And you also were included in Christ when you heard the word of truth, the Gospel of your salvation. Having believed, you were marked in him with a seal, the promised Holy Spirit,* **who is a deposit** *guaranteeing our inheritance until the redemption of those who are God's possession— to the praise of His glory (Ephesians 1:13-14).*

Like Elisha, we must claim our double-portion anointing as we receive the passing of the mantle. Your current anointing will have to be planted in fertile soil so that the seed deposited can bear fruit a hundredfold. *"Most assuredly, I say to you, unless a grain of wheat falls into the ground and dies, it remains alone; but if it dies, it produces much grain" (John 12:24).* You must accept that the latter rain outpouring of the Holy Spirit will bear even greater fruit. It will avail even more power, more authority, and more truth.

The Materials

David was assigned the duty to assemble the materials and given the divine plans to erect the Temple. Nevertheless, he was told that he would not build it. He had to pass the plans and the building materials to Solomon. *"Consider now, for the LORD has chosen you to build a House for the sanctuary; **be strong, and do it.**"* *Then David gave his son Solomon the plans for the vestibule, its Houses, its treasuries, its upper chambers, its inner chambers, and the place of the Mercy Seat; and **the plans for all that he had by the Spirit**... "All this," said David, "the LORD made me understand in writing, by His hand upon me, all the works of these plans." And David said to his son Solomon, "Be strong and of good courage, **and do it**; do not fear nor be dismayed, for the LORD God — my God — will be with you. He will not leave you nor forsake you, until you have finished all the work for the service of the House of the LORD"* (1 Chronicles 28:10-12, 19-20).

David was a man of action. He used God's plans to make the necessary preparations to build the Temple. *"Now for the House of my God I have prepared with all my might"* (1 Chronicles 29:2). Then, in every detail, David described all those things which he had prepared for the House of God. It seems like dèjà vu, like we are seeing the patterns for the Tabernacle given to Moses on the mountain all over again. David went beyond the call and took his commitment personally. *"Moreover, because I have set my affection on the House of my God, I have given to the House of my God, over and above all that I have prepared for the holy House, **my own special treasure** of gold and silver"* (v. 3). My hope for you is that you would share David's heart and, as he did, offer your life as a living sacrifice.

David went on to give praise to God Almighty, assigning all the credit, glory, and honor to Him. *For we are aliens and pilgrims before You, as were all our fathers; Our days on earth are as a shadow, and without hope. O LORD our God, all this abundance that we have prepared to build You a House for Your holy Name **is from Your hand**, and is all Your own* (1 Chronicles 29:15-16). And then he passed on all this abundance to Solomon. THE MANTLE HAS PASSED! *Then Solomon sat on the throne of the LORD as king instead of David his father, and prospered; and all Israel obeyed him* (v. 23).

Once the mantle has passed, be faithful or else!

What is the responsibility of the Joshua/Solomon/Elisha Generation? *Moreover it is required in stewards that one be found faithful (1 Corinthians 4:2)*. In Matthew 25:24 the wicked servant does nothing with his master's deposit because he is afraid. *"I knew you to be a hard man, reaping where you have not sown, and gathering where you have not scattered seed."* Do you remember in Chapter 5 when we introduced the Kingdom mystery of reaping where you have not sown? Good stewardship of the power, authority, and building materials passed on by the Davidic Generation is one of the major areas that this Kingdom mystery comes into play. The Solomon Generation will be given the plans to build the Spiritual Temple. They will be handed most of the materials in preparation for construction, reaping where they have not sown. The Solomon Generation must be faithful stewards and build upon their inheritance. This emphasizes the importance of building precept upon precept. It is imperative, crucial, critical, vital, and essential that this generation be found as faithful stewards of God's plan for the Kingdom.

The Future Solomon Generation

As the Davidic Generation, we must collect the materials. It is our role to bring forth the Gospel of the Kingdom. The purpose of this book (and the books to follow in this series) is to begin to uncover the mysteries of the Kingdom and to make the discoveries clear to the world. During this undertaking, we must always remember that *the spirits of the prophets are subject to the prophets (1 Corinthians 14:32)*. Like David did for the physical Temple, our generation must decipher the divine plan for the Spiritual Temple, and collect the materials to be passed along to the next generation. Then the Solomon Generation must be wise stewards of the divine trust placed in their hands. They must be faithful to do the building.

It is an interesting comparison that Solomon received the materials and brought together the skillful laborers to do the work. However, he received no stones from David. Solomon had to acquire them himself. He commissioned for the stones to be quarried offsite and then brought to the place of assembly, already perfect, ready to be put in place. *And the king commanded them to quarry large stones, costly stones, and hewn stones, to lay the foundation of the Temple (1 Kings 5:17).* Just the same, the Solomon Generation must be carved into stones. To build the Spiritual Temple, the members of His Body must get **hewn into perfect living stones.** Then they will come to the place of assembly and set in position. What an interesting parallel. Because all the stones are hewn before assembly begins, once every stone is complete, final assembly will happen quickly. Be prepared! The events in the Last Days will come swiftly. *The Revelation of Jesus Christ which God gave him so that his servants might have knowledge of the things which will **quickly take place**: and he sent and made it clear by his angel to his servant John (Revelation 1:1 BBE).*

The future Solomon Generation should be careful to NOT repeat the mistakes of their ancestors. *"Therefore understand that the* LORD *your God is not giving you this good Land to possess because of your righteousness, for you are a stiff-necked people. Remember! Do not forget how you provoked the* LORD *your God to wrath in the Wilderness. From the day that you departed from the land of Egypt until you came to this place, you have been rebellious against the* LORD*"* (Deuteronomy 9:6-7). Whether you are called as a fore-runner or you are simply waiting for the mass exodus, you must be prepared for what lies ahead.

If you truly wish to be prepared, you must move beyond the basic elements of the faith. *For everyone who partakes only of milk is unskilled in the word of righteousness, for he is a babe. But solid food belongs to those who are of full age, that is, those who by reason of use have their senses exercised to discern both good and evil. Therefore, leaving the discussion of the elementary principles of Christ, **let us go on to perfection**, not laying again the foundation of repentance from dead works and of faith toward God, of the doctrine of baptisms, of laying on of hands, of resurrection of the dead, and of eternal judgment. And this we will do if God permits (Hebrews 5:13-6:3).*

Consider now, for the LORD has chosen YOU to build a House for His sanctuary. Be strong, and do it!

Chapter Ten

Building the Spiritual Temple

For you are the Temple of the living God. As God has said:
"I will dwell in them and walk among them.
I will be their God, and they shall be My people."
2 Corinthians 6:16

I am confident by now that you have noticed that every chapter begins with a quotation. Every one, save the first, is a direct quote from Scripture. But none other has more bearing on the chapter it heralds than the one above. Don't get me wrong. They are all completely relevant, but this one, in my opinion, most of all.

Why? Why is this one most relevant? Because it not only speaks of God's promise, but His divine plan. *As God has said: "I will dwell in them and walk among them. I will be their God, and they shall be My people."* However, do a little research for yourself. Nowhere in the entire Bible does it actually say this. Nevertheless, logic will testify that Paul would only say "God has said" if he could find it in the Holy Scriptures. And the only "Scriptures" in the First Century was what we call today the "Old Testament." It's a simple point, yet profound. Have you ever given it consideration? In the New Testament, every time we see a reference to something "God said" or that "it is written," it is referring to the words of the Old Testament. Again basic, yet paramount to your full appreciation of Paul's words. *As God has said: "I will dwell in them and walk among them. I will be their God, and they shall be My people."*

It is a curious thing, however, that this verse in 2 Corinthians is the only place in the New Testament where it specifically says "God has said." Sixty-one times Jesus or one of the apostles uses the phrase "it is written." It is used every time to make direct reference to a specific Old Testament Scripture and, in many cases, either Moses, David, or one of the prophets is named as the source. Thirty times the New Testament refers directly to the Old Testament calling it "Scripture." In most cases, when you see the phrase "the Lord said," it is referring either to something Jesus said during his life on earth or is part of some parable. Stephen uses it once in Acts as a direct Old Testament reference, and four times it is a quote from David.

Why belabor this issue? Because *all Scripture is given by inspiration of God, and is profitable for doctrine, for reproof, for correction, for instruction in righteousness, that the man of God may be complete, thoroughly equipped for every good work (2 Timothy 3:16-17).* And also because nowhere in the entire Bible does God actually say in one place "I will dwell in them and walk among them. I will be their God, and they shall be My people." Much like I have been showing you throughout *The Heart of David,* Paul understood the use of prophetic overlay and he employed his vast knowledge of Scripture to help him understand God's deep mysteries. From his command of Scripture, Paul was able to bring multiple ideas together and then organize them to reveal God's prophetic plan; *knowing this first, that no prophecy of Scripture is of any private interpretation, for prophecy never came by the will of man, but holy men of God spoke as they were moved by the Holy Spirit (2 Peter 1:20-21).*

There are many areas of Scripture from which Paul is drawing. It is from these Scriptures, combined with inspiration from the Holy Spirit, that Paul receives his prophetic revelation. *For you are the Temple of the living God. As God has said: "I will dwell in them and walk among them. I will be their God, and they shall be My people."* Below, I believe, are the Scriptures that most likely inspired Paul's prophetic understanding. There are many from which he could have drawn his inspiration, but none more than these. You see, the Tabernacle *was* the institution of God in which He would dwell *among* men. Knowing this, you can appreciate how this idea could foreshadow Paul's claim that God has said, *"I will dwell in them."*

The Blueprint of the Indwelling Spirit

Contemplate the Ark of the Covenant and how it represents God's Presence ("Shekinah" in Hebrew) dwelling in the midst of the Sanctuary (Holy of Holies). Also consider the picture of the cloud by day and the fire by night hovering over and extending down into the Tabernacle. His presence was abiding IN the Tabernacle. For Paul to say that you are the Temple of the living God and that God will dwell IN you, he was seeing what David saw, the Spiritual Temple. Even though the Old Testament does not literally state it, Paul was teaching us that we would be the Spiritual Temple and God would dwell inside of us. *For you are the Temple of the living God. As God has said: "I will dwell in them and walk among them. I will be their God, and they shall be My people."*

Consider the following verses and try to see what Paul could see:

> *(Exodus 29:43-45)* *"And there I will meet with the children of Israel, and the Tabernacle shall be sanctified by My glory. So I will consecrate the Tabernacle of meeting and the altar. I will also consecrate both Aaron and his sons to minister to Me as priests. **I will dwell among the children of Israel and will be their God."***

> *(Leviticus 26:12)* *I will **walk among you** and be your God, and you shall be My people.*

> *(Ezekiel 37:26-28)* *"Moreover I will make a covenant of peace with them, and it shall be an everlasting covenant with them; I will establish them and multiply them, and **I will set My sanctuary in their midst forevermore. My Tabernacle also shall be with them; indeed I will be their God, and they shall be My people.** The nations also will know that I, the LORD, sanctify Israel, when My sanctuary is in their midst forevermore."*

> *(Jeremiah 31:33)* *"But this is the covenant that I will make with the house of Israel after those days, says the* LORD: *I will put* **My Law** *in their minds, and write it on their hearts; and* **I will be their God, and they shall be My people.**

Reading the Blueprint like a Master Builder

God will write His Laws on our hearts. Quite simply, God's Law is His Word that we should meditate on, day and night. *Blessed is the man who walks not in the counsel of the ungodly, nor stands in the path of sinners, nor sits in the seat of the scornful; but his delight is in the Law of the* LORD, *and in His Law he meditates day and night (Psalm 1:1-2).* Here are a few excerpts from Psalm 119 clarifying this simple, yet remarkably important Biblical concept. Observe the following verses and their beautiful relationship between God's Law, His Word, and our Savior.

> *(Psalm 119:172)* *My tongue shall speak of Your word, for all Your commandments are righteousness.*

> *(Psalm 119:16)* *I will delight myself in Your statutes; I will not forget Your word.*

> *(Psalm 119:160)* *The entirety of Your word is* **truth**, *and every one of Your righteous judgments endures forever.*

God's word, in its entirety, is truth and Jesus said, *"I am the way, the* **truth**, *and the life. No one comes to the Father except through Me (John 14:6).* This means Jesus is the entirety of God's Word wrapped up into one perfect example of a man. *Your word is a lamp to my feet and a* **light** *to my path (Psalm 119:105).* God's Word is light and Jesus said, *"I am the* **light** *of the world. He who follows Me shall not walk in darkness, but have the light of life"* (John 8:12).

As we add these ideas together, a clear vision emerges from the fog.

> *(John 1:14)* *And the* **Word became flesh and dwelt among us,** *and we beheld His glory, the glory as of the only begotten of the Father, full of grace and truth.*

Jesus is the Word of God and the Law (Torah) of God, and this Word became a man and dwelt among us. The English word "dwelt" is derived from the Greek word which means *"to fix one's Tabernacle, have one's Tabernacle, abide (or live) in a Tabernacle (or tent), Tabernacle, to dwell."* Literally, it means that the Word of God incarnated as a man and placed His Tabernacle in our midst.

Paul's Masterful use of Scripture

Paul adds these ideas together:

- *I will set My sanctuary in their midst forevermore.*
- *My Tabernacle also shall be with them; indeed I will be their God, and they shall be My people.*
- *I will dwell among the children of Israel and will be their God.*
- *I will walk among you and be your God, and you shall be My people.*
- *I will put My Law in their minds, and write it on their hearts.*

He concludes with this revelation…

For you are the Temple of the living God. As God has said:
"I will **dwell in them** and walk among them.
I will be their God, and they shall be My people."

Can you see how Paul, with the practice of building precept upon precept and line upon line, could add these ideas together and uncover a mystery of the Kingdom? He knew there were mysteries to be solved, and that he not only had the authority, but the responsibility to solve them. And in this day and age, so do you!

Think about it!

What exactly is the Spiritual Temple?

It is fair to say that you ARE the Temple of the living God. However, it is a bit more complex than this. There are more layers to uncover. We must first define the Spiritual Temple in order to reveal the depth of this revelation. *For we know that if our earthly house, this tent, is destroyed, we have a building from God, a House not made with hands, eternal in the heavens (2 Corinthians 5:1).*

For starters, the Spiritual Temple is the true Tabernacle not built with hands. *But Christ came as High Priest of the* **good things to come**, *with the greater and more perfect Tabernacle not made with hands, that is, not of this creation (Hebrews 9:11).* Every Tabernacle or Temple constructed by man is a mere copy or shadow of the real thing. *For Christ has not entered the Holy Places made with hands, which are copies of the true, but into heaven itself, now to appear in the presence of God for us (Hebrews 9:24).* Christ has already been established as the High Priest of the "good things to come." What He offers is a "better sacrifice" **established** on "better promises" in a more perfect Tabernacle erected by the LORD. *Now this is the main point of the things we are saying: We have such a High Priest, who is seated at the right hand of the throne of the Majesty in the heavens, a Minister of the sanctuary and of the true Tabernacle which the LORD erected, and not man (Hebrews 8:1-2).*

A High Priest with a More Excellent Ministry

As we should expect, Jesus' Priestly ministry is the archetype for each one of us who strive to be conformed into His image. As High Priest in heavenly places, Jesus is already performing the duties that He has bestowed upon us. His ministry is the "heavenly reality" that casts shadows of "good things to come" over all who wish to follow in His perfect footsteps. Inevitably, we will step into the fullness of our calling to take part in His priestly ministry. *But now He has obtained a more excellent ministry, inasmuch as He is also Mediator of a better covenant, which was* **established** *on better promises (Hebrews 8:6).* The covenant based on Jesus' blood atonement is better for sure, because it is "ESTABLISHED" on better promises. However, if you are willing to search deeply into the meaning of the words behind the words, and you are willing to be genuine in your conclusions, you will discover another beautiful overlay.

The Greek word translated into *"established"* in English is the word *"nomotheteo"* {nom-oth-et-eh'-o}. It means *1) to enact laws 1a) laws are enacted or prescribed for one, to be legislated for, furnished with laws 2) to sanction by Law, enact.* By this point in our journey, I hope you would agree that the only legitimate Laws worthy of "sanctioning" or "legislating" are not man-made laws, even if the laws are developed by men who claim to have been operating by the Holy Spirit. The only Laws worthy of sanctioning are God's Laws (the Torah) given to Moses on Mount Sinai. In other words, Jesus is Mediator of a better covenant, which was legislated, sanctioned, or established on the Mosaic Covenant, but **this time with much better promises.** The "better promises" make it a "better covenant." What are the better promises? With the promise of the Holy Spirit and the gift of Christ's righteousness, God's laws are no longer too difficult. They are near you in your mouth and in your heart, and you do not have to depend on your own strength to do them. *I can do all things **through Christ** who strengthens me. (Philippians 4:13).* Holy Spirit empowered obedience is far superior to depending on our own strength, which is what we had to do before Christ. Spirit-inspired, faith-based obedience is contrary to standing in our own righteousness. This disease of self-righteousness was the major problem suffered by God's people before Christ shed His blood. *For they being ignorant of God's righteousness, and seeking to establish their own righteousness, have not submitted to the righteousness of God (Romans 10:3).* If we are willing to submit to His righteousness, and if we dare to believe that we can **literally** follow in His footsteps, we too can become "Royal Priests" (1 Peter 2:9) of a more excellent ministry, a perfect ministry.

After the writer of Hebrews substantiates that Jesus is the Mediator of a *better covenant, which was established on better promises,* he goes on to clarify the problem with the first covenant (the first covenant made with the entire Nation of Israel, the Mosaic Covenant). The problem was not with the covenant itself. The writer of Hebrews continues: *For if that first covenant had been faultless, then no place would have been sought for a second. Because finding fault with **them,** He says... (8:7-8a).* What follows in verses Hebrews 8b-12 is a beautiful reminder of what God had said about the new covenant in Jeremiah 31:31-34. Encapsulated in Hebrews 8:10, the LORD summarizes the remedy to the problem; *"I will put My laws in their mind and write them on their hearts; and I will be their God, and they shall be My people."* The Mosaic

Covenant was not the problem. The people were the problem; hence the term "them" and not "it" in designating where the fault lies, and why the remedy would be to change the hearts of the people. They were ignorant of God's righteousness and continually sought to establish their own righteousness, thereby not submitting to the righteousness of God. The fault was with "them" and not the first covenant.

What does this all mean? It means that when Christ shed his blood and imparted His righteous TO YOU, it is supposed to produce something IN YOU! Should it produce, in you, the attitude that Jesus' blood **"replaced"** the necessity for God's Law, and that this is the "better covenant" established on "better promises"? Or, should it produce in you the attitude that Jesus' blood imparted to you the supernatural ability to **"obey God's Laws,"** and that clothed with His righteousness, you can now walk like Christ (who was perfect because He obeyed all His Father's commandments)? I think you know the correct answer. (Note: Even though obedience is only possible through "His righteousness," **YOU** still must do "the walking.") In the King James, both the prophet Isaiah and John, the beloved disciple, agree. Isaiah 30:21 reminds us that whether you turn to the right or to the left, your ears will hear a voice behind you, saying: *"This is the way, walk ye in it!"* Second John 1:6 reports that: *"This is love, that we walk after His commandments. This is the commandment, that, as ye have heard from the beginning, ye should walk in it."*

Jesus already ministers on our behalf in a heavenly Tabernacle. His ministry, however, is as *"High Priest of the good things to come."* His present service is preparation for something good that is **coming** — meaning, at the time Hebrews was written, some 30 years after Christ's ascension, it had not yet come — and we have no evidence that it has come since. When it does come, we, as a Holy and Royal Priesthood, will serve like Christ as ministers of the true Sanctuary. *And as it is appointed for men to die once, but after this the judgment, so Christ was offered once to bear the sins of many. To those who eagerly wait for Him He will appear a second time, apart from sin, for salvation (Hebrews 9:27-28).* My deepest heartfelt desire is that *The Heart of David* will help prepare you for this most excellent ministry.

The Restoration:
Rebuilding the Tabernacle of David

Jesus fulfilled (and is fulfilling) His role. So it is time for you to fulfill your role before He appears a second time? This is the good thing to come. Jesus is the Word of God, the perfect essence of every divine instruction. Filled with the Spirit of God, He became flesh and dwelt, or Tabernacled, among man: *But this Man, after He had offered one sacrifice for sins forever, sat down at the right hand of God, from that time waiting till His enemies are made His footstool (Hebrews 10:12-13)*. What is Jesus waiting for in heaven? He is currently serving at the right hand of the Father, a minister of the true Sanctuary (Holy of Holies). However, He is waiting for something. In Hebrews it says He is *waiting till His enemies are made His footstool*. In the book of Acts, however, Peter teaches us from another perspective. *"Repent therefore and be converted, that your sins may be blotted out, so that **times of refreshing** may come from the presence of the Lord, and that He may send Jesus Christ, who was preached to you before, **whom heaven must receive until the times of restoration of all things,** which God has spoken by the mouth of all His holy prophets since the world began"* (Acts 3:19-21).

We have already discussed the idea of the restoration of the heart in Chapter 2, and the restoration of all things in Chapter 4. It is most appropriate again here in Chapter 10. Jesus is waiting in heaven until the restoration of all things. When asked by His disciples in Matthew 17:10-11, *"Why then do the scribes say that Elijah must come first?" Jesus answered and said to them, "Indeed, Elijah is coming first and will restore all things."* I believe it is obvious from our previous study, and also here again, that Jesus is ministering in heaven **until Elijah comes FIRST to restore all things**. After Jesus was sacrificed once for all time, He now waits patiently in heaven to reap the harvest of His labor. He is waiting until both God's institution and man's condition are restored to perfection. I know this flies in the face of the doctrine of "imminent return" that is so popular today in evangelical circles. But "imminent return" (the teaching that Christ could return at any moment with no prerequisites) just doesn't seem to line up with the whole of Scripture, but instead just isolated verses. As His Body and future Bride, it is our job, inspired by Christ as our model and imbued with the power of the Holy Spirit, to bring the enemies of the Most High into subjection and to subdue them under His power. The enemy of the Most High is sin. In other words, we must make sin His footstool. This is the restoration and it is the job that "Elijah" must perform **FIRST** before Christ's return. (Note: Is it any wonder that Satan keeps attacking those of us in the Body, tempting us to keep on sinning? He knows God's Word is true and, as long as he can keep us imperfect, he can delay his date with the lake of fire.)

In Chapter 2 we focused mainly on man's heart as the object of restoration. Here, in our discussion of the Spiritual Temple, we will direct our focus on the restoration of God's institution or Government. The Greek word for restoration is apokatastasis {ap-ok-at-as'-tas-is} meaning: *1) restoration 1a) of a true theocracy 1b) of the perfect state before the fall.* We must reestablish, and then come into complete submission to God's theocracy (the Government of Heaven). Only then will we be restored to a state of sinless perfection. As you can see, it is both God's institution and man's condition that will be restored, and Jesus tarries until all such is fulfilled.

Throughout this book we have been discussing the magnitude of your high calling. You have a choice to make. Believe the bad report of faithless spies and die in the Wilderness. Or believe the good report and press on to the high calling and a more excellent ministry.

God's Institution

Earlier in Chapter 7, we discovered the prophetic picture of Israel's dreadful decision to remove the Ark of the Covenant from the Sanctuary. This is an eerie forecast of God's Spirit and power being divided from His institution. This separation has plagued God's people for generations ever since. In the Church today, however, the long term effects of this separation masks itself as denominationalism: **God's Spirit and Truth being treated as chattel, guarded by self-appointed denominational lords who dole out paltry morsels of what they determine can be digested by a truth-starved flock.** Denominationalism remains the single greatest cause of diversity and enemy of unity among God's chosen people. The Church certainly contains the Spirit of God, but the institution of God is divided up among thousands of man-made denominations. We must come together in unity to rebuild His government. *Of the increase of His government and peace there will be no end, upon the throne of David and over His Kingdom, to order it and establish it with judgment and justice from that time forward, even forever. The zeal of the LORD of hosts will perform this (Isaiah 9:7).*

God's institution AND government need to be reestablished. But instead of a physical Temple, the institution to which we are now referring contains a Spiritual Temple; a Temple not made with earthly hands, but with glorified hands. Jesus will remain in heaven until the Government of Heaven, along with its Spiritual Temple, is reestablished on earth. This theocracy will be built with God's laws and instructions (Torah) as its framework and the Spiritual Temple at the center of His restored institution.

> **(Acts 15:14-17)** *"Simon has declared how God at the first visited the Gentiles to take out of them a people for His name. And with this the words of the prophets agree, just as it is written: 'After this I will return and will **rebuild the Tabernacle of David**, which has fallen down; I will rebuild its ruins, and I will set it up; so that the rest of mankind may seek the LORD, even all the Gentiles who are called by My name, says the LORD who does all these things.'"*

In the Scripture above, during the assembly known as the "Jerusalem Council," was James speaking of rebuilding a Temple of inanimate stones? In confidence, I can say NO! Instead, he used the words of the prophet Amos to confirm the relationship between God's chosen people and the building of the Spiritual Temple.

> **(Amos 9:9-12)** *"For surely I will command, and will **sift the house of Israel among all nations**, as grain is sifted in a sieve; yet not the smallest grain shall fall to the ground. All the sinners of My people shall die by the sword, who say, 'The calamity shall not overtake nor confront us.' On that day I will **raise up the Tabernacle of David**, which has fallen down, and repair its damages; I will raise up its ruins, and rebuild it as in the days of old; that they may possess the remnant of Edom, and all the Gentiles who are **called by My name**, says the LORD who does this thing."*

So, in Acts 15, James taught from Amos 9. He referred to a Temple that would one day be restored; a Spiritual Temple made up of God's chosen people whom He would "sift" from among the nations. This is you and I, my friends. [Note: By the time the Jerusalem Council met in the First Century, the Second Temple had not yet been destroyed and was still standing in Jerusalem. The destruction of the Second Temple would take place years later in 70 AD. So, it is fair to say that James was not referring to "rebuilding" a physical Temple (the Third Temple). This does not, however, mean that there will not be an actual rebuilding of the physical Temple. It is the opinion of this author that there will be a Third Temple erected in Jerusalem.]

To Raise up the Tabernacle of David

What then is the Tabernacle of David? This is a prophetic reference to the Spiritual Temple. As you know, David is the kingly line from which Messiah would come. And in addition, David is the one who, in a prophetic moment, conceived the idea of building a "new" Temple in which the LORD would dwell. Of course, it was Solomon who eventually built the Temple with all its glory. Yet even at its best, during the height of its marvelous splendor, Solomon's work was never more than a shadow of the true Tabernacle in heaven.

In the book of Acts 6:13-14, Stephen shed some light on this topic. *"This man does not cease to speak blasphemous words against this holy place and the Law* (the Torah); *for we have heard him say that this Jesus of Nazareth will destroy this place* (the Temple) *and change the customs which Moses delivered to us."* After this false accusation against him, Stephen defended himself. He used his vast knowledge of the Law and his sincere faith to defend this false allegation. To prove that his faith was not contrary to God's Law, in his defense he depended on the Torah itself as he recounted the life of Abraham, Joseph, and Moses. In other words, he established that the foundation of His faith came from the Law of God and, therefore, proved he was not speaking blasphemous words against the Law of God or the Temple. He concluded his defense by demonstrating that both the Tabernacle in the Wilderness and the Temple built by Solomon were mere shadows of the true Tabernacle in heaven.

➤ (Acts 7:44-50) *"Our fathers had the Tabernacle of witness in the Wilderness, as He appointed, instructing Moses to make it according to the pattern that he had seen, which our fathers, having received it in turn, also brought with Joshua into the land possessed by the Gentiles, whom God drove out before the face of our fathers until the days of David, who found favor before God and asked to find a dwelling for the God of Jacob.* **But Solomon built Him a House. However, the Most High does not dwell in Temples made with hands,** *as the prophet says: 'Heaven is My throne, and earth is My footstool. What House will you build for Me? says the* LORD, *or what is the place of My rest? Has My hand not made all these things?'"*

Stephen understood that David had not only passed on a plan to build a physical Temple for the LORD, but had obviously impressed upon Solomon that this was a mere shadow of God's prophetic plan for a Temple not made with hands. Solomon acknowledged this when he had completed the work of erecting the Temple. First he testifies of its completion. *"I have surely built You an exalted House, and a place for You to dwell in forever"* (1 Kings 8:13). However, soon after, in his prayer of dedication, Solomon humbly acknowledges its insufficiency. *"But will God indeed dwell on the earth? Behold, heaven and the heaven of heavens cannot contain You. How much less this Temple which I have built!"* (1 Kings 8:27).

Patterns for the Future

Think about it! Once again, let's depend on patterns to create our prophetic model of the future and draw some conclusions about building the Spiritual Temple. This will help us establish the framework for creating perfect ministry in Chapter 11. It took seven years for Israel to conquer the "giants" in the Promised Land and then erect the Tabernacle in Shiloh (Joshua 14-18). It took seven years to build Solomon's Temple (1 Kings 6:38), and it was dedicated during the Feast of Tabernacles which is a seven day Feast in the seventh month (2 Chronicles 7:8-10). Recall that mankind is on one long seven-year (seven thousand years) prophetic journey from Captivity, to the Wilderness, into the Promised Land, and then on to eternity. On the final prophetic journey from the Wilderness, it will take seven years after we cross into the Promised Land to conquer sin and build the Spiritual Temple. Those first seven years in the Wilderness correspond to the first seven years of Joseph's ministry. Those were the years of the double-portion harvest and the storing away for lean times to come. (Who is that "faithful and wise servant who gives the people food in due season"? Stay tuned to chapter 11!)

David was given the plan to build and made provision for the items within the physical Temple. Solomon, his son, took his fathers plan and actually had the stones cut (1 Kings 6:17). Solomon laid those stones in place according to his father's plan. With a transformation in the hearts of the people that serve the living God, the Body of Christ will become the living stones from which this Temple will be assembled.

> *(1 Peter 2:1-9) Therefore, laying aside all malice, all deceit, hypocrisy, envy, and all evil speaking, as newborn babes, desire the pure milk of the Word, that you may grow thereby, if indeed you have tasted that the Lord is gracious. Coming to Him as to a living stone, rejected indeed by men, but chosen by God and precious, **you also, as living stones, are being built up a Spiritual House, a Holy Priesthood, to offer up spiritual sacrifices acceptable to God through Jesus Christ.** Therefore it is also contained in the Scripture, "Behold, I lay in Zion a Chief Cornerstone, elect, precious, and he who believes on Him will by no means be put to shame." Therefore, to you who believe, He is precious; but to those who are disobedient, "The Stone which the builders rejected has become the Chief Cornerstone," and "A stone of stumbling and a rock of offense." They stumble, being disobedient to the Word, to which they also were appointed. But you are a chosen generation, a royal priesthood, a holy nation, His own special people, that you may proclaim the praises of Him who called you out of darkness into His marvelous light!*

Okay. I admit that this gets a bit confusing. Earlier we learned that Jesus serves as the High Priest ministering in a heavenly Tabernacle not made with hands. Yet, we also see how the Body of Christ is the Temple of living stones, being built up a Spiritual House, a Holy Priesthood, to offer up spiritual sacrifices acceptable to God through Jesus Christ. Which is it? Is the Spiritual Temple already in heaven where Jesus serves as High Priest or do we as members of the Body of Christ still need to build the Spiritual Temple in which we serve as priests? The answer is BOTH! It is in heaven and we still have to build it. Stick with me on this one.

The Mystery of the Spiritual Temple

The Spiritual Temple already exists in heaven. Everything on earth serves as a copy or shadow of heavenly things. That is why, if you recall, Moses was divinely instructed when he was about to make the Tabernacle. *"See that you make all things according to the pattern shown you on the mountain."* If the Spiritual Temple already exists in heaven, why do we still need to build one? It is difficult to conceive, but let's give it a try. In order to unravel this mystery, we first must start with a major premise drawn from Scripture. Then we must have faith to believe it is true. The premise is this.

As members of the Body of Christ, it is our duty to build the Spiritual Temple!

Let's explore some New Testament passages concerning the Spiritual Temple. See with me if you agree that, first of all, building it is our duty, and secondly, that it is a corporate undertaking, one worthy of your utmost attention.

➤ *(Ephesians 2:19-22) Now, therefore, you are no longer strangers and foreigners, but fellow citizens with the saints and members of the household of God, having been built on the foundation of the apostles and prophets, Jesus Christ Himself being the Chief Cornerstone, in whom the whole building, being joined together, grows into a Holy Temple in the Lord, in whom you also are being built together for a dwelling place of God in the Spirit.*

251

It should be beyond obvious already that together, as a Body with Christ, we are becoming the Spiritual Temple in which God will dwell. Each of us has a role to play in bringing this about. *For as we have many members in one body, but all the members do not have the same function, so we, being many, are one body in Christ, and individually members of one another (Romans 12:4-5).*

If you are a forerunner, you should be chomping at the bit by this time. You should be totally fired up to accomplish something great for God. Remember, your life is not your own. *Or do you not know that your body is the Temple of the Holy Spirit who is in you, whom you have from God, and you are not your own? For you were bought at a price; therefore glorify God in your body and in your spirit, which are God's (1 Corinthians 6:19-20).* On our journey through God's prophetic plan for history, if we hold firm till the end, it will be in the Promised Land that we begin to assemble the Spiritual Temple, the House of the living God. *But Christ as a Son over His own House, whose House we are if we hold fast the confidence and the rejoicing of the hope firm to the end (Hebrews 3:6).*

As I emphasize our personal responsibility in building the Spiritual Temple, let me remind you that without the power of the Holy Spirit working in us, none of this is possible. It is the power of God that animated the Tabernacle in the Wilderness and it is the power of God that inspires and empowers the Body of Christ to build the Spiritual Temple. As Psalm 127:1 says, *Unless the LORD builds the House, they labor in vain who build it;* and like Paul says in Colossians 1:29: *To this end I also labor, striving according to **His working** which works in me mightily.* It is the power of God working in us that will enable us to reach the high calling. Nevertheless, it is still our own responsibility to be good stewards of the building materials with which we have been entrusted.

Remember the Kingdom principle of building precept upon precept? When we apply this principle to building the Spiritual Temple, we will acknowledge that Christ serves as the foundation, and that we must build upon Him wisely.

> *(1 Corinthians 3:9-17) For we are God's fellow workers; you are God's field, you are **God's building**. According to the grace of God which was given to me, as a wise master builder I have laid the foundation, and another builds on it. **But let each one take heed how he builds on it.** For no other foundation can anyone lay than that which is laid, which is Jesus Christ. Now if anyone builds on this foundation with gold, silver, precious stones, wood, hay, straw, each one's work will become clear; for the Day will declare it, because it will be revealed by fire; and the fire will test each one's work, of what sort it is. If anyone's work which he has built on it endures, he will receive a reward. If anyone's work is burned, he will suffer loss; but he himself will be saved, yet so as through fire. **Do you not know that you are the Temple of God and that the Spirit of God dwells in you?** If anyone defiles the Temple of God, God will destroy him. For the Temple of God is holy, which Temple you are.*

Let each one take heed as to how he builds on the foundation. We are all living stones being built up into a Spiritual House and Jesus is the Chief Cornerstone.

Our Major Premise:
As members of the Body of Christ,
it is our duty to build the Spiritual Temple!

Our Conclusion:
Let each one take heed as to how he builds on the Foundation.

For a preliminary summary of the Spiritual Temple, we can make a few assertions. When Jesus Tabernacled among us in the First Century, He was not the Spiritual Temple. He was, however, the Chief Cornerstone or the Foundation. As an individual member of the Body of Christ, you are not the Spiritual Temple either. And you do not become the Spiritual Temple the moment you are born again, when Jesus first comes into your heart. What unfolds, however, when you consider your role as a distinct member of a larger body, and the vital importance of unity, is that you realize that building the Spiritual Temple is a corporate accomplishment and a vital component to the

End of the Age. Together with your brothers and sisters in the faith, you are a living stone being used to build up into a Spiritual House. We are the living stones which fit together to form the Spiritual Temple, and Christ is the Chief Cornerstone.

Another Two-edged Sword

So far we discovered that in the future, all of us, as living stones, are going to be assembled into a Spiritual Temple and a Holy Priesthood intended to offer up spiritual sacrifices. We also learned that Jesus already serves as the High Priest in a heavenly Spiritual Temple. This Temple, however, was not made with hands. Christ is Minister of the Sanctuary and of the true Tabernacle which the LORD erected, and not man. Let us attempt to fuse this apparent contradiction by synthesizing one consistent idea from these two thoughts.

1. We are **being built** into the Spiritual Temple.
2. The Spiritual Temple apparently **already exists**.

The Holy Spirit indicating this, that the way into the Holiest of All was not yet made manifest while the first Tabernacle was still standing. It was symbolic for the present time in which both gifts and sacrifices are offered which cannot make him who performed the service perfect in regard to the conscience; concerned only with foods and drinks, various washings, and fleshly ordinances **imposed until the time of reformation.** *But Christ came as High Priest of* **the good things to come,** *with the greater and more perfect Tabernacle not made with hands, that is, not of this creation (Hebrews 9:8-11).*

Synthesizing One Consistent Idea from the Two

In order to synthesize one consistent idea from the two, we will make practical use of a mystery we already uncovered. Do you remember the Kingdom mystery we exposed earlier in this book in which seemingly contradictory messages in the Scripture are actually consistent messages on opposite sides of the same coin? On one side of the coin we have Jesus already serving as High Priest in a heavenly Tabernacle not made with hands. He is the Minister of the sanctuary and of the true Tabernacle, which the LORD erected. Mark 14:58 says, *"We heard Him say, 'I will destroy this Temple made with hands, and within three days I will build another made without hands.'"* John 2:21 clarifies what Jesus meant with His bold declaration about building another Temple by saying that *He was speaking of the Temple of His body.* On one side of the coin, we already have Jesus serving as High Priest in a heavenly Tabernacle. On the other side, however, He is serving as High Priest over good things that are **yet to come.**

Summary

One side of the coin:
    Jesus already serves in a Spiritual Temple erected by the Lord, which is His own body.

The other side of the same coin:
    Jesus serves as High Priest of good things to come.

What are the good things to come? The good things to come are the times of refreshing and the restoration of all things. This is the part where we, as living stones, get built into a Spiritual Temple and into a Holy Priesthood, intended to offer up spiritual sacrifices. In unity of the faith, we become one with each other and one with Christ (one body). All of us are members of the Household of God, Christ Himself being the Chief Cornerstone. Joined together, the whole building grows into a Holy Temple in the LORD, a dwelling place of God in the Spirit. Do you now understand that you are the Temple of God and that the Spirit of God dwells in you? Your body is the Temple of the Holy Spirit, your Body being the corporate body of the Church.

The Fusion of Ideas

I'll attempt to give you my best summary of this two-edged sword, and both sides of the coin. I apologize in advance for the insufficiency of my explanation, as I am a man trying to explain heavenly things. At the present time, I, like Paul, can only see through a glass darkly.

Look at the Temple the way you would look at Christ. He always existed in the spiritual realm. Through Him all things were created. But in a sense, He was not "Jesus" until He came in the flesh. He was the Word, the Son of God, one of the three members of the Divine Family, But He was not Jesus yet. Even though in the present age you can look back and refer to all the prophecies about Christ, as if they were referring to Jesus, He, as a human being, did not exist until He was conceived in His mother's womb.

Consider it this way. The blood of Jesus covers the sins of every Believer — past, present, and future. Even those who died before He ever completed His work on the cross are covered by the blood that was not yet spilled when they were alive. Essentially, Jesus was already Jesus. This is because He was going to be Jesus and God is not subject to a linear timeline, as we are. Applying this same reasoning to the Spiritual Temple, we can say:

The Spiritual Temple already exists... because it will exist!

Although this concept is seemingly very metaphysical and "New Age-y," I'm confident it's Biblical. Effectively, the Temple He already serves in is the one we must build. Remember, God's timeline is not linear like man's. God always was, always is, and always will be. He is not trapped in linear (one dimensional, unidirectional) time, as we are. God does, however, give us clues and patterns of what will come by casting shadows down from the real things in heaven, which already exists. In turn, we use the shadows cast from heaven, as blueprints, to recreate the real things on earth. For instance, this is why He gives us archetypes as patterns of Christ's ministry in the Old Testament. Joseph is a perfect example of an archetype of Jesus. Joseph's ministry foreshadowed Christ's ministry, who, in turn, foreshadowed our ministry. Meanwhile, from God's perspective, it was all already done from the foundations of the world. In the next chapter we will explore the life of Joseph, using it as a model for perfect ministry.

In the same way, God gave Moses the Tabernacle in the Wilderness and said to be sure to build it according to the pattern shown him on the mountain. During the Sermon on the Mount, Jesus gave us the pattern for building the Kingdom of Heaven, God's government with the Spiritual Temple at its center. Both the Tabernacle in the Wilderness and Kingdom of God with the Spiritual Temple were/are built using blueprints given on the mountain. Following the examples of the Tabernacle in the Wilderness and the Sermon on the Mount, we should build the Spiritual Temple to precise specifications.

Stay with me now. Even though from the beginning of time, God knew that His Son would die for the sins of the world and He knew who would be saved for an eternity by His blood, Jesus still had to do it. He actually had to do the work that His Father already knew He would do. Let's consider this perspective when contemplating the Spiritual Temple. We know that Jesus already serves as High priest in the Spiritual Temple, but we still have to build it. *But Christ as a Son over His own House, whose House we are if we hold fast the confidence and the rejoicing of the hope firm to the end (Hebrews 3:6).* It is at the end of the Millennial Kingdom that it all comes together and is typified by the concept of marriage. I hope this unifies your perception of the Spiritual Temple.

Concept of Marriage

As you will see in more detail at the conclusion of *The Heart of David*, the ultimate realization of the Spiritual Temple is at the end when, as one unified bride, we become one flesh with the Messiah. Together as ONE in Christ, we become the Spiritual Temple.

> ➤ *(Revelation 21:1-3) Now I saw a new heaven and a new earth, for the first heaven and the first earth had passed away. Also there was no more sea. Then I, John, saw the Holy City, New Jerusalem, coming down out of heaven from God, prepared as a bride adorned for her husband. And I heard a loud voice from heaven saying, "Behold, the Tabernacle of God is with men, and He will dwell with them, and they shall be His people. God Himself will be with them and be their God."*

If I might digress for a moment, I'd like to share a short poem I composed to my wife for one of our anniversaries. During that time, I was in deep prayer and consideration about the concepts that needed to come forth in *The Heart of David*. While contemplating the call to build the Spiritual Temple, I found myself imagining what it might be like, at that time, for those so in love with their earthly brides.

<u>*Living Stones*</u>

They asked and He replied,
In the resurrection
You are neither married nor given to marriage…
"So sad" you might say
For you and I who love so deeply.
But there is a House for us to dwell together.
And it takes many stones to build,
All laid perfectly in place,
One stone near the other,
A unique role each plays
Building this place,
A Spiritual House of living stones.
All different, yet still the same.
One body,
Completely dependent on each stone
To set in place perfectly.
A mysterious marriage of form and function
In this place,
Where unity is the vow of perfection,
Permanence born out of a world of shadows
And weightless vapors.
So, from this world,
When love's fate entwines
Two lives as one
As yours and mine;
There remains one way to stay
An inseparable one
In that place.
And that is…To lay
My living stone on yours
For all eternity to taste,
Our living stones together
As One In Place.
I will forever lie next to you, my love.

So, what is our role until this prophetic moment, until *"the Tabernacle of God is with men"?* We are to be transformed into the fullness and image and stature of Christ, and then assemble the Spiritual Temple (bring the government of heaven to earth). Certainly it is a monumental task and a high calling, one worthy of our full attention and greatest effort. Thankfully, with the help of the Holy Spirit, it is a mission that He has equipped us to complete, should we choose to accept it.

Sharper than a Two-edged Sword

The concepts and principles presented throughout *The Heart of David* are difficult at best; and they are very challenging to your walk as a disciple of Christ. Your reaction to them will tell you a lot about yourself. There are a number of key **doctrinal issues** that have been raised in *The Heart of David*. Some of them are admittedly controversial, and I would like to gauge your reaction to them. Let me choose two of these issues for our example. These two principles are inseparably woven together.

The first issue we will evaluate is that of **obedience to the Law** of God — the Torah that Moses was given at Mt. Sinai and instructed to write down. I have upheld throughout this book that born again Christians should endeavor to keep the Law, not unto salvation of course, but *because of salvation*. The second issue, to put to the test, is the idea of **sin-less perfection**. I maintain that it is possible for some remnant of the Body of Christ to be conformed into the image of Christ before His second coming. Both concepts certainly fall outside of modern-day, mainstream Christian theology. Nevertheless, they are easily supported by Scripture, in my humble opinion.

Curious enough, God supplied a built-in "battery tester" when He inspired the Holy Scriptures. He provided a gauge to measure our response and to expose our reaction to His divine truths. With it, He can reveal the thoughts and intents of the heart.

> ➤ *(Hebrews 4:12-13) For the Word of God is living and powerful, and sharper than any two-edged sword, piercing even to the division of soul and spirit, and of joints and marrow, and is a discerner of the thoughts*

and intents of the heart. And there is no creature hidden from His sight, but all things are naked and open to the eyes of Him to whom we must give account.

Your reaction to God's Word will expose your inner thoughts. Assuming, of course, that we have already provided sufficient evidence that these two doctrinal statements are valid, let's plug our controversial issues into the battery tester and see what happens.

The Battery Tester

Doctrine: We should keep God's commandments because the Law has **NOT** been done away with. Obedience to the Law of Moses is beneficial and possible.

Scripture: *For this is the love of God, that we keep His commandments. And His commandments are not burdensome (1 John 5:3).*

Reaction: We can't keep all of the Law. It's too difficult.

Discerns: A heart issue (an uncircumcised heart).

Doctrine: Perfection. You can become sinless before Jesus returns.

Scripture: *Therefore you shall be perfect, just as your Father in heaven is perfect (Matthew 5:48).*

Reaction: Sinlessness in not possible until we die.

Discerns: A faith issue (the shed blood of Christ is not enough).

We must not only believe that Jesus was who HE says HE was and did what HE said HE would do. We must also believe WE are who He says WE are and that WE can become who He says WE can become. We are no longer citizens of earth, but heavenly citizens with an ultimate calling. *Therefore, holy brethren, partakers of the heavenly calling, consider the Apostle and High Priest of our confession, Christ Jesus... (Hebrews 3:1).*

God's Word has exposed your nakedness and it is to Him that you must give account. *Therefore, as the Holy Spirit says: "Today, if you will hear His voice, do not harden your hearts as in the rebellion, in the day of trial in the Wilderness" (Hebrews 3:7-8).* Dear brothers and sisters in Christ; please do not harden your hearts to His high calling on your life!

It is time for us, as children of the Most High, to bring God's Spirit back into His institution, and bring the government of heaven to earth. We are to reestablish one body in one Spirit, with no denominationalism, just as you were called in one hope of your calling; one Lord, one faith, one baptism, serving one God and Father of all, who is above all, and through all, and in you all. Witness the shadow of this ultimate restoration, as Solomon restored the Ark of the Covenant to its rightful place in the Holy of Holies. *Then the priests brought in the Ark of the Covenant of the* LORD *to its place, into the inner sanctuary of the Temple, to the Most Holy Place, under the wings of the cherubim (2 Chronicles 5:7).* We must build the Spiritual Temple, so YAHWEH can establish a permanent place for His Name to dwell forevermore. *And I heard a loud voice from heaven saying, "Behold, the Tabernacle of God is with men, and He will dwell with them, and they shall be His people. God Himself will be with them and be their God" (Revelation 21:3).*

I know the call to build the Spiritual Temple is a tremendous challenge to your faith. But as you have come this far, I know you are up for the challenge. I believe it is an assignment worthy of your total commitment. Your heart beats to the tune of a different drummer now. The spirit of Elijah is calling. Today, if you hear his voice, hearken to the call of the forerunner. And now, *leaving the discussion of the elementary principles of Christ, let us go on to perfection (Hebrews 6:1).*

Chapter Eleven

Perfect Ministry

"Who then is a faithful and wise servant, whom his master made ruler over his household, to give them food in due season?"
Matthew 24:45

S o what does it all boil down to? You have endured ten demanding chapters. They've challenged your faith as you walk as a disciple of Christ and, ultimately, you have come face to face with your high calling. It may still seem surreal to you, but the testimony of your heart is telling you deep inside that it is true. You know it is true! You can't escape it now! If you prayed the Prayer of David with the heart of David, you are called to build the Spiritual Temple. You are called to partake in the office of the Messiah, to complete the work that He started. You are called to perfect ministry.

Ephesians, the book of unity and oneness, says it best. In chapter 4, Paul inspires unity by commanding us to "walk worthy of the high calling with which we were called." Paul says that we should be one body, in one Spirit, with one hope, worshiping one Lord, in one faith, under one baptism, because there is only *one God and Father of all, who is above all, and through all, and in you all (v. 6).* In order to unite God's chosen people into one; the Son of God came to earth to fill the office of Messiah. He came bearing great gifts for His future bride. He gifted some as Apostles, some Prophets, some Evangelists, some Pastors and some Teachers. The reason He gave these gifts to the Body of Christ is to equip us to participate in His duties in the office of Messiah, ultimately completing the goals of His ministry.

Collectively, these five subordinate offices define the head office of the Messiah. Each of us, called to one or more of these offices, must combine our efforts until corporately we all come "to a unity of the faith, to the knowledge of the Son of God, to a perfect man, and to the measure of the stature of the fullness of Christ." In other words, *until we grow up in all things into Him who is the head — Christ (v. 15)*. This is when we, as heirs of His inheritance, manifest as the sons of God. Remember, we learned from Galatians 3 that *if you are Christ's, then you are Abraham's seed, and heirs according to the promise (v. 29)*. Yet Galatians 4 clarifies: *Now I say that the heir, as long as he is a child, does not differ at all from a slave, though he is master of all, but is under guardians and stewards until the time appointed by the Father (vs. 1-2)*. The time appointed by the Father is when the sons of God are revealed. In other words, the sons of God are revealed when we grow up in all things to be like Him, to the measure of the stature of the fullness of Christ. The Son of God came to fulfill the office of Messiah and, corporately, when we manifest as the sons of God we will participate in that office.

The right to be called "Sons of God" Title or Position?

Think about it!   How do we obtain the title of "sons of God"? It is a pretty uncomplicated answer. *For you are all sons of God through faith in Christ Jesus (Galatians 3:26); for as many as are led by the Spirit of God, these are sons of God (Romans 8:14)*. Simple, would you agree? However, there is a wide chasm between "obtaining a title" and "manifesting a position." *For the earnest expectation of the creation eagerly waits for the **revealing** of the sons of God*. The King James says *"For **manifestation** of the sons of God" (Romans 8:19)*. After we obtain the title, we must then manifest the position. To manifest means: "That which was previously hidden from view is now made visible to all." This is that for which all of creation is waiting, for the sons of God to become visible.

The Temporary Dwelling
& the Office of Messiah

The presence and the power of God reside in His Tabernacle. Jesus came and tabernacled among us and, as humans, we currently occupy the same temporary tabernacle. Jesus descended from His divine form and took on an outward appearance, which would be familiar to us, so He could establish the office of Messiah. He did not complete His ministry, but fulfilled one part as the "suffering servant" of Isaiah 53. He left us until we become conformed into His image, establish His Kingdom on earth, and ultimately complete His ministry to the world. After the restoration of all these things, He can return for His spotless bride as a reigning King. Both Jesus and His bride must demonstrate the faith to live in a temporary dwelling, while patiently waiting for God's permanent resting place. Abraham laid out this Biblical blue-print perfectly. *By faith Abraham obeyed when he was called to* ***go out*** *to the place which he would receive as an inheritance. And he went out, not knowing where he was going. By faith he dwelt in the Land of promise as in a foreign country, dwelling in tents with Isaac and Jacob, the heirs with him of the same promise; for he waited for the City which has foundations, whose builder and maker is God (Hebrews 11:8-10).* By faith, Abraham had to leave his dwelling and go out to receive his inheritance. He lived in a temporary tabernacle and never established a permanent dwelling, waiting for God to establish His permanent home. God's permanent home will be the Spiritual Temple in the City of God.

Jesus did the same when he shed His divinity and became man, descending to fill the office of Messiah. Like Abraham, He **went out** (of heavenly places) by faith and dwelt in a temporary tabernacle (He tabernacled among us). All He did, He did for us, so *we* could receive our inheritance, *a City whose builder and maker is God.* Jesus did His part, and then ascended into heaven where He serves in the Spiritual Temple as High Priest. He waits patiently until the restoration of all things — which is our part of the ministry. By faith, we must shed our humanity, become the sons of God, and ascend to fill the office. In essence, we are called to complete the ministry of Messiah. *For though* *we walk in the flesh, we do not war according to the flesh. For the weapons of our warfare are not carnal but mighty in God for pulling down strongholds, casting down arguments and every high thing that exalts itself against the knowledge of God, bringing every thought into captivity to the obedience of Christ, and being ready to punish all disobedience **when your obedience is fulfilled** (2 Corinthians 10:3-6).*

We can rely on the use of Biblical blueprints, once again, to discover God's plan for mankind. More importantly, we can gain insight into the power and authority we are given, and the revelation of what He expects of us, as we fulfill our part of His plan. In Ephesians 1, Paul encapsulates the vital role we play. He prays that we may receive the Spirit of wisdom and revelation in the knowledge of God's plan, and that we may come to recognize the expectation of His high calling on our lives, along with the magnitude of our inheritance. He wants us to be aware of the exceeding greatness of God's power that is bestowed upon we who believe. God has made the same mighty power available to us that He wrought in Christ when He raised Him from the dead. This idea alone is staggering! Say it with me:

I am indwelt with the power that raised Christ from the grave & have been given an important role in God's plan for mankind!

As we progress through this chapter, we will define perfect ministry and we will use Joseph, the son of Jacob, as our model. We will discover the ultimate purpose of his calling and make the all important connection between his ministry, the ministry of Jesus Christ and, finally, the ministry of the Church. Along the way, we may get a glimpse at the magnitude of authority laid in our hands through the work of the cross. On our journey we will also discover that the most deadly enemy to authority does not come from external challengers to power, but from internal opposition. Pride goes before the destruction of any man who attempts to substitute building his own Kingdom for using his calling and resources to advance God's Kingdom. We must discover the delicate balance between humbly accepting the awesome power and authority placed in our keeping, and getting puffed up with "our own" great ministry to the world. There are two types of toxic pride and they both quench the Spirit. One proclaims "I will" or "I can" with the focus being on "I." The other complains "I can't" or "That's not possible"; thereby denying the power of God by believing everything depends on his own limited capabilities. Paul says to Timothy that these types of people have a "form of godliness (outward religion), but deny the source of true power (genuine faith)." He says that from such people, "Turn away!"

Whose report will you believe?

In John 14:12 the Lord said, *"Most assuredly, I say to you, he who believes in Me, the works that I do he will do also; and **greater works than these he will do**, because I go to My Father."* That's right. You won't just be "like Christ." You have been assigned to perform even greater works and have an even greater ministry. Amazing, huh! You are to have a greater ministry to the world than Jesus Himself.

However, as we progress towards the end of the book, I must ask you one vital question:

> *Who has believed our report? And to whom has the arm*
> *of the LORD been revealed?* **(Isaiah 53:1)**

God has placed a high calling on your life. He has prepared unimaginable riches for you, which in ages past were hidden from mankind. But they are now made available through His Spirit. What is made available? The deep mysteries of God revealed to you for **YOUR** glory. No one can say it better than Paul.

> ➤ *(1 Corinthians 2:7-10) But we speak the wisdom of God in a mystery, the hidden wisdom which God ordained before the ages for **our glory**, which none of the rulers of this age knew; for had they known, they would not have crucified the Lord of glory. But as it is written: "Eye has not seen, nor ear heard, nor have entered into the heart of man the things which God has prepared for those who love Him." But God has revealed them to us through His Spirit. For the Spirit searches all things, yes, the deep things of God.*

The question remains, do you believe His report? We know that twelve spies went in to spy out the Promised Land and only two returned with a good report. I will believe the report of the LORD. Whose report will you believe? Believe in Him and believe His report. Don't be blinded by pride. Don't let pride harden your heart.

> ➤ *(John 12:37-40) But although He had done so many signs before them, they did not believe in Him, that the word of Isaiah the prophet might be fulfilled, which he spoke: "LORD, who has believed our report? And to whom has the arm of the LORD been revealed?" Therefore they could not believe, because Isaiah said again: "He has blinded their eyes and hardened their hearts, lest they should see with their eyes, lest they should understand with their hearts and turn, so that I should heal them."*

Believe the report of the LORD! You have a high calling on your life. Remember, we are joints heirs with Christ and share a common position. We have a responsibility to fulfill, and the redemption of the world depends on it!

The Manifestation of the Sons of God

All of creation is waiting for God's chosen people to manifest the position to which they have already been given title. God's creation itself is waiting to be delivered from the bondage of corruption into the freedom from sin that will finally be attained when God's children manifest their full inheritance. *The Spirit Himself bears witness with our spirit that we are children of God, and if children, then heirs — heirs of God and joint heirs with Christ, if indeed we suffer with Him, that we may also be glorified together. For I consider that the sufferings of this present time are not worthy to be compared with the glory which shall be revealed in us.* **For the earnest expectation of the creation eagerly waits for the revealing of the sons of God.** *For the creation was subjected to futility, not willingly, but because of Him who subjected it in hope; because the creation itself also will be delivered from the bondage of corruption into the glorious liberty of the children of God. For we know that the whole creation groans and labors with birth pangs together until now (Romans 8:16-22).*

268

All of creation is eagerly waiting for the manifestation of the sons of God. Why? Creation is waiting because we have a mission to complete. We have a perfect ministry to fulfill, a common ministry with Jesus Christ. All of creation is enthusiastically waiting for us to be conformed into the image of Christ, so that it too can be delivered from the bondage of sin. But first, we must fulfill our role as joint heirs with Christ, the administration of perfect ministry. This is our incredible privilege and crucial responsibility. To help understand the role and enormity of this perfect ministry, God gave us Joseph as the ideal archetype. With a "perfect ministry," he redeemed the world.

Joseph - The Faithful & Wise Servant

In Psalm 145, the LORD refers to **Himself** as the One who gives food in due season. *The LORD upholds all who fall, and raises up all who are bowed down. The eyes of all look expectantly to You, and You give them their **food in due season** (vs. 14-15).* In Matthew's Gospel, however, the Lord said that He is looking for a **faithful servant** to give the people food in due season. *"Who then is a faithful and wise servant, whom his master made ruler over his household, to give them **food in due season?** Blessed is that servant whom his master, when he comes, will find so doing. Assuredly, I say to you that he will make him ruler over all his goods"* (Matthew 24:45-47).

The shift in responsibility to feed the people in due season, from Divine to human hands, identifies God's prophetic plan. He will eventually assign man to fulfill His ministry.

The LORD is looking for faithful and wise servants to feed his people in times of great need. In so doing, He will make them rulers over many things. *His lord said to him, 'Well done, good and faithful servant; you were faithful over a few things, I will make you ruler over many things. Enter into the joy of your lord'* (Matthew 25:21). This entire ministry is reflected in the life of Joseph, who demonstrated the perfect blueprint of the faithful and wise servant. From his ministry, we can establish our high calling.

Even though Jesus never mentions Joseph in Matthew 24, it is obvious that Joseph is the faithful and wise servant to whom Jesus is referring.

Joseph is the servant who was made ruler over the master's household. This will be very clear when we go back to the story of Joseph and find his ultimate prophetic significance. In addition, as we reveal Joseph's life as the framework for prophecy, we will again witness David's role as a true visionary. When David wrote Psalm 145 about the LORD giving the people food in due season, he knew the ministry of Joseph. David could envision how the LORD'S ministry of giving the people food in due season was exemplified in Joseph's life. Joseph did precisely that. And David could see how this exact ministry needed to be fulfilled again in the future by those wise enough to follow after Joseph's example.

Did you know that the story of Joseph's life accounts for more chapters in the Bible than the life of any other person other than Jesus Himself? Joseph is the key prophetic figure in all of Scripture. His life is the framework for prophecy. As an archetype of Christ (and anyone called to walk in Christ's ministry), Joseph foreshadowed both roles that Christ would play, that of the suffering servant and that of the reigning king. Joseph was the suffering servant when he was sold into slavery and persecuted, though innocent. He represented the reigning King when he was made ruler over all of Egypt.

Framework for Prophecy

Through Joseph's life, we can witness the prophetic significance of God's plan for the End of the Age. We learned in the last chapter that the seven day week is a prophetic picture for seven thousand years of history, six days of work and one day of rest. For the wise, the End of the Age can be summed up in one sentence.

The End of the Age is represented by the last two days of the week, a Friday and Saturday, and whoever will manage them (prepare) wisely.

For the rest of the world (the not so wise), the End of the Age can be summed this way:

The End of the Age is represented by the last day of the week only, a Saturday, and the struggle to survive because of a lack of preparation.

In other words: **Surviving Sabbath!**

God promised the people that He would provide a double-portion on Friday so they would have enough to eat on Saturday (the Sabbath). They were NOT to go out and collect manna on the Sabbath day. The manna was the "bread from heaven" that supernaturally provided for the sustenance of the people. Without it, the people would have perished. *Then the LORD said to Moses, "Behold, I will rain bread from heaven for you. And the people shall go out and gather a certain quota every day, that I may test them, whether they will walk in My Law or not. And it shall be on the sixth day that they shall prepare what they bring in, and it shall be **twice as much** as they gather daily" (Exodus 16:4-5).* So daily, the people gathered what they needed to survive. *And Moses said, "Let no one leave any of it till morning" (v. 19).* When the people refused to obey, the manna left over until morning was filled with maggots. *And so it was, on the sixth day, that they gathered twice as much bread, two omers for each one. And all the rulers of the congregation came and told Moses. Then he said to them, "This is what the LORD has said: 'Tomorrow is a Sabbath rest, a holy Sabbath to the LORD. Bake what you will bake today, and boil what you will boil; and lay up for yourselves all that remains, to be kept until morning.'" So they laid it up till morning, as Moses commanded; and it did not stink, nor were there any worms in it. Then Moses said, "Eat that today, for today is a Sabbath to the LORD; **today you will not find it in the field.** Six days you shall gather it, but on the seventh day, which is the Sabbath, there will be none." Now it happened that some of the people went out on the seventh day to gather, **but they found none.** And the LORD said to Moses, "How long do you refuse to keep My commandments and My Laws? **See! For the LORD has given you the Sabbath; therefore He gives you on the sixth day bread for two days.** Let every man remain in his place; let no man go out of his place on the seventh day." So the people rested on the seventh day (vs. 22-30).*

This, as you will see, was precisely the ministry of Joseph. He was the faithful and wise servant. Joseph was the wise manager of his master's house who collected a double-portion on Friday so he could feed the people on Saturday. At the End of the Age, those who are not prepared will literally starve to death, unless someone is prepared to feed them. Through this mechanism, those following in Joseph's footsteps will redeem the world.

Joseph's Life - the Framework for Prophecy

You probably already know that Joseph was gifted to relay God's interpretation of dreams. It was Joseph's discernment about the meaning of Pharaoh's dreams that caused Pharaoh to make him ruler over Egypt. Joseph discerned that there were two seven-year periods crucial to the survival of Egypt. The first seven years were that of a double-portion harvest. Years eight through fourteen were to bring the worst famine in the history of mankind. With inspiration from the true and living God, Joseph gives Pharaoh his life saving advice.

"Store up, he says, during the years of plenty and take from your stores in the years of famine."

Pharaoh was so impressed with Joseph's interpretation that he made him second in command over all of Egypt. He assigned Joseph to design, institute, and coordinate the plan to save Egypt from the seven years of famine. In doing so, Joseph's plan also saved Israel and the rest of world from certain starvation. You will see shortly that these two seven-year periods are an exact blueprint for the End of the Age.

> ➤ *(Genesis 41:36-41, 44)* *"Then that food shall be as a reserve for the land for the seven years of famine which shall be in the land of Egypt, that the land may not perish during the famine."* So the advice was good in the eyes of Pharaoh and in the eyes of all his servants. And Pharaoh said to his servants, "Can we find such a one as this, a man in whom is the Spirit of God?"* **Then Pharaoh said to Joseph, "Inasmuch as God has shown you all this, there is no one as discerning and wise as you. You shall be over my house,** and all my people shall be ruled according to your word; only in regard to the throne will I be greater than you." And Pharaoh said to Joseph, "See, I have set you over all the land of Egypt." Pharaoh also said to Joseph, "I am Pharaoh, and **without your consent no man may lift his hand or foot in all the land of Egypt."*

When we use the story of Joseph as a prophetic model, Pharaoh represents the LORD and Joseph is the wise servant who is made ruler and given

272

complete authority over the LORD'S house. It is Joseph's role, as a representative of the "LORD," to give the people food in due season and redeem them from certain death. As followers of Christ, we have been given the same magnitude of authority. We should acknowledge that at the End of the Age we will fill the same role of redeeming the world from certain death.

Preserver of Life

The story continues when Joseph comes face to face with his brothers who, years earlier, out of jealousy, sold him into slavery. He is met with a mix of emotions. Feelings of anger, sadness, grief, sorrow, and heartache over the years of separation from his father and the loss of his mother, are balanced with feelings of mercy, compassion, forgiveness, and joy that he is finally being reunited with his family. Joseph recognized God's plan for him as the preserver of life. Speaking to his brothers in Genesis 45, he said, "*But now, do not therefore be grieved or angry with yourselves because you sold me here; for God sent me before you* **to preserve life**. *For these two years the famine has been in the land, and there are still five years in which there will be neither plowing nor harvesting.* **And God sent me before you to preserve a posterity for you in the earth, and to save your lives by a great deliverance.** *So now it was not you who sent me here, but God; and He has made me a father to Pharaoh,* **and lord of all his house,** *and a ruler throughout all the land of Egypt*" (vs. 5-8).

The Faithful & Wise Servant

Who then was the faithful and wise servant, whom his master made ruler over his household? Who was that blessed servant who gave the people **food in due season;** and who was made ruler over all his master's possessions? The answer is Joseph; but in the future, it is anyone who wishes to emulate his ministry. Joseph recognized that he was sent before his brothers (the tribes of Israel) to save their lives in such a great deliverance. As a result, he not only insured their survival, but he also offered them prosperity through his authority from Pharaoh. '*Bring your father and your* *households and come to me; I will give you the best of the land of Egypt, and you will eat the fat of the land' (Genesis 45:18).* In the process, Joseph made a way for the rest of the world to be preserved as well.

Lives for Food - Redeeming the World

Paul said in Philippians 2:10-11 *that at the name of Jesus every knee should bow, of those in heaven, **and of those on earth**, and of those under the earth, and that every tongue should confess that Jesus Christ is Lord, to the glory of God the Father.* What will it take for every knee on earth to bow to our Lord and Savior? We know that when He returns as a triumphant King, to rule and reign for one thousand years, there will be no mistaking who is the true and living God. The LORD is One and there is no other. But, by that time, it will be too late for those who did not believe.

What will it take at the End of the Age to gather in the single greatest harvest of souls? Once again, let's depend on blueprints and patterns to predict God's plan. God used food — time and time again — to demonstrate his power over life and death. He provided manna and quails from heaven to feed Israel in the Wilderness. During the great famine, Joseph provided grain from Egypt to feed Israel. In 2 Kings 4:43-44, Elisha fed 100 men with 20 loaves and had some left over. And Jesus multiplied a few loaves of bread and a few fish to feed five thousand, and again four thousand.

When God lets a man go hungry, He immediately gets his attention, and it becomes easy for His righteous laborers to take authority. Even the most stubborn unbelievers will become willing to voluntarily surrender their lives, without the shedding of blood, in exchange for not having to watch their loved ones starve to death. They will come face to face with the all-important question: Why do you have food and how is it that you were prepared for the famine? The answer is that we serve a mighty God, the only true and living God, and so can you. Watch how this prophetic model played out in the life of Joseph.

Then Joseph provided his father, his brothers, and all his father's household with bread, according to the number in their families. Now there was no bread in all the land; for the famine was very severe, so that the land of Egypt and the land of Canaan languished because of the famine. **And Joseph gathered up all the money that was found in the land of Egypt and in the land of Canaan, for the grain which they bought;** *and Joseph brought the money into Pharaoh's house. So when the* **money failed** *in the land of Egypt and in the land of Canaan, all the Egyptians came to Joseph and said, "Give us bread, for why should we die in your presence? For the money has failed."* Then Joseph said, **"Give your livestock, and I will give you bread for your livestock, if the money is gone."** *So they brought their livestock to Joseph, and Joseph gave them bread in exchange for the horses, the flocks, the cattle of the herds, and for the donkeys. Thus he fed them with bread in exchange for all their livestock that year. When that year had ended, they came to him the next year and said to him, "We will not hide from my lord that our money is gone; my lord also has our herds of livestock.* **There is nothing left in the sight of my lord but our bodies and our lands.** *Why should we die before your eyes, both we and our land?* **Buy us and our land for bread,** *and we and our land will be servants of Pharaoh; give us seed,* **that we may live and not die,** *that the land may not be desolate." Then Joseph bought all the land of Egypt for Pharaoh; for every man of the Egyptians sold his field, because the famine was severe upon them. So the land became Pharaoh's. And as for the people, he moved them into the cities, from one end of the borders of Egypt to the other end. Only the land of the priests he did not buy; for the priests had rations allotted to them by Pharaoh, and they ate their rations which Pharaoh gave them; therefore they did not sell their lands. Then Joseph said to the people,* **"Indeed I have bought you and your land this day for Pharaoh.** *Look, here is seed for you, and you shall sow the land. And it shall come to pass in the harvest that you shall give one-fifth to Pharaoh. Four-fifths shall be your own, as seed for the field and for your food, for those of your households and as food for your little ones." So they said,* **"You have saved our lives; let us find favor in the sight of my lord, and we will be Pharaoh's servants"** *(Genesis 47:12-25).*

When the famine became so devastating and the people ran out of food, they first spent all their money to buy food. Then they exchanged their personal belongings for food. Next, they traded their land. And lastly, they resorted to trading their very lives, their actual freedom *"that we may live and not die."* Without a single battle, without even one skirmish, the world surrendered itself to Pharaoh. They not only did this willingly, but with great appreciation. *So they said, "You have saved our lives; let us find favor in the sight of my lord, and we will be Pharaoh's servants."* Consider again the question from Jesus, *"Who then is a faithful and wise servant, whom his master made ruler over his household, to give them food in due season?"* Let's consider our answer using Joseph as our prophetic model for the End of the Age. Here is the blueprint. Pharaoh is the master representing the Lord, and Joseph is the servant representing us as Jesus' disciples. In the same way, at the End of the Age, we as faithful and wise servants will bring in a great harvest because we have prepared ourselves to *give them food in due season.*

During His earthly ministry, Jesus said in John 4:35: *"Behold, I say to you, lift up your eyes and look at the fields, for they are already white for harvest!"* He also said in Luke 10:2: *"The harvest truly is great, but the laborers are few; therefore pray the Lord of the harvest to send out laborers into His harvest."* How do we increase the number of laborers? The intent of *The Heart of David* is to inform the laborers of their duties and to prepare them for the power and authority that has been bestowed upon them, as they accept their commission as forerunners of the End of the Age. And then, once prepared, *"this Gospel of the Kingdom will be preached in all the world as a witness to all the nations, and then the end will come"* (Matthew 24:14). Do you recall the great Kingdom mystery of reaping where you have not sown, which you learned earlier in Chapter 5? *"For in this the saying is true: 'One sows and another reaps.'" "I sent you to reap that for which you have not labored; others have labored, and you have entered into their labors"* (John 4:37-38). To prepare for the End of the Age, you simply must build upon the precepts (labors) of the laborers that have come before.

Who is the breadmaker?

"Men listened to me and waited, and kept silence for my counsel. After my words they did not speak again, and my speech settled on them as dew. They waited for me as for the rain, and they opened their mouth wide as for the spring rain. If I mocked at them, they did not believe it, and the light of my countenance they did not cast down. I chose the way for them, and sat as chief; so I dwelt as a king in the army, as one who comforts mourners" (Job 29:21-25).

In this small excerpt, Job recalls the days before His great trial. Notice the tremendous level of influence and authority that he had. Brothers and sisters, in Christ you have even more potential. I want to show you a famous story from Scripture demonstrating power and authority. But this time I want to expose you to a slightly different perspective. And when I do, I want you to remember and internalize God's promise. *"Every place on which the sole of your foot treads shall be yours"* (Deuteronomy 11:24).

Give Them Food in Due Season

On two occasions, Jesus found Himself with a great multitude of hungry people, a situation similar to that of Israel's shortly after they crossed the sea into the Wilderness. About one month after the Exodus, the rebellious sons of Israel found themselves in a circumstance requiring a great act of faith. They had previously witnessed the ten plagues, the parting of the Red Sea, and the supernatural destruction of Egypt's army. Now they were out of food and they were hungry. In Exodus 16, with little faith and in fear of starvation *the whole congregation of the children of Israel complained against Moses and Aaron in the Wilderness. And the children of Israel said to them, "Oh, that we had died by the hand of the LORD in the land of Egypt, when we sat by the pots of meat and when we ate bread to the full! For you have brought us out into this Wilderness to kill this whole assembly with hunger." Then the LORD said to Moses, "Behold, I will rain bread from heaven for you. And the people shall go out and gather a certain quota every day, that I may test them, whether they will walk in My Law or not"* (vs. 2-4).

On both occasions with Jesus, just like in the days of Moses, there was an option for His disciples to display great faith and the opportunity for them to administer a great miracle. In the Wilderness of Sinai, God used the circumstance to test the people. But there were really two tests. One was to test their faith, and the other was to test their obedience. Their faith was tested simply because there was no food to eat and no prospects of getting any. Their obedience was tested because, after God provided bread from heaven, they were instructed to gather only what they needed, and twice as much on Friday. If they gathered more than needed, other than for the provision for the Sabbath, the excess would rot. God knew that those who gathered more than they needed for that day were not trusting in the LORD to provide for tomorrow. This is why we pray in Matthew 6:11: *Give us this day our daily bread.* In Hebrews 3, we can see just how precise the relationship is between obedience and faith.

> ➤ *(Hebrews 3:16-19) For who, having heard, rebelled? Indeed, was it not all who came out of Egypt, led by Moses? Now with whom was He angry forty years? Was it not with those who sinned, whose corpses fell in the Wilderness? And to whom did He swear that they would not enter His rest, but to those* **who did not obey?** *So we see that they could not enter in* **because of unbelief.**

Concerning both times when Jesus and His disciples had the need to feed the multitudes in a desolate place, He also was providing a test. In this case, it was a test for His disciples, not the people at large. What would you have done or said had you been put in the following situation? And more importantly, what will you do in the future when you ARE put in this situation? There were five thousand people to feed and not enough food to do so. In addition, there was no prospect of getting any food in the location where they were gathered. *Then Jesus lifted up His eyes, and seeing a great multitude coming toward Him, He said to Philip, "Where shall we buy bread, that these may eat?" But this He said to* **test** *him, for He Himself knew what He would do. Philip answered Him, "Two hundred denarii worth of bread is not sufficient for them, that every one of them may have a little"* (John 6:5-7).

In Matthew's Gospel, the event is recalled this way. *When it was evening, His disciples came to Him, saying, "This is* **a deserted place,** (symbolic of the Wilderness) *and the hour is already late. Send the multitudes away, that they may go into the villages and buy themselves food." But Jesus said to them, "They do not need to go away.* **You give them something to eat."** *And they said to Him, "We have here only five loaves and two fish"* (Matthew 14:15-17).

On the next occasion, this time faced with the prospect of feeding four thousand people, Jesus gives His disciples another chance to demonstrate their faith. *Now Jesus called His disciples to Himself and said, "I have compassion on the multitude, because they have now continued with Me three days and have nothing to eat. And I do not want to send them away hungry, lest they faint on the way."* Then His disciples said to Him, **"Where could we get enough bread in the Wilderness to fill such a great multitude?"** *(Matthew 15:32-33).* A great multitude of people are hungry in the Wilderness and an opportunity to demonstrate great faith exists. But again, the disciples bungle away the chance. Can you recognize how both occasions with Jesus mirror the events in the Wilderness of Sinai following the Exodus?

In summary, Jesus said:

"Where shall we buy bread, that these may eat?"

"They do not need to go away. You give them something to eat."

And the disciples craft the feeble reply:

"Where could we get enough bread in the Wilderness to fill such a great multitude?"

Now I pose this question to you: *"Who then is a faithful and wise servant, whom his master made ruler over his household, to give them food in due season?"* In other words, who is the breadmaker? That's right, it's YOU! I hope by now, with all that you have learned, that when the need arises, you will not fumble away the opportunity to feed the hungry people in due season.

The Lost Opportunity

On both occasions, the followers of Jesus had the opportunity to step out in faith and say, "We will provide the bread from heaven to feed the multitudes." However, they were still new in their training and, more critically, were not yet empowered with the indwelling of the Holy Spirit. But **we** have been Spirit filled, and therefore have absolutely NO EXCUSE! So at the End of the Age when the Lord asks, *"Where shall we buy bread that these may eat?"* Or the Lord tells you, *"They do not need to go away. You give them something to eat."* Your testimony as a forerunner will be:

**I am the faithful and wise servant
who my Master made ruler over His household,
and I will give the people food in due season.**

Like Joseph's interpretation of Pharaoh's dreams, at the End of the Age there will be two seven-year periods. The first seven-year period will be like a Friday (with its double-portion harvest and extraordinary abundance). The latter seven-years will be like a Saturday (with no harvest and famine). Throughout the first seven years, the wise servants will store up from the double-portion harvest. During that time, I believe we will become the spotless bride, conformed into the perfect image of Christ. And yes, during the first seven years, we will store up literal food for the people. We will also cultivate the faith needed to call down bread from heaven during the period when there is no harvest. I believe this time of need (famine) is the latter seven-year period, and that it corresponds to the Tribulation period, which is the last seven years before Jesus returns. The Tribulation is characterized by Christ Himself in this way:

> ➤ *(Matthew 24:29-31)* *"Immediately **after the tribulation of those days** the sun will be darkened, and the moon will not give its light; the stars will fall from heaven, and the powers of the heavens will be shaken. Then the sign of the **Son of Man will appear** in heaven, and then all the tribes of the earth will mourn, and they will see the **Son of Man coming on the clouds** of heaven with power and great glory. And He will send His angels with a great sound of a trumpet, and they will **gather together His elect** from the four winds, from one end of heaven to the other."*

I personally agree with Christ on the timing of "the Rapture" (the gathering together of His elect). The Rapture comes AFTER the Tribulation, during which we must give the people food in due season. Like Joseph, we will give the people bread to eat and, just like in the days of Joseph, the people will say, *"Buy us and our land for bread, and we and our land will be servants of Pharaoh."* They will testify, *"You have saved our lives; let us find favor in the sight of my lord, and we will be Pharaoh's servants."* In the story of Joseph, the people surrendered their lives to Pharaoh because of Joseph. Prophetically speaking, Pharaoh represents God the Father and Joseph represents the Savior. At the End of the Age, because of our testimony in Jesus Christ (the Joseph role), the people will thankfully and willingly hand their lives over to the LORD. **They will be fed bread for life and, ultimately, find the Bread of Life.**

The Bread of Life

The manna from heaven was symbolic of the true bread from heaven, the Bread of Life. *Then Jesus said to them, "Most assuredly, I say to you, Moses did not give you the bread from heaven, but My Father gives you the true bread from heaven. For the Bread of God is He who comes down from heaven and gives life to the world ." Then they said to Him, "Lord, give us this bread always." And Jesus said to them, "I am the Bread of Life. He who comes to Me shall never hunger, and he who believes in Me shall never thirst..."* (John 6:32-35). Feeding the people in due season will bring in a great harvest. However, like Joseph, you must be prepared. *"Most assuredly, I say to you, he who believes in Me has everlasting life. I am the Bread of Life. Your fathers ate the manna in the Wilderness, and are dead. This is the Bread which comes down from heaven, that one may eat of it and not die. I am the Living Bread which came down from heaven. If anyone eats of this Bread, he will live forever; and the Bread that I shall give is My flesh, which I shall give for the life of the world"* (John 6: 47-51).

Once the harvest is complete, there will be no more bread from heaven. *Then the manna ceased on the day after they had eaten the produce of the Land; and the children of Israel no longer had manna, but they ate the food of the Land of Canaan that year (Joshua 5:12).* Until the Lord returns a second time, we will have access to call down "manna from heaven." After He returns, anyone not having already eaten from the Bread of Life will have no chance to rule and reign with Him.

Pride

We are going to wrap up this chapter by explaining how we will transition in our high calling from bearing the *title of* "Sons of God" to manifesting the *position as* "Sons of God." This title is free for all who believe that Jesus is Lord. Filling the position, however, comes only to those willing to press on and make great sacrifices.

> ➤ (Phillipians 3:13-14) *Brethren, I do not count myself to have aprehended (taken hold of it); but one thing I do, forgetting those things which are behind and reaching forward to those things which are ahead, I press toward the goal for the prize of the upward call of God in Christ Jesus.*

To become conformed into His image, you must engage in the mature pursuit of Christ-like perfection and the bold display of authority that comes with it. But in doing so, you must offer your life as a living sacrifice. You must first be conformed to His death. *That I may know Him and the power of His resurrection, and the fellowship of His sufferings, being conformed to His death, if, by any means, I may attain to the resurrection from the dead. Not that I have already attained, or am already perfected; but I press on, that I may lay hold of that for which Christ Jesus has also laid hold of me (Philippians 3:10-12).* Paul recognized that his new life in Christ was a race that he needed to run every day. Even after many years of ministry, he had not yet attained perfection. Unlike most Christians today, Paul completely understood that attaining sinless perfection was the ultimate life goal of every true follower of Christ. He kept his eyes firmly on the prize of this high calling all the way to the end.

Always remember that you must, like Paul, and even Jesus himself, remain genuinely humble as you walk in your high calling. Toxic pride will destroy your witness and negate your efforts. *Let this mind be in you which was also in Christ Jesus, who, being in the form of God, **did not consider it robbery to be equal with God,** but made Himself of no reputation, taking the form of a bondservant, and coming in the likeness of men. And being found in appearance as a man, He humbled Himself and became obedient to the point of death, even the death of the cross (Philippians 2:5-8).*

We are called to become like Christ Jesus. Yet we see that Jesus did not think it was robbery to consider Himself equal to God. Should we maintain the same belief that Jesus had? The Bible says absolutely! *For "who has known the mind of the LORD that he may instruct Him?" But we have the mind of Christ (1 Corinthians 2:16).* Paul encourages all Believers to adopt this mature position. *Therefore let us, as many as are mature, have this mind; and if in anything you think otherwise, God will reveal even this to you. Nevertheless, to the degree that we have already attained, let us walk by the same rule, let us be of the **same mind** (Philippians 3:15-16).*

Staying Humble

How could Jesus know He was equal to God and stay humble at the same time? The answer is: Death! In pursuit of His ministry, He humbled

Himself even unto death. Why? Because Jesus knew and understood that *pride goes before destruction, and a haughty spirit before a fall (Proverbs 16:16)*. In pursuit of Christ-like perfection, we must do the same. We must remain humble. Paul knew this was a great risk and recognized how God protected him from his potential worst enemy. He had the opportunity to boast because of the abundance of revelations given to him, but instead he attributes all the credit to God.

> ➤ *(2 Corinthians 12:1-10) It is doubtless not profitable for me to boast. I will come to visions and revelations of the Lord: I know a man in Christ who fourteen years ago — whether in the body I do not know, or whether out of the body I do not know, God knows — such a one was caught up to the third heaven. And I know such a man — whether in the body or out of the body I do not know, God knows — how he was caught up into Paradise and heard inexpressible words, which it is not Lawful for a man to utter. Of such a one I will boast; yet of myself I will not boast, except in my infirmities. For though I might desire to boast, I will not be a fool; for I will speak the truth. But I refrain, lest anyone should think of me above what he sees me to be or hears from me. And lest I should be exalted above measure by the abundance of the revelations, a thorn in the flesh was given to me, a messenger of Satan to buffet me, lest I be exalted above measure. Concerning this thing I pleaded with the Lord three times that it might depart from me. And He said to me, "My grace is sufficient for you, for My strength is made perfect in weakness." Therefore most gladly I will rather boast in my infirmities, that the power of Christ may rest upon me. Therefore I take pleasure in infirmities, in reproaches, in needs, in persecutions, in distresses, for Christ's sake. For when I am weak, then I am strong.*

The revelations that God had given Paul were so spectacular that when he speaks of them he goes so far as to refer to himself in the third person. He says, "I know a man in Christ who fourteen years ago," but he is actually referring to himself who received the revelation. Paul so wants to give all the glory to God that he refers to "the man" as if it were not himself. Wow! That's humility. He says, "Of such a one I will boast; yet of myself I will not boast, except in my infirmities." He goes on to say that

God has left a thorn in his flesh to keep him dependent on the Lord, lest he should be exalted above measure by the abundance of the revelations given him. In his weakness, he glorifies God so that the power of Christ may rest upon him.

High Calling - High Risk

Christ Jesus called Himself the "Son of God" and He also called us "Sons of God." In this shocking call to equality, it is easy to see why developing toxic pride is so tempting. Pride is a potential hazard, and is most likely the biggest obstacle between us and our high calling. Of course, we know that Jesus did not fall into this temptation. But, He was accused of it nevertheless. In John 10:30 Jesus said, "*I and My Father are one.*" The Jews wanted to stone Him for blasphemy, "*because You, being a Man, make Yourself God*" (*v. 33*). Jesus inquired: Are you saying I am a blasphemer, '*because I said, 'I am the Son of God?'* (*v. 36*). Remember, even though Jesus did not consider it robbery to be equal to God, He was still submitted to His heavenly Father. The following is the model for submission that will help all of us avoid the risk of deadly pride in our pursuit of the high calling.

> ➢ **(Matthew 26:39)** "*Nevertheless, not as I will, but as You will.*"

> ➢ **(John 5:19)** *Then Jesus answered and said to them, "Most assuredly, I say to you, the Son can do nothing of Himself, but what He sees the Father do; for whatever He does, the Son also does in like manner.*"

> ➢ **(John 5:30)** "*I can of Myself do nothing. As I hear, I judge; and My judgment is righteous, because I do not seek My own will but the will of the Father who sent Me.*"

Absolute submission to His heavenly Father protected Jesus from becoming like Lucifer, who was the poster child for pride. Lucifer's pride came before his destruction. "*How you are fallen from heaven, O Lucifer, son of the morning! How you are cut down to the ground, you who weakened the nations! For you have said in your heart: 'I will ascend into heaven, I will exalt*

my throne above the stars of God; I will also sit on the mount of the congrega-
tion on the farthest sides of the north; I will ascend above the heights of the
clouds, I will be like the Most High.' Yet you shall be brought down to Sheol,
To the lowest depths of the Pit" (Isaiah 14:12-14).

Lucifer said, "I will be like the Most High." What's wrong with that, you might ask? Jesus was equal to His Father and we are called to be like Jesus. So why is Lucifer's claim considered prideful? Isn't Lucifer simply being confident that the Word of God is true? The answer is clearly "No!" in Lucifer's case, because of his narcissistic attitude! Lucifer said, "I will ascend into heaven; I will exalt my throne; I will sit on the mount; I will ascend above the clouds; and I will be like the Most High." This "I will" attitude is born of the pride that came before his destruction. Remember what Paul said in His pursuit of Christ-like perfection. *Him we preach, warning every man and teaching every man in all wisdom, that we may present every man perfect in Christ Jesus. To this end I also labor, striving according to His working which works in me mightily* (Colossians 1:28-29). Paul says "I labor," but more importantly acknowledges that it is God's power which is working in him. This is very different than saying, "I will exalt my throne above the stars of God."

Recall that this same Luciferian pride plagued Israel in the Wilderness. *For they being ignorant of God's righteousness, and seeking to establish their own righteousness, have not submitted to the righteousness of God* (Romans 10:3). If we return one more time to the story of Job, we will witness the same type of lethal, self-righteous "drib drab" coming from the counsel of Job's so-called friend. Zophar advises Job that if he would just get his life in order, then he would find favor in God's eyes. This is a far cry from Christ-like humility which acknowledges that *"I can of myself do nothing."*

Zophar's "friendly counsel," given to Job some four thousand years ago, is the same "self-deterministic" advice found throughout countless quasi-spiritual self-help books published today.

> ➤ *(Job 11:13-19) "If you would prepare your heart, and stretch out your*
> *hands toward Him; if iniquity were in your hand, and you put it far*
> *away, and would not let wickedness dwell in your tents; then surely you*
> *could lift up your face without spot; yes, you could be steadfast, and*

not fear; because you would forget your misery, and remember it as waters that have passed away, and your life would be brighter than noonday. Though you were dark, you would be like the morning. And you would be secure, because there is hope; yes, you would dig around you, and take your rest in safety. You would also lie down, and no one would make you afraid; yes, many would court your favor."

Yes, we are called to become "like Messiah," and we are given the right to become "Sons of God." However, please don't fall victim to the pride that says "I will do it myself." This is the same pride that got Lucifer kicked out of heaven and condemned to the lake of fire. And it will destroy you also.

The Other Side of Pride

So far, we have exposed the side of pride that says, "I will." I will exalt myself above the heaven; I will sit on the high mountain; and I will become like the Most High God. We contrasted this to the humility required for the Spirit to work in our lives. He will lift us up. He calls us sons of God. He empowers us to become like Messiah, and to be conformed to His image. This can ONLY happen by His power working in us, individually and corporately.

If we ignore this high calling, or do not make it the top priority it should be, we also risk the sin of pride. Not the "I will" type of pride, but the "I can't" or "I won't" type. If we won't respond to the high calling by proclaiming, "Here I am, LORD," then we are making our own plans for ourselves. We are making our own opinions of what is possible preeminent over His high calling for our lives. This is the other side of pride. If you suffer from this type, my admonition to you is this; **"To him who knows to do good and does not do it, to him it is sin."** My advice is this; **"Time is short! Whatever the Lord wills, do it!"** James would agree.

➤ *(James 4:13-17) Come now, you who say, "Today or tomorrow we will go to such and such a city, spend a year there, buy and sell, and make a profit"; whereas you do not know what will happen tomorrow. For what is your life? It is even a vapor that appears for a little time and then van-*

286

ishes away. Instead you ought to say, "If the Lord wills, we shall live and do this or that." But now you boast in your arrogance. All such boasting is evil. **Therefore, to him who knows to do good and does not do it, to him it is sin.**

What labor needs to be performed to further the Kingdom? Are you willing to do the work necessary to get the job done? Are you willing to exercise the authority placed in your keeping?

> ➢ *(Hebrews 2:6-8) But one testified in a certain place, saying: "What is man that You are mindful of him, or the son of man that You take care of him? You have made him a little lower than the angels; you have crowned him with glory and honor,* **and set him over the works of Your hands. You have put all things in subjection under his feet."** *For in that He put all in subjection under him, He left nothing that is not put under him. But now we do not yet see all things put under him.*

From God's heavenly perspective, the work is already completed. However, He has given you total authority in Christ Jesus and has generously supplied His Spirit to your advantage. He's done this so you can meet the demands of your high calling and see that the work is completed from your earthly perspective as well. Will you answer the call? Remember, to him who knows to do good and DOES NOT do it, to him it is sin. We now know that this sin is the other side of pride. I truly believe, in reaction to His generous gift, the only appropriate response is this.... Say it with me my friends: **Lord, Here Am I, Send Me!**

Chapter Twelve

The Last Great Day

*On the Last Day, that Great Day of the Feast, Jesus stood and cried out,
saying, "If anyone thirsts, let him come to Me and drink."*
John 7:37

F or the purpose of bringing our time together to an end, we are now
going to fast forward past the Lord's return, through His one thousand year reign, and all the way to the end of His Millennial Kingdom.
We will refer to the period that begins after the Millennial Kingdom has
ended as "The Last Great Day." You may be shocked to discover that
there is a reference, in the New Testament, to a very significant Feast day
that is prophetic of this time period. *On the Last Day, that Great Day of
the Feast, Jesus stood and cried out, saying, "If anyone thirsts, let him come to
Me and drink"* (*John 7:37*). John places the timing of this famous teaching
of Jesus on the Feast of the Last Day. When you read his Gospel, it is sur-
prising if you even notice that John mentions this Feast. Most Believers
know nothing about it. It is even more astonishing when you discover this
Feast's incredible prophetic significance.

Now the Jews' Feast of Tabernacles was at hand (John 7:2). The begin-
ning of John 7 tells us that Jesus was in Jerusalem to keep the Feast of
Tabernacles. The Feast of Tabernacles is one of the three pilgrimage
Feasts requiring a trip to Jerusalem.

> ➤ **(Deuteronomy 16:16)** *"Three times a year all your males shall appear
> before the LORD your God in the place which He chooses: at the **Feast
> of Unleavened Bread**, at the **Feast of Weeks**, and at the **Feast of
> Tabernacles**; and they shall not appear before the LORD empty-handed."*

Unleavened Bread is the seven day Feast following the Passover. The Feast of Weeks is what you know as Pentecost. The Last Great Day is the last day of the Feast of Tabernacles, and as a man submitted to His Father's Law (Torah), Jesus was in Jerusalem for the Festival. It is interesting to note that John calls the Feast of Tabernacles "the Jews' Feast." This raises a curious question: Why would John call any Biblical Feast *"the Jews' Feast"* when the Scriptures clearly describe all the commanded Feasts in Leviticus 23 as "Feasts of the LORD"? In John 5:1 and 6:4, he also refers to a commanded Feast as *"a Feast of the Jews."* In other words, John is describing a Biblical Feast in a way that Almighty God never did. In Leviticus 23:1-2, *The LORD spoke to Moses, saying, "Speak to the children of Israel, and say to them: 'The **Feasts of the LORD**, which you shall proclaim to be holy convocations, these are **My Feasts**.* God calls them, ***"The Feasts of the LORD"*** and says, ***"These are My Feasts."*** He does NOT call them the "Feasts of the Jews."

Two possible reasons come to mind as to why John would refer to the LORD'S Feasts in such a way. The first possibility is that John refers to the Feasts as "Jewish" because the First-Century Jews were the only people, at that time, who were still honoring God's Feasts. Even though the Feasts were commanded for all of Israel, the Jews, who represent only a small fraction of the entire people of Israel (read Appendix C for Israel's true identity), were the ones who had returned to the Land after being dispersed. They were the only recognizable group from all of Israel who were keeping the Feasts. In fact, the Jewish people are still the only group on earth who still honor these Holy Days en masse. Of course, after reading *The Heart of David*, as Christians, I hope you will be joining them.

The second possibility is that it is simply a transcriptional addition. Instead of writing "the Feast of Tabernacles," John writes "the **Jews'** Feast of Tabernacles." We translate our modern versions of the New Testament from Greek transcriptions of Greek writings. It is certainly possible that Greek scribes, long removed from keeping the Feasts themselves (likely due to widespread anti-Semitism in early Church history), simply described the Feasts this way for the sake of clarity. This could have happened for the same reason that someone not from the United States of America might say, "The Americans' Forth of July celebration." Other examples that might be used to add clarity are the ways Americans often refer to things like "The Chinese New Year" or "Canadian Thanksgiving." The Chinese do not call their New Years Day "Chinese New Year"; nor do the Canadians call their Thanksgiving Day "Canadian Thanksgiving." Likewise, it would have been strange for John, a First-Century Jew, to have referred to his national Holy Days in such a way. Don't you think? Therefore, "Jews'" may simply be a descriptive word, innocently added during transcription, by a non-Jew, to offer what he thinks will add clarity to the passage. But instead, it has historically made it appear like the "Feasts of the LORD" are only "Feasts of the Jews." Subsequently, most non-Jewish followers of Jesus (Y'shua), the "Jewish" Messiah, have excluded these important dates from their calendars.

I am not sure which, if either, case is true. Nevertheless, the Feasts are for all of God's people, not just Jews. This is not just my humble opinion. The Almighty makes this very clear in Leviticus 23 when He states, "These are My Feasts" and commands that "You shall proclaim them to be holy convocations."

The Feast of Tabernacles is a seven day Feast with a special eighth day added. Leviticus 23:36 instructs that on the eighth day you shall have a holy convocation. A holy convocation is a gathering together or great assembly. *Also on the fifteenth day of the seventh month, when you have gathered in the fruit of the Land, you shall keep the Feast of the LORD for seven days; on the first day there shall be a Sabbath-rest, and on the eighth day a Sabbath-rest... It shall be a statute forever in your generations (Leviticus 23:39, 41).* So the eighth day of the Feast is a commanded rest. Society today, including the Church, is largely unaware that this day exists, let alone when it occurs each year.

Two Sabbath-Rests

God said that on the first day of the Feast of Tabernacles there shall be a Sabbath-rest. And on the eighth day, He instructs us to take another Sabbath-rest. **"It shall be a statute forever in your generations."** Both days, the first day of the Feast and the first day after the Feast, are called Sabbaths "forever." Now let's take a look at the significance of these two Sabbaths with a prophetic telescope so we can gaze into the future.

Do you remember our previous reference to the seven day week of Creation? There were six days of Creation and one Sabbath day, six days of work and one day of rest. *But, beloved, do not forget this one thing, that with the Lord one day is as a thousand years, and a thousand years as one day (2 Peter 3:8).* We have six thousand years of man and then Messiah reigns for one thousand years in His Millennial Kingdom, the Sabbath Kingdom. Stay with me now. The Feast in which we rehearse Christ's return is the Feast of Trumpets. The Feast of Trumpets is followed by Yom Kippur (the Day of Atonement) ten days later, signifying the atoning blood. Five short days after Yom Kippur, the Feast of Tabernacles begins. This Feast rehearses the one thousand year Sabbath millennium in which Messiah will tabernacle among us and rule as King.

The First Sabbath-Rest

The Millennial Kingdom is symbolized by the Sabbath-rest on the first day of the Feast of Tabernacles. At the very end of one thousand years (the end of the seventh day), Satan is released one final time before he is cast into the lake of fire and brimstone where he *will be tormented day and night forever and ever (Revelation 20:10).*

The Second Sabbath-Rest- The Last Great Day

The first day after Satan is cast down is marked by yet another Sabbath-rest. This is indicative of eternity which we will spend as one with Messiah in the presence of the Father. This second Sabbath-rest associated with the Feast of Tabernacles is the eighth day, or the Last Great Day.

I will establish My Name forever!

We know as Believers that our ultimate inheritance is not land. Again, we can turn to the blueprint of the past to discover God's plan for our future. God instructed Israel to carefully observe all His commandments after they crossed over the Jordan to receive their inheritance. He knew that there would be great temptation to follow after other gods, so He warned His chosen people to destroy every place the pagans worshiped, every altar, every sacred pillar, and every wooden image. They were to destroy anything that might remind them of the name of false gods. God said: *"You shall not worship the* LORD *your God with such things. But you shall seek the place where the* LORD *your God chooses, out of all your tribes,* **to put His Name for His dwelling place;** *and there you shall go"* (*Deuteronomy 12:4-5*). God is looking for a place where He can establish His Name forever.

In Search of a Permanent Place to put His Name

First, God instructed Israel to build a Tabernacle in the Wilderness where He would put His Name. Through this Tabernacle, He dwelt in the midst of the people. But that was not forever. Then David conceived to build a great Temple of stone and cedar, and Solomon is chosen by the LORD to complete it. But Solomon knows that no physical Temple could confine Almighty God. *And the Temple which I build will be great, for our God is greater than all gods. But who is able to build Him a Temple, since heaven and the heaven of heavens cannot contain Him?* (*2 Chronicles 2:5-6a*). Yet, when Solomon finished building the Temple, God declared that He would put His Name there forever. *"For now I have chosen and sanctified this House,* **that My Name may be there forever;** *and My eyes and My heart will be there perpetually* (*2 Chronicles 7:16*). Could this promise be fulfilled through a Temple made of inanimate stones? The wisdom of Solomon says "no." Nothing constructed of dead stones could contain a living and Almighty God. *I have surely built You an exalted House, and a place for You to dwell in forever... But will God indeed dwell with men on the earth? Behold, heaven and the heaven of heavens cannot contain You. How much less this Temple which I have built!* (*2 Chronicles 6:2, 18*).

Bearing in mind that a stone Temple in the city of Jerusalem could not contain God, what did He mean when *the Lord said to David and to Solomon his son, "In this House and in Jerusalem, which I have chosen out of all the tribes of Israel, I will put My Name forever?"* (*2 Kings 21:7b*). God used the Temple that Solomon built to foreshadow the ultimate place in which He would establish His Name forever. This would be in a Temple not made with hands on Mount Zion, and in the city of the living God, the New Jerusalem.

> ➤ **(Revelation 3:12)** *"He who overcomes, I will make him a **pillar in the Temple** of My God, and he shall go out no more. And I will write on him the Name of My God and the name of the city of My God, the New Jerusalem, which comes down out of heaven from My God. And I will write on him My new Name."*

The city is the New Jerusalem and the House is the Spiritual Temple built one living stone upon another. *"He who has an ear, let him hear what the Spirit says to the Churches. To him who overcomes I will give some of the hidden manna to eat. And I will give him a **white stone**, and on the stone **a new name** written which no one knows except him who receives it"* (Revelation 2:17).

I previously dedicated an entire chapter to defining our role in building the Spiritual Temple. This can be summed up in one verse.

> ➤ **(1 Peter 2:5)** *You also, as **living stones**, are being built up a Spiritual House, a holy priesthood, to offer up spiritual sacrifices acceptable to God through Jesus Christ.*

I hope you can appreciate how consistent this is with Revelation 2:17 above. Now we must blend some of these ideas together. What and where is this Spiritual Temple? When will it be finished, and when will those who overcome get their new name? Is this new name the same name that God said He would establish forever? If our assessment is correct, these answers will harmonize perfectly with the prophetic patterns of the Eighth Day, the Last Great Day.

Let's recap

Before Saul was King, the Ark of the Covenant was irresponsibly taken from the Holy of Holies and used in an attempt to defeat the Philistines. The plan backfired. Israel was defeated and the Ark was captured. After the Ark was recovered, it was never returned to the Sanctuary in the Tabernacle built by Moses. The Ark of the Covenant remained outside the Holy of Holies for many years. When David was King, he conceived to build a new Temple for the LORD instead of bringing the Ark back to the original Tabernacle. In a dramatic affirmation God says "OK!" but the LORD elects Solomon to build it instead of David. The LORD promised to choose a city in which to build a House to put His Name forever. Ultimately, Solomon restored the Ark to the Holy of Holies in the new Temple in Jerusalem. This entire picture is a mere foreshadow of the true restoration that will happen in the future on the Last Great Day.

Reuniting God's Spirit with His Institution

The Tabernacle in the Wilderness and Solomon's Temple both served as forecasts of "good things to come." They were merely shadows cast from the real thing. When the Ark was irresponsibly removed from the Tabernacle in the Wilderness to be used in battle, man's blunder allowed the Ark to be captured. This symbolized a separation of God's power from His institution. It would be through Solomon's Temple that God would foreshadow reuniting them. God uses man's inadequacies to advance His plan.

When the Temple was complete, it was time to restore the power of God, represented by the Ark of the Covenant, to His institution, which was represented by the Temple. As you might predict, this restoration took place in the seventh month of the year; it was the same month as the Feast of Tabernacles and the Last Great Day. This is a beautiful foreshadow of the ultimate restoration that will take place at the end of the Millennial Kingdom. *Then the priests brought in the Ark of the Covenant of the LORD to its place, into the inner sanctuary of the Temple, to the Most Holy Place, under the wings of the cherubim (2 Chronicles 5:7).* But again, this prophetic moment was just a shadow of the true restoration.

All Things Made New

Now I saw a new heaven and a new earth, for the first heaven and the first earth had passed away. Also there was no more sea. Then I, John, saw the Holy City, New Jerusalem, coming down out of heaven from God, prepared as a bride adorned for her husband. And I heard a loud voice from heaven saying, "Behold, the Tabernacle of God is with men, and He will dwell with them, and they shall be His people. God Himself will be with them and be their God. And God will wipe away every tear from their eyes; there shall be no more death, nor sorrow, nor crying. There shall be no more pain, for the former things have passed away." Then He who sat on the throne said, "Behold, I make all things new." And He said to me, "Write, for these words are true and faithful." And He said to me, "It is done! I am the Alpha and the Omega, the Beginning and the End. I will give of the fountain of the water of life freely to him who thirsts" (Revelation 21:1-6).

In the First Century, while celebrating the Last Great Day as a rehearsal for eternity, Jesus taught, *"If anyone thirsts, let him come to Me and drink. He who believes in Me, as the Scripture has said, 'out of his heart will flow rivers of living water.'"* In His revelation to John about eternity that follows the Millennial Kingdom, the Last Great Day, He says, *"I will give of the fountain of the water of life freely to him who thirsts."* On the cross Jesus said, *"It is finished!"* and that was true regarding the mission of His First Coming. However, *"It is truly finished!"* only after the New Jerusalem has come down out of heaven, and there is a new heaven and a new earth. All things are made new. It is the Last Great Day, or in other words, the start of eternity.

Rivers of Living Water

It was while keeping the eighth day of Tabernacles that Jesus taught us to drink from the fountain of living water. *On the Last Day, that Great Day of the Feast, Jesus stood and cried out, saying, "If anyone thirsts, let him come to Me and drink." He who believes in Me, as the Scripture has said, 'out of his heart will flow rivers of living water.'" But this He spoke concerning the Spirit, whom those believing in Him would receive; for the Holy Spirit was not yet given, because Jesus was not yet glorified* (John 7:37-39). In the First Century, there was no Scripture yet in existence that actually said, *"Out of his heart will flow rivers of living water."* So John clarifies to what Jesus was referring by explaining that it is the Spirit that flows as rivers of living water. *"But this He spoke concerning the Spirit."*

Jesus first taught this concept to the Samaritan woman at the well in John 4:10. *"If you knew the gift of God, and who it is who says to you, 'Give Me a drink,' you would have asked Him, and He would have given you **living water**."* She is confused because Jesus has nothing with which to draw the water. He teaches her in verse 14 that if she drinks water from the well she will thirst again; *"but whoever drinks of the water that I shall give him will never thirst. But the water that I shall give him will become in him a fountain of water springing up into everlasting life."*

Think about it!

Marriage

In search of an answer to unite End of the Age concepts of the Temple and a permanent place for God to place His Name, I arrive at one underlying theme...**Marriage**

Revelation 19:7-9 describes the bride who has made herself ready for her wedding. *"Let us be glad and rejoice and give Him glory, for the **marriage of the Lamb has come**, and His wife has made herself ready. And to her it was granted to be arrayed in **fine linen**, clean and bright, for the fine linen is the **righteous acts** of the saints." Then he said to me, "Write: 'Blessed are those who are called to the **marriage supper of the Lamb!**'" And he said to me, "These are the true sayings of God."* How has she made herself ready? Throughout *The Heart of David* we have emphasized the Church's call to perfection. The only way to achieve perfection is to press on to the high calling. The Greek word underlying that for which is described as "righteous acts of the saints" is "dikaioma" {dik-ah'-yo-mah}. It is defined by that which has been "established or ordained by Law." To no surprise, the acts of the saints are weighed against obedience to God's commandments. *Here is the patience of the saints; here are those who **keep the commandments of God and the faith of Jesus** (Revelation 14:12).* This is how the bride gets prepared. The Church will become the spotless bride, conformed into the image of Christ. However, this manifestation of the "sons of God" is possible only by becoming completely submissive to the Father's commandments. However, the wedding supper of the Lamb does not take place immediately upon the return of the Bridegroom. Jesus must take care of some final business. He must first destroy the armies of Satan and cast him into the bottomless pit so that he should deceive the nations no more until the thousand year reign of Messiah has ended. After we rule and reign with Christ in His Kingdom for one thousand years, the enemy is released one final time before he is cast into the lake of fire forever. Jesus makes His final judgment of the dead, and then takes His place, as the Bridegroom, alongside His bride at the altar. The marriage supper of the Lamb has come.

A Bride with a New Name

The ultimate fulfillment of everlasting life and oneness with God is the marriage of Christ with His bride. This event is encapsulated in one prophetic day. The wedding takes place after the final prophetic fulfillment of the Feast of Tabernacles, after the Messiah has reigned one thousand years. This final union takes place on the eighth day, the Last Great Day, when all things are made new.

> ➤ *(Revelation 21:1-3) Now I saw a new heaven and a new earth, for the first heaven and the first earth had passed away. Also there was no more sea. Then I, John, saw the Holy City,* **New Jerusalem,** *coming down out of heaven from God,* **prepared as a bride** *adorned for her husband. And I heard a loud voice from heaven saying, "Behold, the* **Tabernacle** *of God is with men, and He will dwell with them, and they shall be His people. God Himself will be with them and be their God."*

In Revelation 19, we read that the bride was made ready. But it is not until after the one thousand year Kingdom has ended that the marriage supper of the Lamb takes place. Notice, however, that the **bride** is now identified as the **Holy City,** the New Jerusalem. Isn't that curious? New Jerusalem, prepared as a bride, comes down and a voice from heaven says, *"the* **Tabernacle** *of God is with men."* The Greek word for Tabernacle in this verse is "skene" {skay-nay'}. It is the word used for the Tabernacle that Moses built using the pattern shown him on Mount Sinai, which later served as the blueprint for the entire Temple in Jerusalem.

In the beginning God said, "*It is not good that man should be alone; I will make him a helper comparable to him... Therefore a man shall leave his father and mother and be joined to his wife, and they shall become one flesh*" (Genesis 2:18, 24). Paul revealed the deep spiritual meaning of becoming one flesh in Ephesians 5:32 when he taught: "*This is a great mystery, but I speak concerning Christ and the Church.*" The Church is the bride of Christ and the two will become one flesh, and serve as the Spiritual Temple. However, on the Last Great Day, the New Jerusalem coming down out of heaven is also prepared as the bride of Christ adorned for her Husband. This can only mean one thing:

The entire city of the New Jerusalem prepared as His bride is the Spiritual Temple!

Calling the New Jerusalem the Spiritual Temple is a radical departure from traditional thought. Let me prove it further with solid Scriptural evidence. In Chapter 10, we already established that the Church is being built into the Spiritual Temple and we will confirm it again here.

> ➢ *(Ephesians 2:19-22) Now, therefore, you are no longer strangers and foreigners, but fellow citizens with the saints and members of the Household of God, having been **built on the foundation of the apostles** and prophets, Jesus Christ Himself being the Chief Cornerstone, in whom the whole building, being joined together, **grows into a Holy Temple in the** LORD, in whom you also are being built together for a dwelling place of God in the Spirit.*

The Body of Christ is the Temple and is being built on the foundation of the apostles and prophets, Christ being the Chief Cornerstone. Amazingly, in Revelation 21:9b-10, an angel says to John, "*Come, I will show you the **bride, the Lamb's wife**.*" *And he carried me away in the Spirit to a great and high mountain, and showed me the great city, the holy **Jerusalem**, descending out of heaven from God.* Do you see this? The angel tells John he will see the bride of Christ, and is then shown the New Jerusalem. While describing details about this city in verse 14, the angel says, "*Now the wall of the city had twelve **foundations**, and on them were the **names of the twelve apostles** of the Lamb.*" The Church is the future bride of Christ and is being built on the foundation of the apostles into a Holy Temple in the Lord. The New Jerusalem is the future bride of Christ and its walls are being built on the foundation of the apostles. The natural conclusion of our Scriptural evidence is that the walls of the New Jerusalem must certainly define the outer courts of the Spiritual Temple.

Some faithful saints will even be selected to be pillars in the Temple. The word used for Temple in Revelation 3:12 below is the Greek word "naos" {nah-os'}. It is used Biblically to identify the Temple in Jerusalem. It is translated as such in most English translations, but actually refers **only** to the sacred edifice or Temple Sanctuary itself, which consists of the Holy Place and the Holy of Holies — not the entire Temple. When the entire Temple in Jerusalem is being referred to, the Greek word "hieron" {hee-er-on'} is used. Hieron embraces the entire aggregate of buildings, balconies, porticos, and outer courts. *"He who overcomes, I will make him a **pillar in the Temple** (naos, sanctuary) of My God, and he shall go out no more. And I will write on him the Name of My God and the name of the city of My God, the New Jerusalem, which comes down out of heaven from My God. **And I will write on him My new Name** (Revelation 3:12).*

The New Name

God will write His new Name on His people who have become the Spiritual Temple. It is in this Spiritual Temple that God's Name will finally be established forever. The final fulfillment of this promise will take place on the Last Great Day, the **"Eighth Day."** If you're following Biblical patterns, the eighth day is precisely when you would expect a new Name to be given. The eighth day is the exact day that Jesus, or more accurately "Y'shua," was given His name.

Christ's Birth Prefigures the End

Joseph was informed by an angel of the LORD that Mary had conceived a child by the Holy Spirit. *"And she will bring forth a Son, and you shall call His name JESUS* (Y'shua in Hebrew meaning salvation), *for He will save*

His people from their sins" (Matthew 1:21). After He was born, Joseph and Mary, in obedience to the Law of Moses, took Jesus and circumcised Him on the **"eighth day."** *And when eight days were completed for the circumcision of the Child, His name was called JESUS, the name given by the angel before He was conceived in the womb (Luke 2:21).* According to Genesis 17:9-14, all male children shall be circumcised on the eighth day. In Judaism, it is still the tradition to not name a male child until the time of his circumcision. Many scholars agree that Jesus was actually born in the fall, during the Feast of Tabernacles, when He came and tabernacled among us. *And the Word became flesh, and did Tabernacle among us, and we beheld his glory, glory as of an only begotten of a father, full of grace and truth (John 1:14 YLT).* What a beautiful picture this paints. Jesus was born on the first day of the Feast of Tabernacles. This is a day set apart for a Sabbath-rest, and He is our rest. The eighth day, the Last Great Day of the Feast, is a day symbolic of new beginnings. All things are made new. On that day, He was circumcised and given His name, Jesus (Y'shua). He is our eternal salvation. Y'shua means "YAHWEH'S salvation."

When John saw the New Jerusalem come down out of heaven, he conspicuously commented about the absence of a Temple. The word traditionally translated as "Temple" in this passage is "naos" in the Greek. This word actually refers to the Sanctuary, or inner Temple, and not to the entire Temple, which would be "hieron" in the Greek. So for clarity, I will use Sanctuary in the translation to help draw out the deeper meaning of John's words. John saw the New Jerusalem come down out of heaven and said:

> ➤ *(Revelation 21:22-24) But I saw no **Sanctuary** in it, for the Lord God Almighty and the Lamb are its Sanctuary. The city had no need of the sun or of the moon to shine in it, for the glory of God illuminated it. The Lamb is its light. And the nations of those who are saved shall walk in its light, and the kings of the earth bring their glory and honor into it.*

John saw the New Jerusalem (the outer walls of the Spiritual Temple) descend from heaven. But John did not see the Sanctuary, which consists of the Holy Place and the Holy of Holies. The reason he did not see the Sanctuary was because the LORD God Almighty and the Lamb (Christ) are the Sanctuary.

Solomon asked in 2 Chronicles 6:18, *"But will God indeed dwell with men on the earth?"* During His first coming, Christ tabernacled among us (dwelt with men on earth), and His shed blood became the remedy for our sins. *Behold, God is my salvation, I will trust and not be afraid; 'For YAH, the LORD, is my strength and song; He also has become my salvation.' (Isaiah 12:2).* YAH is the poetic short form of God's Name "YAHWEH." YAHWEH has become our salvation. The Hebrew word for Salvation is "yeshuw`ah" {yesh-oo'-aw} which happens to be the Hebrew name of our Lord and Savior (Y'shua). YAHWEH has become our Y'shua. In the end, after Y'shua is married to His bride, every tongue will confess, *"Behold, **the Tabernacle of God is with** men, and He will dwell with them, and they shall be His people. God Himself will be with them and be their God"* (Revelation 21:3). **God is with men.** We will live for all time with a new Name in the perfect union of marriage as one with Christ. As a bride takes on the name of her husband, we too will take His Name, Y'shua, which declares, YAHWEH has become my salvation. *So all this was done that it might be fulfilled which was spoken by the LORD through the prophet, saying "Behold, the virgin shall be with child, and bear a Son, and they shall call His name **Immanuel**," which is translated, **"God with us"*** (Matthew 1:22-23).

The Church, as the New Jerusalem, has become the bride and is now serving as the Spiritual Temple of God. The LORD God Almighty and the Lamb are in the midst of the Temple serving as the Sanctuary. The nations of those who are saved shall walk in its light and the kings of the earth shall bring honor into it.

> ➤ *(Revelation 22:1-3) And he showed me a pure river of water of life, clear as crystal, proceeding from the Throne of God and of the Lamb. In the middle of its street, and on either side of the river, was the Tree of Life, which bore twelve fruits, each tree yielding its fruit every month. The leaves of the tree were for the **healing of the nations**. And there shall be no more curse, but the Throne of God and of the Lamb shall be in it, and **His servants shall serve Him**.*

What puzzles me however, and what I want to offer you only as food for thought at this time, is this mystery. It says in Revelation 21:3, *Behold, the Tabernacle of God is **with men**.* By that time, the Church is the bride of Christ. It is already serving as the Spiritual Temple (the Tabernacle of God). This being so, then who are these "men"? Who are the nations of those who are saved who bring honor into the city? Could this be referring to the Church, which by this time is already one with Christ as His bride? If so, why must they eat from the Tree of Life for their healing? By this time, why would the perfect bride of Christ still need healing? All of these are questions to stimulate your spiritual juices. I don't pretend to have all the answers. In future books, we hope to explore the various possibilities.

A Name Forevermore

In eternity, the nations need to eat from the Tree of Life to be healed and, I suppose, to stay alive. Only those obedient to God may do so. *Blessed are those who do His Commandments, that they may have the right to the Tree of Life, and may enter through the gates into the City. But outside are dogs and sorcerers and sexually immoral and murderers and idolaters, and whoever loves and practices a lie (Revelation 22:14-15).* I am fairly certain that those needing to eat from the Tree of Life are NOT today's members of the Body of Christ. By that time, the Church has already become the bride of Christ. It now serves the Father day and night, as one with Jesus, and *they shall see His face, and **His Name shall be on their foreheads** (Revelation 22:4).* The bride of Christ, as the servant of the LORD, performs the duties of the Spiritual Temple. They are finally imprinted with God's Name, YAHWEH, on their foreheads forevermore.

יהוה

This is the final prophetic fulfillment of David's bold prayer; **"LORD, I will build You a House."** It is also the final prophetic fulfillment of God's promise to David that, *"In this House and in Jerusalem, which I have chosen out of all the tribes of Israel, I will put My Name forever!"*

> *"My Tabernacle also shall be with them; indeed I will be their God,*
> *and they shall be My people. The nations also will know that I, the LORD,*
> *sanctify Israel, when My sanctuary is in their midst forevermore."*
> **Ezekiel 37:27-28**

For all eternity the bride of Christ will share His ministry to the nations saying, "Come!" *And the Spirit and* **the bride say**, *"Come!" And let him who hears say, "Come!" And let him who thirsts come. Whoever desires, let him take the water of life freely (Revelation 22:17).* As living stones, along with Christ, we have been built into the Spiritual House from which flows the water of life. *And he showed me a pure river of water of life, clear as crystal, proceeding from the Throne of God and of the Lamb (Revelation 22:1).* God has restored His Spirit to His institution for all time. On His Bride, and on His Temple, and on His Holy City, YAHWEH, through the marriage supper of the Lamb, has established His Name forever. David understood that the only way to establish the Father's Name (YAHWEH) forevermore was through the Son (Y'SHUA), YAHWEH'S salvation.

"This is the gate of the LORD (YAHWEH),
through which the righteous shall enter.
I will praise You, for You have answered me,
and have become my salvation (Y'SHUA)."
Psalm 118:20-21

YAHWEH has become our Y'SHUA (Salvation)

A Final Word

More than three thousand years ago, in a moment of enormous prophetic significance, God's Spirit was divided from His institution. Today, with the heart of David freshly transplanted within you, you are being equipped to reestablish His institution on earth. This will eventually usher in the Lord's return to inhabit His Temple. *"Behold, I send My messenger, and he will prepare the way before Me. And the Lord, whom you seek, will suddenly come to His Temple, even the Messenger of the covenant, in whom you delight. Behold, He is coming," says the LORD of hosts (Malachi 3:1).* You are being transformed from glory to glory because He is returning for a sinless bride, one without spot or wrinkle. Prepare to raise up a Spiritual House for the Lord because the Temple that He is returning to inhabit is one not made with hands. And there YAHWEH will write His Name for all time.

*Behold, what manner of love the Father hath bestowed upon us, that we
should be called the **Sons of God**: therefore the world knoweth us not,
because it knew Him not. Beloved, now are we the Sons of God, and it doth
not yet appear what we shall be: but we know that, when He shall appear,
we shall be like Him; for we shall see Him as He is.*
KJV **1 John 3:1-2**

Pray the Prayer of David with purpose and endurance; "LORD, I WILL
BUILD YOU A HOUSE." Persevere and believe that Almighty God is craft-
ing you, by the power of the Holy Spirit, and through your steadfast faith-
based obedience, into the perfect image of Christ Jesus Himself. May this
be your testimony! *Here is the patience of the saints; here are those who **keep
the commandments** of God __and__ the **faith of Jesus** (Revelation 14:12).* And
then, as Moses did in Exodus 14:3:

Stand still, and see the salvation of the LORD!

Into Eternity...

Breath of Life or Winds of Warning

In whose hand is the life of every living thing,
and the breath of all mankind?
Job 12:10

An epilogue is a short addition or concluding section at the end of a literary work. It often deals with the future of its characters. You hold the enviable position of being "the characters" in this literary work. Your eternal function as stones in the Spiritual Temple has been determined from the foundations of the world. Every step on your journey from Captivity, through the Wilderness, and into the Promised Land, and everything you must become to fulfill your destiny, to fill your position as "sons of God," will usher in one extraordinary event. *Then they will see the Son of Man coming in a cloud with power and great glory (Luke 21:27).*

Controversies over theology about the timing of the Second Coming have in many ways left Believers confused, or at best complacent, in their understanding concerning the Lord's return. Most Believers can neither defend nor deny any of the proposed theories. Major theorists hale from at least five different camps: pre-tribulation, mid-tribulation, post-tribulation, pre-wrath, and amillennial. These theories place the timing of the Rapture of the Church, if any, somewhere in relation to the Second Coming of the Lord. It is not the purpose of this book to explore these various possibilities. There are many scholarly-type works for you to examine advocating each of these positions.

I would, however, ask you to consider a few questions when evaluating the validity of each claim. Does the position take into consideration the Torah-centric patterns demonstrated in the Word of God, like those revealed throughout this book? For instance, does the theory emphasize *defining* and *preaching* the Gospel of the Kingdom to the entire world? Does the position take into consideration the prophetic significance of the Feasts of the LORD, why they are rehearsed, their timing, and their future fulfillment? Notice in the following Scriptures that His return takes place at the sound of the last trumpet. When you read Appendix B at the end of this book, you will discover that one of the Feasts of the LORD is called the "Feast of Trumpets." What do you suppose the Feast of Trumpets, commanded in Leviticus 23, is rehearsing? In addition, does the position on end times (or the Rapture) consider the life of Joseph in creating a model for the End of the Age? I believe we have demonstrated with certainty that Jesus considered Joseph's life as the key prophetic blueprint from which we can forecast the events of the End of the Age. Do any of these viewpoints follow in His footsteps? And lastly, does the theory honor the purity of God's Word, or does it need to explain away Scripture that doesn't "fit" the model. For one example, consider the simple question. Are the Rapture of the Church and the Second Coming the same event? I leave it up to you to draw your conclusion from Scripture itself.

> *(Revelation 1:7) Behold, He is **coming with clouds, and every eye will see Him**, even they who pierced Him. And all the tribes of the earth will mourn because of Him. Even so, Amen.*

> *(Matthew 24:30-31) "Then the sign of the Son of Man will appear in heaven, and then all the tribes of the earth will mourn, and they will see **the Son of Man coming on the clouds** of heaven with power and great glory. And He will send His angels with a great sound of a trumpet, and they will **gather together His elect** from the four winds, from one end of heaven to the other."*

> *(1 Thessalonians 4:16-17) For the **Lord Himself will descend from heaven** with a shout, with the voice of an archangel, and with the trumpet of God. And the dead in Christ will rise first. Then we who are*

*alive and remain **shall be caught up together** with them in the clouds to meet the Lord in the air. And thus we shall always be with the Lord.*

➤ *(1 Corinthians 15:51-52) Behold, I tell you a mystery: We shall not all sleep, but we shall all be changed — in a moment, in the twinkling of an eye, at the **last trumpet**. For the trumpet will sound, and the dead will be raised incorruptible, and we shall be changed.*

➤ *(Revelation 10:7) But in the days of the **sounding of the seventh angel** (the last trumpet), when he is about to sound, the mystery of God would be finished, as He declared to His servants the prophets.*

We will leave Scripture to define Scripture. We all need to become students of God's Word so *that we should no longer be children, tossed to and fro and carried about with every wind of doctrine (Ephesians 4:14).*

The Prophetic Significance of the Feasts

In 1 Thessalonians 5:1, Paul wrote, *concerning the **times and the seasons**, brethren, you have no need that I should write to you.* "Seasons" is a reference to God's calendar, the yearly Feast cycle, which is regulated by coordinating solar and lunar cycles.

➤ *(Genesis 1:14) Then God said, "Let there be lights in the firmament of the heavens to divide the day from the night; and let them be for signs and seasons, and for days and years."*

The meaning of each of the LORD'S Feasts holds vital prophetic significance. Understanding them helps us discern the signs of the "times." Not understanding them brings reproof. When Jesus was asked for a "sign" by the religious leaders of His day, He rebuked them: *Hypocrites! You know how to discern the face of the sky, but you cannot discern the signs of the times (Matthew 16:3).*

Concerning the Feasts of the LORD, if the modern-day Church was being addressed instead of First-Century religious leaders, what would it sound like: *"Brethren, you have no need that I should write to you";* you fully understand God's calendar and the prophetic significance of His Feasts? Or, "*Hypocrites!*" You understand the things of the world, but you know not the "seasons" of God; "*you cannot discern the signs of the times!*" I believe that the modern-day Church would receive the latter word. In Leviticus 23, God says that His Feasts are forever, but unfortunately, the Church is largely unaware that they exist, let alone when they occur each year.

Winds of Warning

In the fall of 2005 in South Florida, we had an eerie reminder that when God says "forever," He means forever. When He commands a Sabbath-rest on one of His Feasts, He wants us to stop everything we would normally be doing and focus our attention on Him. On the morning of October 24, 2005, during the seventh day of the Feast of Tabernacles, Hurricane Wilma ripped through South Florida. That evening, at sundown, began the eighth day, the Last Great Day, a commanded rest from God. In South Florida, millions of people were forced to unplug from the world and be still. During the height of the storm, I am sure that even the most stoic unbelievers were crying out "Oh God!" or "Dear Lord!"

Interestingly, Wilma means "protector." To protect means "to preserve; to keep or maintain intact." Spiritually speaking, what was being preserved or kept intact on this Last Day of the Feast of Tabernacles in 2005? When I looked up the concepts of "to preserve" or "to keep" in the Bible, I discovered a fascinating correlation. In Scripture, the Greek word for preserve or keep is "tereo" {tay-reh'-o} which means:

- *To attend to carefully, take care of, guard, observe, keep*

For this is the love of God, that we keep {tay-reh'-o} *His commandments. And His commandments are not burdensome (1 John 5:3).* In some supernatural way, we were being guided to obey God's commanded Sabbath-rest, a separation from the world on the Last Great Day. Immediately following the storm, the world no longer had anything to offer us. It was like a "mini" wilderness. Ask anyone who experienced Wilma and her aftermath; South Florida was turned into a small, post-apocalyptic war zone. Everything was disrupted. No one could proceed with "business as usual."

We are called to be holy, set apart from the world, and Wilma was all too happy to accommodate. It was a temporary separation, maybe a small foreshadow of things to come, but one we ought to consider with great care.

Another Greek word used four times in Scripture denoting the idea of "keep" or "preserve" is "suntereo" {soon-tay-reh'-o} which is a compound word including "tereo" {tay-reh'-o} and the preposition "with." When used, it invokes the idea of something being kept or preserved with:

- *To preserve (a thing from perishing or being lost)*
- *To keep within one's self, keep in mind (a thing, lest it be forgotten)*

"Nor do they put new wine into old wineskins, or else the wineskins break, the wine is spilled, and the wineskins are ruined But they put new wine into new wineskins, and both are **preserved** {soon-tay-reh'-o}" *(Matthew 9:17)*. Your life, just like an old wineskin, cannot contain the new Spirit within you unless you put off the old man *and that you put on the new man which was created according to God, in true righteousness and holiness (Ephesians 4:24)*. A new wineskin is like a new heart. *"I will give you a new heart and put a new Spirit within you; I will take the heart of stone out of your flesh and give you a heart of flesh" (Ezekiel 36:26)*. God's Spirit can only dwell in, and His ways can only be preserved by, a new man with a new heart. Mary was told by shepherds that she had given birth to the Christ, the Savior of the world, *but Mary* **kept** {soon-tay-reh'-o} *all these things and pondered them in her heart (Luke 2:19)*. Mary preserved what she had learned with her heart. Just the same, with a circumcised heart we might preserve God's commandments. In Hurricane Wilma, God would preserve His commanded Sabbath on the Last Great Day. He did this by taking away everything the world had to offer and by giving us the opportunity to turn our hearts toward Him and ponder His ways, even the unbeliever who might cry out "Oh God!"

We also need to look at the Hebrew. What we find in Hebrew is that "preserve" or "keep" is mainly translated from two different Hebrew words. Natsar {naw-tsar'} which means:

- *To guard, watch over, keep, preserve, observe, guard with fidelity*
- *Watchman*

*For there shall be a day when the **watchmen** {naw-tsar'} will cry on Mount Ephraim, 'Arise, and let us go up to Zion, To the LORD our God' (Jeremiah 31:6).* Natsar is the primitive root for Notzri. This is the Modern Hebrew word for Christian. Christians or Notzrim (plural) are watchmen, pre-servers or protectors of God's ways. We should be protecting God's Laws by writing them on our hearts and then, of course, obeying them.

The other Hebrew word is shamar {shaw-mar'} which essentially means the same thing as natsar with some variations:

- *To preserve, keep, guard, observe, give heed, keep watch, protect, save life*
- *Watchman*
- *To observe, celebrate, keep Sabbath, covenant or commands*

*Even the stork in the heavens knows her appointed times; and the turtledove, the swift, and the swallow **observe** {shaw-mar'} the time of their coming. But My people do not know the judgment of the LORD (Jeremiah 8:7).* So Wilma, the protector, flew in and preserved God's appointed time, His Feast, His commanded Sabbath-rest – at least in South Florida. There was simply no option. Everyone had to shut it down. There were no lights, no phones, no TV, no computers, no internet, and no DVD's. There was nothing to distract us from his appointed time, only the beautiful stars under a quiet night sky. Today, Christians are charged with the responsi-bility of watching over God's ways, preserving His appointed times. Even the stork in the heavens knows, yet unfortunately God's people, the watchmen, had to be usurped by a *lady* named Wilma.

What an appropriate picture Wilma would paint on the Last Great Day, the eighth day, a day that symbolizes the future when all things pass away. In Hebrew, the number eight always alludes to a departure from this world and entry into the world to come – new beginnings. *Now I saw a new heaven and a new earth, for the first heaven and the first earth had passed away (Revelation 21:1).*

Become a "true watchmen" with the heart of David.

*Give me understanding, and I shall **keep** {naw-tsar'} Your Law; Indeed, I shall **observe** {shaw-mar'} it with my whole heart.* **Psalm 119:34**

Life & Warning

In Hebrew, the word ruwach {roo'-akh} is used for each of the words Spirit, breath and wind. The Spirit that gives life also brings judgment. *In whose hand is the life of every living thing, and the* **breath** {roo'-akh} *of all mankind? (Job 12:10).* It's your choice. Submit to the Spirit that formed you from dust, *the* **Spirit** {roo'-akh} *of God hath made me, and the breath of the Almighty hath given me life (Job 33:4);* or be chastened by the same Spirit carried on the winds of warning. *You blew with Your* **wind** {roo'-akh}, *the sea covered them; they sank like lead in the mighty waters (Exodus 15:10).* In the future, why don't we give up the ways of the world and protect that for which God has made us. The alternative: *By the blast of God they perish, and by the* **breath** {roo'-akh} *of His anger they are consumed (Job 4:9).*

I could easily be guilty of over-spiritualizing the explanation of Wilma's name and the interpretation of her timing. However, having been engaged in so many hours of contemplation over the subject matter of this book, and having kept the Feasts in my home over the past five years, my spiritual antennae were up. I am looking for prophetic signs of God's next move on the earth, so Wilma's timing was prophetically relevant to me. I hope you agree that the signs of the times indicate that we are close to the Day of the LORD, and that soon the time will come when we must shed this temporary tabernacle in which we now dwell.

We are told in Scripture to dwell in a sukkah (a temporary tabernacle) for seven days during the Feast of Tabernacles. So in celebration of the Feast, we erected a sukkah in our backyard. But, in 2005, as the seventh day was drawing to a close, and the Last Great Day of the Feast was almost upon us, I watched our sukkah be easily crushed like so many matchsticks. Oh, how this world and our physical bodies, our current temporary dwellings, will pass away in like manner. So it seemed symbolically appropriate when our sukkah was so easily dismantled and dispatched by Wilma's prophetic winds.

Conclusion...

Eternity:
The Beauty of Patterns & Hebrew Symbolism

With the right key, reading Biblical blueprints becomes a joy. The Last Great Day takes place on the eighth day and the number eight in Hebrew is symbolic of new beginnings and eternity. In Judaism, this eighth day of Tabernacles is called "Shemini Atzeret," the Eighth Day of Assembly. Jewish tradition celebrates this Feast day as "Simchat Torah." This is a Hebrew term meaning **"Rejoicing in the Law,"** or in other words, "Delighting in God's Commandments." Each week in synagogues world-wide, a few chapters of the Torah are read publicly, starting in Genesis 1 and progressing through the year to Deuteronomy 34. Simchat Torah marks the completion and renewal of this annual cycle of weekly Torah readings, as both the last portion of Deuteronomy and the beginning of Genesis are read. This is a reminder that the Torah is a cycle that never ends. The Scriptures contain patterns and mysteries ready to reveal prophecy throughout the ages. All those holding to the testimony of Jesus Christ should fall in love with prophecy. We must continue to study Torah and teach it to our children, as long as it is called "today," so that the Truth can be revealed. For the angel of the LORD said, *"Worship God! For the testimony of Jesus is the spirit of prophecy"* (Revelation 19:10).

Simchat Torah- Rejoicing in the Torah

Both John the Baptist and Jesus came preaching: *"Repent, the Kingdom of Heaven is at hand!"* When Elijah returns he will preach the same message with different words; *"Remember the Law of Moses!"* On the Last Great Day, it is fair to say, that all of God's people will be "Simchat Torah" — rejoicing in His Law. God's Commandments are no longer too difficult. They will be near you in your mouth and in your heart; remembering them will be a joy.

Now all has been heard; here is the conclusion of the matter:
Fear God and keep his Commandments, for this is the whole duty of man.
NIV *Ecclesiastes 12:13*

The End

Appendixes

Appendix A: Resource Guide

- ## A Rood Awakening!
For more than a decade, Bible teacher and author Michael Rood has traveled the globe exhibiting Bible-confirming archaeology and proclaiming that the "Feasts of the LORD" are precise prophetic shadow pictures by which our Creator has revealed the Messiah, as well as His plan for the created universe. Through multi-media seminars, which excited audiences have appropriately dubbed "A Rood Awakening!" as well as books, audio and video teachings, and an internationally-broadcast weekly TV program in English and Spanish, Michael has invited hundreds of thousands of people around the world to "Leave your western Gentile mentality behind, and explore the Scriptures from a Hebrew, or Jewish, perspective." His mission is to help all Believers discover their Hebrew roots and return to the faith of the First Century followers of Messiah Y'shua (Jesus). Contact us for a free resource catalog which includes a DVD sampler. **www.aroodawakening.tv**

- ## First Fruits of Zion
First Fruits of Zion proclaims the Torah and its way of life, fully centered on Messiah, to today's People of God. **www.ffoz.org**

- ## Hebraic Heritage Ministries International
Hebraic Heritage Ministries International has a data base of members from all 50 states and over 55 foreign countries. We network people and ministries all around the world who are studying the Hebraic Roots of Christianity. We can help you find resource materials to aid you in your study, as well as help you locate people in your area who share the same heart. **www.hebroots.com**

- ## Lion & Lamb Ministries
Lion & Lamb Ministries is a non-profit organization with an end time prophetic message in a Messianic Jewish context. **www.lionlamb.net**

- ## Messianic Israel Alliance
All that we do is focused on one point – preparing the way for Messiah's return. Therefore our mission is: To equip YAHWEH'S people for the restoration of all things (Acts 3:21). Scripture is clear that Messiah will not return until all things spoken by the prophets come to pass. This is a huge undertaking, and one that will not be accomplished until His people rise up and accept their calling and role in His Kingdom. Our mission is to equip Believers for this mighty work. **www.mim.net**

I

- **Outreach Israel Ministries**
  Outreach Israel Ministries (OIM) has been commissioned to minister, to educate, connect, and to reach out to people throughout the world, about all Israel, both the People and the Land, until the "restoration of all things" (Acts 3:21). www.outreachisrael.net

- **TNN Online**
  Our goal is to discuss all manner of Biblically related issues, primarily Messianic apologetics. We are a division of Outreach Israel Ministries.
  www.tnnonline.net

- **The Holy Land Experience**
  The Holy Land Experience is a living Biblical history museum that takes you 7,000 miles away and 2,000 years back in time to the land of the Bible. Its unique combination of sights, sounds, and tastes stimulate your senses. Together with its many educational materials, The Holy Land Experience is a valuable resource for any Believer.
  www.theholylandexperience.com

- **The Word of Righteousness**
  Our mission is to acquaint Christians with what the Apostle Paul meant by Divine grace. Grace is not an alternative to righteous behavior, but forgives us, and then makes righteous behavior possible. www.wor.org

- **The Torahwalk Club**
  Join our email prayer group and worship and praise with instrumental and vocal CD's. www.weareyisrael.net / torahwalk@weareyisrael.net

- **We Are Yisrael Worship**
  We are available to travel and provide your group with a program of contemporary and traditional Hebraic worship and teachings. www.weareyisrael.net

- **Sinai Calvary Ministries**
  We are devoted to preaching the Gospel of the Kingdom to the entire world.
  Available in Print: *The Heart of David* (Book 352 pages)
  ArtworkCollection: *The Journey & the Destination / The Dwelling Place*
  Coming soon: *The Heart of David* (Audio)
  The Heart of David Study Guide
  The Heart of David Journal
  The Heart of David Daily Devotional
  Check online for availability. www.theheartofdavid.com

The Heart of David Artwork Collection

The Dwelling Place
Artist: Jutta Herold

(Also available as laminated posters)

The Dwelling Place
postcards and greeting cards
are available on our website.

Visit us online for our
complete gallery of Christian
and Prophetic artwork
available by our artists.

Ordering information at **www.TheHeartOfDavid.com**

The Journey & the Destination
Artist: David Utrera
Available in color and black/white

Three-in-One Framed

Individually framed or laminated posters also available.

Also Available:

The Journey & the Destination postcards and greeting cards available on our website.

Lessons for Health Living
Practical instructions for Biblically based health & nutrition.
A 5 DVD set (10 hours) featuring Drs. Jeff & Andrea Hazim.

Ordering information at www.**TheHeartOfDavid.com**

Appendix B: The Feasts of the LORD
Stephen Duame

Since the fall of Adam the world has been sick. Judaism sees this need to make things right again. They call this spiritual repair "Tikkun Olam" which means "perfecting the world." Christianity frames this "repair" in terms of redemption. Redemption is the opportunity for something that was forfeited to be re-purchased by the original owner. There are four major foundational patterns in Scripture, which prophetically depict the process of restoring things to their original state. In the elegant beauty of truth, they are all presented in the Bible as a process of seven steps. These Biblical patterns are part of the fabric of national order and family life. Like the sunrise and sunset, they regulate a healthy national heartbeat. But underneath the surface of these "family friendly" events is the master plan of divine warfare. They reveal the incredibly complex and profound strategy designed by God to bring a final end to suffering and death. In them, God reveals His plan to restore mankind to righteousness and the promised paradise.

These four major patterns are:
1. The week of creation (Six days of work and then the Sabbath)
2. The journey from Egypt to Canaan
   (Captivity, Wilderness, Promised Land)
3. The Tabernacle
4. The Feasts of the LORD

For the purpose of this essay, we will focus on the Feasts of the LORD. The weekly Sabbath and the Feast Sabbaths, both infuse holiness into time. They are eternal cycles that will regulate time forever. The Feasts of the LORD reveal an incredibly rich and intricate yearly cycle. They reveal the patterns of all life – whether agricultural, biological or spiritual. Be it corporate or individual, all life follows these patterns. The seven Biblical Feasts are observed at three distinct seasons of the year.

Each season represents one phase in the progression of life - re-birthing, nurturing, and fruiting.

In Scripture, repetitive cycles are highly prophetic, but not all prophetic events are cyclical. There are also events that will only take place one time. These events are also predicted in the Bible. The complex events of the End-of-the-Age are an intersection of familiar cyclical events, like the Feasts, as well as events that will occur only one time. Prophetic events have been rehearsed for millennia in what the Bible calls "shadows of things to come." In all of these events we are learning more about the one who created them, God. This is how relationships are built - through learning patterns of behavior. The Feasts of the LORD teach us both about God and how to repair our world.

Only one chapter in the Bible, Leviticus 23, lists and details ALL the Feasts of the LORD. Below are brief profiles of each Feast. Each one has so many facets and applications that it is extremely hard to summarize them. As an aid to help you remember something about each Feast, it is helpful to pick one facet and assign a single word that represents it best. Following one prophetic line, each Feast below has been given a related key word:

Passover
The 14th day of the 1st month of the Biblical calendar
Key word: Death

We commonly refer to this Feast as Passover, but the actual Hebrew word is pesach - the substitute victim of the death decree. This special offering of the lamb brings both physical freedom for everyone, and spiritual redemption for the firstborn. We should note that Passover is not the beginning of life, for there is life in Egypt. It was a comfortable life for a time, but like a womb, there is limited opportunity for growth. There are birth pangs (10 plagues) which eventually result in a birth, an exodus to another world. Out of death comes new life.

Passover is filled with important symbolism. It is both the most formal family event of the year, and also the most prophetically significant Feast. It is the first event of the sacred year. Passover requires a reservation, it cannot be done spontaneously. Careful preparation is needed to find a spotless lamb for a household, and the portions must be measured precisely. Males must be "circumcised" and all "leaven" removed.

Unleavened Bread
The 15th through the 21st day of the 1st month of the Biblical calendar
Key word: Burial

Unleavened Bread is the seven-day Feast associated with Passover, and is characterized by eating matzah, or bread without yeast (leaven). Our bread was unleavened because we left Egypt in haste. Leaven is a type of sin in our Passover scenario. This Feast properly focuses our attention on the heart of man's problem – sin. It emphasizes the need to make great efforts to remove sin, not just from our lives but from our households, and even from within the borders of our nation. We endure a type of death for one week by not enjoying the full taste of life. In this Feast we reckon the "fallen nature" of our "old self" dead, and we live a week of sinlessness. This is a type of water baptism. As Israel went through the sea, the old (Egyptian army) died, and Israel was prepared for the new life that would follow. While we rehearse a state of sinlessness here, there remain five more steps in our journey to perfection.

Firstfruits
The 1st day following the 1st Sabbath after Passover
Key word: Resurrection

Rebirth is symbolized by bringing a firstfruits portion of the first barley harvest. As Israel came out of the water they were born again. God receives the firstfruits offering and grants us the firstfruit of the Spirit as a deposit. This serves as a reminder of the fullness that is coming.

Weeks
Seven weeks plus one day following Firstfruits
Key word: Power

From the barley firstfruits we count fifty days and then offer the wheat firstfruits. By counting, we are connecting to and extending the Feast of

Passover. Over these seven weeks our consciousness is elevated, and we are being transformed from slaves to sons. We are preparing ourselves to appear before the LORD. At the original Feast of Weeks, the Israelites came to Mt. Sinai and received the Torah. The Torah, the embodiment of knowledge and truth (Rom 2:20), is both a national constitution and a marriage Ketubah (certificate). After Jesus' resurrection, He instructed His disciple to wait for the "gift" that would come (Pentecost). Two loaves made of the firstfruits of the wheat harvest were offered. These TWO loaves are clearly symbolic of the SPIRIT and TRUTH, the "gifts" given to us by God. These gifts equip us for the long hot summer of growth. Over the summer, our progress is often marred by failures. The spirit is willing but the flesh is weak. We may lose our way... until the trumpet calls!

Trumpets
The 1st day of the 7th month of the Biblical calendar
Key word: Repentance

The Feast of Trumpets is a call to a new beginning, often a prodigal return. It sounds the alarm for an earnest and sincere preparation for the coming new dispensation (year or Kingdom). More specifically, Trumpets begins the countdown of the "ten days of awe" leading to the High Holy Day - the Day of Atonement. The blowing of trumpets is to remind us of our sin and our need for repentance. It is to remind us of our obligation to remind God to fulfill His covenant and promises to us (Israel).

Yom Kippur
The 10th day of the 7th month of the Biblical calendar
Key word: Reconciliation

This represents the completion of our week of "work." It is the High Priest's most laborious day. It is the day that the Priests obtain a covering and removal of sins for the people. It is a day of fasting and humiliation, the most solemn and fearful day of the year. The outcome is never assured. If successful, this final atonement achieves reconciliation to the Father. Ultimately, Yom Kippur typifies the work of the divine family reconciling the human family to God. The Son, taking on flesh, lives perfectly and then offers Himself as the unblemished Passover Lamb. He passes the work of nurturing and building to the Holy Spirit for the long "summer." This work now culminates in the finishing touches of Yom Kippur. All human needs are met and provided for in atonement. This includes (but is not limited to): the covering of sins, appeasing God's wrath, forgiveness of debt, release from broken promises, and healing. The two sets of clothes, golden and white linen; the components of the Ark, gold and wood; and the two bloods from the two different sacrificial animals; all indicate the blending of the divine and the human. As the body of Messiah, we must clarify the mystery surrounding Yom Kippur. We are not only the recipients of atonement, but as priests in the order of Melchizedek, confident to enter the "most holy place" (Heb 10:19), we too must "work" on Yom Kippur.

Tabernacles
The 15th through the 22nd day of the 7th month
of the Biblical calendar
Key word: Rest

Fruitfulness, victory, harvest, rest, joy, oneness, thanksgiving, indwelling, and perfection are some of the words that characterize the Feast of Tabernacles. We enjoy the fruitfulness of the year (week, dispensation), while we also look back in thankfulness to important aspects of our journey. Specifically, we remember the booths (temporary bodies) we lived in when we were in the Wilderness. It was in the Wilderness (of our need, of our humanity) that we laid the foundations of resting in the land (our God-likeness). The booth we built and perfected during the week of work now can be filled with the presence and glory of God. It is around this "Tabernacle" of God that all the nations will one day dwell in security, eating from the tree of life and drinking from the well of living water.

Appendix C: Who Is Israel?
Stephen Duame

To know God one must know Israel. When you hear the word "Israel," what do you think of? Do you think of: "the country," "the current nation-state," "the Jews," "the 12 tribes," "Jacob's new name," "the covenant people of the Bible", "the Church." etc.? Maybe you think about volatile politics, conflicts between Jews and Arabs, or wars over ancient borders. This is a confusing subject because "Israel" has come to mean so many things to so many people. In this essay, I will define "Israel" in a way most people have never fully considered. For now, resist the temptation to define Israel with any previous prejudice, whether good or bad, and be open to something new.

Israel is the personality, the purposes, and the process, by which God opens His heart to man. There is no other context through which the world can correspond with God. The world has the Judaeo-Christian Scriptures, written by Israelites. Israel is the sum total of God's will for mankind, past and future. The Scriptures chronicle the only credible history of man and man's relationship with God by detailing the birth and the progressive development of the Nation of Israel. The Bible identifies a single man, who was born some 3500 years ago in what is now Iraq, as the spiritual father of all mankind. These ideas might be easy to dismiss as fantasy storytelling were it not for the overwhelming influence that Judaeo-Christian cultures have on the world. Even such things as how we mark time (which we may take for granted) - the "seven day week" and "yearly reckoning," which are accepted universally, have come from the Judaeo-Christian Scriptures. Even though it is slightly inaccurate, our calendars read 2006. The world counts years since the birth of another Israelite (Jesus Christ). The world is slowly, becoming Israel. The degree, to which the world does not personify Israel today, is the degree to which God has temporarily removed Himself from the affairs of the world.

For many, maybe you, this Israel may seem too big, too un-provable, and too useless to the practical affairs of today. For you, a much smaller religion would be warmer, more friendly and useful. Yes, that may be true, and even needed for a time. But if we were to downsize this Israel, keep truth, but limit it and shape it into something more manageable, accessible, and inviting; it would only be a matter of time before someone would be sure to recognize the limitations in our more friendly religion. He would naturally start another religion (or denomination) to compensate for what he sees as some under-emphasized or overlooked truth. And then someone else would find something else important. Ah, another religion! You can see the point. They may all theoretically be espousing the truth (and with good intentions), while strongly disagreeing with each other, because each has only a piece of the puzzle, and so cannot see the big picture. Righteous wars, if we may call them that, are fought over ideas that are too small, ideas that don't, or can't, harmonize with "all truth."

If spirituality is our goal, the world today offers many assisting voices. Humans are uniquely spiritual creatures. But for most of us, pure individual spirituality, in any flavor, would not satisfy a deep human need to be social. Our spirituality would, quite naturally, lead us to seek out others of like mind to form some social expression of our spirituality. Utilizing another unique human gift, that of organization and administration, our spiritual evolution might naturally derive doctrine and customs until we create something quite satisfying and enduring—our own religion. Religion meets the needs of man. But why invent your own religion when there are so many established flavors to choose from? Eighty percent of humanity is religious, and would claim to be associated with one of the world's twenty major religious groups. And there are thousands of more specialized religious sub-groups from which one may choose. Even those who profess Jesus are offered an incredible variety of ways to "follow" Him. According to the *New Edition of World Christian Encyclopedia*, there are currently 33,830 specific Christian denominations!

If "religion" is your goal, the world today offers many inviting choices. But are spirituality and religion your primary goal? In religion, you can find community, encouragement, guiding principles, long standing tradition, intellectual stimulation, social action, and even, if desired, a professional career path. Most of us are hugely vested in some religion. Family, friendships, lifestyle, our sense of identity and purpose, social standing and, critically important, affirmation of being in right standing with God, are all wrapped up in our religion. This is the world that most people exist in, spirituality packaged for livability. We create longstanding traditions and the safe institutions that support them. This is what humans do; and at a basic level there is nothing wrong with it—unless we get so caught up that we miss the real God. So, how connected are you with your religion?

Beyond spirituality and religion, we have a paramount, but very abstract reality we'll call "truth." In fact, truth can be defined as exactly that—"reality." Knowing truth and seeking truth should be one of the supreme goals of life. It might be assumed that everyone engaged in the discussion about "Israel" is doing so in a quest for truth, but that would not be reality. There are many lesser motivations that foster interest in Israel. Defending one's personal or institutional position must not be equated with defending or seeking truth. Don't just assume that some-one else, long ago, resolved the truth about Israel, and your job now is to defend those long held traditions. The word "tradition" comes from the Latin meaning "the act of handing over"; it is up to us to decide if we want to receive what is handed to us...or not. Traditions can be wonder-ful, but there are times when we need to reexamine the basis for long standing beliefs, especially when it comes to something as important as "Who is Israel?"

Knowing truth goes beyond spirituality and even religion. Instinctively, we sense that truth should be the ultimate goal; it is the ulti-mate blessing, the ultimate gift granted to free and glorify mankind. Only in spirit AND TRUTH can we worship God. Only then, with a mind transformed by truth, we will find God. In this "tent of meeting," speak-ing the language of truth, we will commune with God.

Truth seeking is a messy, difficult, and costly process. If you would short-circuit that struggle, and instead hope for peace and safety via some other easier path, then an expedition to find the real Israel may not be for you. You may want to leave it to someone else. And that may be okay for now; not everyone is a pioneer who cares to walk on the "bleeding edge." But you can at least understand, appreciate, and sympathize with the struggle. If it's not for you, then please don't become an obstacle. Let an honest search for truth proceed. Wait for the final report before making your judgment, even if preliminary information you receive sounds like heresy to your religion. Either join in the effort, or keep an open mind and an open ear for developing news. All truth must come; and Israel is the only path we can take to apprehend it.

A very important person once said, "The truth will set you free." It's true! Resolving "all truth," that is, "thinking truthfully" or "knowing reality," is the only path to paradise. God is, in fact, saying to mankind, until you see things the way I see things, I will not release you from your "fallen-ness." Whatever you think the World-to-Come may be like, it will not come until God has adequate, proven partners in its management. You may not have realized that the stakes are so high, or that our participation would be such a determining factor in the world's future. Knowing Israel is not ultimately an academic exercise. Israel's past is the model of the world's future. Only by knowing Israel do we know God, thereby qualifying as legitimate managers of the world's future. Yes, the stakes are this high!

If we institutionalize this relationship, if we define the rules of engagement and extend them to the expanding human family, for endless ages, we would define the embodiment of knowledge and truth. We would define reality. That reality is called "Israel." Religion can satisfy man's needs to a point, even faulty and limited religion appear adequate for a time, but upon closer examination, there is no truly truthful religious experience outside of Israel. For some, that may be a very radical idea. It may provoke strong objection and pluralistic demands. They may say, "God can't be limited to such a narrow and singular idea. God is much more diverse than that."

Israel is difficult to know because knowing Israel is difficult. A comprehensive knowledge of Israel is at the upper level of human capacity to perceive spiritual things. It is for the mature. Why has man not resolved Israel? Because the implications are too staggering, too demanding. Most human hearts and minds will not go to the highest demands of Israel. But the glorious truth is that we, as humans, have been given the right to be sons of God. It is difficult, but rest assured; it is also possible. That is what the story of Israel tells us; a wounded man can prevail.

We haven't made an attempt to define Israel yet, so we should offer a short disclaimer here to avoid unnecessary concern. In some cases we have to separate modern Jewish culture, or even Judaism, from Israel. Every nation or ethnic group has a culture that is a product of collective experiences and traditions. Modern Jewish traditions do not always reflect the Biblical or Godly foundations of Israel. Very often they do, but it should be noted that modern Judaism is not necessarily synonymous with Israel.

Israel in the context portrayed above is a concept - an idea as big as the universe itself. To know Israel, that is where we must start. There was a man named Israel, there is one country on earth called Israel, and they are, most assuredly, connected to the overall concept of Israel, but let's resist the impulse to so quickly connect the spiritual idea of Israel to some physical reality. Doing so would be a mistake if we really want to gain a truthful understanding of Israel. Even the Patriarchs realized this, and did not, in their day, begin to build a material institution. However, it probably can be said that a "truthful" understanding of Israel is not the objective of the majority of mankind. Israel may be important to you for reasons other than truth. We must get to the genuine physical manifestation(s) of Israel eventually; but there are very strong personal and institutional pressures to kidnap both the idea and the physical existence of Israel, and use it to leverage some sociopolitical advantage.

Abraham, Moses, and Jesus all added flesh to the fabric of Israel. God invites all men to come and walk again with Him, to learn from Him, and to grow in the likeness of Him through the revelation of Israel. Israel has been misunderstood and abused, as it has been easier for mankind, to fight over it (or against it) than it has been to comprehend it. The influence of Israel far exceeds its landmass or the numeric value of those who currently carry its name.

Let us make our first attempt to define "Israel." It's a bit abstract, but helpful nonetheless: **Israel is the universal government of God. We are all Israelites; we all live within the territory of Israel and under the laws of Israel, whether we realize it or not, whether we want to or not.** Certainly, we will get much more specific as we go along, as this is not the whole truth, but the first truth about Israel that we need to understand.

What is Israel? Anyone who reads the Bible knows that Israel is the context in which God revealed Himself to the world. But Israel is more then a context; to know God, one must know Israel. There are diverse attitudes concerning Israel and they take on different forms. If Israel is uniquely tied to God and God's "light" (revelation, purposes and demands) for mankind, it would follow that God's enemies would uniquely single out Israel for special wrath and distain. This is a curious and tragic fact of history. From Haman to the Amalakites to Hitler, the world has witnessed extreme hatred for Israel quite often. But there is another form of hostility which should be distinguished from "blind hatred." This hostility might more accurately be categorized as a type of family rivalry. Those involved actually recognize value in Israel and its blessings, and want to participate in them.   Family rivalry, in effect, can be just as deadly and vicious, but it has a different motivational foundation. Take for examples, Isaac and Ishmael, Jacob and Esau, and Joseph and his ten brothers. These "family members" actually competed for God's favor. They saw and accepted that God's favor does flow through Israel (or Abraham), and so devised theology to bolster their claim. Family infighting started as early as the first two brothers, Cain and Able. Incredibly, there are only about 15 million "Jewish" people on earth today (recognized Jewish blood descendants of Abraham/Isaac/Jacob). One would think that these people would be the most popular, honored culture on earth, but such is not the case. Amazingly, history indicates the opposite. Quite a long time ago, it became popular to separate Israel's favor from Israel's people. It would have been nice if God had made this issue much clearer, but He didn't. So the struggle, and the question, continues: Just who is Israel?

In the "family" camp today, we could place Judaism, Christianity, and even Islam. These all claim to be physical or spiritual sons of Abraham. In our search for Israel, we want to be careful to seek truth, as opposed to common perception or sacred tradition. For instance, you might assume that Judaism is Israel, but even that point can be argued. If you know your Bible, you will recall that the kingdom of Solomon, the best picture of national Israel, was split into northern and southern kingdoms. The Bible refers to the much larger northern kingdom as Israel, and the southern kingdom as Judah. Though mixing occurred both before and after the split, the Jews of today are largely descendants of the southern two tribes, Judah and Benjamin. The northern tribes are often referred to as the "ten lost tribes," as history does not clearly record what became of them. So Judaism today and the Jews who have formed the modern State of Israel, while unquestionably the genetic sons of Jacob (Israel), technically, may not be the Biblical Israel.

It is an extremely complicated topic, and we cannot possibly even mention all the related issues. Rather, we will try to frame our debate around a single key issue. To set the stage, we will review four common Biblically-based perceptions of Israel held by Judaism and Christianity. The summaries below are written with very broad strokes and are continuing to evolve in the winds of time. We confess beforehand that these generalizations, as all generalizations, are imperfect.

Four Views of Israel

No. 1) Faithful (observant) Judaism sees a nationalistic Israel, restored and peaceful under the rule of a conquering world leader. They see the ancient Davidic/Solomonic kingdom as the prototype of the coming restored Kingdom ruled by an "anointed" (Messiah) human king, a descendant of King David. This Kingdom's capital will be an expanded Jerusalem, established within a much enlarged territorial Israel (enlarged from the borders of present day Israel). It will have a rebuilt Temple and a functioning Levitical priesthood ministering via a judicial system based on the Mosaic Law. Out of the leadership of this Kingdom (nation), a restored, obedient world will experience peace and paradise forever. This is a natural, physical Israel, whose members are generally blood descendants of Jacob. To distinguish it from other views, we'll refer to this Kingdom as the, **"Royal House of David."** For the most part, the views of Faithful Judaism are all legitimate Biblical prophetic ideas.

Faithful Christianity has at least three significant and differing concepts of Israel that are useful for our discussion here.

No. 2) The majority of Christians through the ages have believed in supersessionism, making it the dominate view of Christianity. The more common term for this belief is "**Replacement Theology.**" It's called "replacement," because it states that the Church has completely replaced Israel as God's "chosen" agency on earth. All favor and promises prophesied in the Old Testament are now transferred to the Church. God used an ancient people, the Israelites, and an ancient nation, Israel, to express and demonstrate, in literal terms, the will and revelation of God to man. In this theology, Israel was the "school room" in which God used very "literal" teaching objects to impart "spiritual" principles. With the coming of Jesus, God signaled the end of "school Israel" and the beginning of the "new spiritual Israel." Now, Judaism could be reprocessed, sort of like putting Judaism into a juicer where all the pure spiritual juice is separated from the physical "pulp." For instance, replacement theology teaches that we don't need the Sabbath any longer, because man, through Jesus, fully understands the principle of Sabbath "rest." The pulp is discarded as useless—no, not useless, worse than useless—pulp Judaism is now considered poisonous to true faith. Paul's (misunderstood) words, in Galatians 5:2 confirmed this. *NIV Mark my words! I, Paul, tell you that if you let yourselves be circumcised, Christ will be of no value to you at all.*

Faith alone is now the new and only way to be reconciled to God, and enter His Kingdom. To adherents of replacement theology, territorial national Israel, the people in the blood line, the Temple, etc., are no more significant than any other of the world's cultures. To attribute significance to the return of the Jews to the Land and the rebirth of national Israel (which happened in the 20th Century), or looking forward to the restoration of the Mosaic Law and the rebuilding of the Temple, is a grave mistake. Interestingly, while replacement theology calls for the purging of all things Jewish, it claims it is exclusively "Israel." Perhaps not intentional in most cases, replacement theology very often elicits subtle or even overt anti-Semitism. At the heart of its systematic theology you will always find the use of an exegetical technique called (hyper) allegorization or spiritualizing of Scripture.

No. 3) Other Christians see the Church as a new and separate entity completely distinct from Israel. This leaves Israel pretty much intact retaining much of its special-ness. By rejecting Jesus, Israel was broken off from the tree and has been set-aside until the "times of the Gentiles" are over. These Christians generally still consider Israel a special nation both in its favor and in its prophetic role at the End-of-the-Age. They see the time when Israel will accept Jesus as the Messiah and will be graphed back into the tree. Here it gets a little fuzzy, but they largely see a Torah-less Christianity eventually merging with, and even taking on some of, Judaism's physical culture, with its capital in Jerusalem, services in the Temple, and an active priesthood. This improved Israel is reshaped by Messiah Jesus as a grace oriented, non-sacrificial blend of Judaism and Christianity under a "new" covenant.

No. 4) For our fourth Israel, we spotlight a new phenomenon in Christianity appearing over the last thirty years—a pro-Torah return to the Jewish (or Hebrew) roots of Christianity. (Many adherents do not even want to be labeled as "Christian.") This group, while numerically small today, is keeping in step with the Spirit, by pioneering important new spiritual ground. They see the shortcomings of the traditional views expressed above and have set about to resolve them. They identify a perfect precedent for a new radical theology—the original "Church." They notice that the founders of the Church—Jesus, Peter, James, John, and Paul, and the community in which they existed, were orthodox Jews living orthodox lifestyles. How could this be? **The founders of the original "Christian" movement had a very specific lifestyle, which if lived today would be considered heretical by mainstream Christianity.** It's bizarre, but ask any honest Christian scholar and they will explain why you cannot live like Jesus did and still be a good Christian. However, a thorough and sincere reexamination of Scripture does reveal that a Torah-based orthodox lifestyle, as walked-out by the early messianic Jewish community (it wasn't called "Christianity" back then), was not, and is not today, inconsistent with true Christianity

Modern pro-Torah Christians set about to track the history of pagan and anti-Semitic influences that crept into the Church. In their quest, they rediscovered Torah and its vital and direct connections to the New Testament. They rediscovered Sabbath and the Feasts of the LORD. They began to synchronize prophecy to Torah concepts. They came to acknowledge the value of Judaism and the traditions it has maintained, and some even chose to study Judaism's source literature, such as the Talmud. They redesigned more authentic worship, as would have been familiar to Jesus and the Apostles, incorporating the use a Torah scroll, weekly Torah readings, prayer shawls, and established written prayers in the siddur (prayer book). Not afraid of (or antagonistic towards) physical Israel anymore, they rediscovered the truths of the "two houses" (two kingdoms) of Israel. They found evidence that today's Judaism and Jewish tradition have very likely been handed down to us by a very small remnant of the whole house of Israel. They learned the prophecies which predict the End-of-the-Age and the reuniting of the two houses. Many surmised that this new sense of identity with Israel indicates that they, themselves, are actually physical descendants of the lost tribes of Israel. They began to reach out to the Jewish people as brothers, in support of their many political struggles for the Land of Israel, and against anti-Semitism.

This phenomenal movement is continuing to get stronger and will (I predict) grow incredibly in the coming years. The natural result of these radical changes is a theology that virtually matches Judaism (after deficiencies on both sides are corrected), except for the identity of Messiah. In fact, there is such a disillusion with Christian tradition and doctrine that an overreaction has developed. The rallying cry of this group is "one house", the whole house of Israel. They see Israel like Judaism sees Israel—the Royal House of David Restored. All believers are Israelites, even with an inheritance in the Land. Judaism with its Mosaic traditions is the rightful model for all God's people. Someday, Judaism will see Y'shua (the original, restored name of Jesus) as Messiah. Until then, Christians and Jews have more in common than they have differences. The sentiments and even much of the prophecy of pro-Torah Christianity is good; they are heading in the right direction, but even their doctrine of Israel misses the mark.

Israel & Prophetic Leadership

There are sincere God loving people in all these groups, and there is truth in all of these views of Israel, however, none of them adequately explain the full picture of Israel. Whatever you want to call it, they have all built, and vigorously defend, an incomplete idea of Israel. Each one defines an

Israel that is not fully Biblical—and therefore not truly Israel. But understanding Israel is essential to understanding prophecy, which is essential to
understanding truth. The difficulty in understanding Israel stems from
human issues of both heart and mind, and therefore, the resolution of
Israel is indicative of a proper attitude towards God. Whether through
the eyes of your heart or through the eyes of your mind, it is given that
each will seek the level of Israel to which he is called. The world desper-
ately needs prophetic leadership, and that leadership will be granted to
men and women who understand Israel at the highest level.
Understanding Israel is a requirement for leadership. The final ranks of
Israel, at all levels, are being filled today. Whether you are a Jew by blood
or a Christian who believes in eternal security, nothing should be taken for
granted. Resting passively and ignorantly in some theological assurance
alone will prove to be very unwise, no matter whom you are. Leadership
will be bestowed on those who know where we, as a people, are going and
what needs to be done to get us there. So, let's now begin to describe a
view of Israel that is fully Biblical, and will give us the tools for wise participation in the prophetic days ahead.

Two Israels

The issue really hinges on one key idea: **Are there one or two Israels?**
Taken broadly, you can see two distinct views of Israel from the descrip-
tions above. We don't want to quibble over words here. Someone might
want to label what we're about to describe as a single Israel with two
dimensions, and that would be perfectly fine. But for this dialog, we pre-
fer the clarity of "two Israels."

It is no coincidence that God provided this "two Israels" model over
and over. Abraham, the father of all the faithful, had two sons, Ishmael
and Isaac, from two different mothers. Jacob, the man given the name
Israel, had a family of sons that eventually excised Joseph from the family.
This set the stage for the Judah—Ephraim, two house split. Even the
pure original form of Christianity (the community of Jewish disciples of
Y'shua) was excised from Judaism to form a second house, both claiming
rights to Israel. There is a message in all this beyond the obvious family

infighting. The message in these patterns is that there really are two distinct concepts of Israel. In their immature state, each perceives the other to be foreign, so they have fought one another through the ages.

From the very first verse of the Bible we are exposed to the idea of two centers, or jurisdictions of authority: Heaven and Earth. Gleaning from the whole of Scripture, we can formulate the following conditions. **God rules from heaven by delegating universal stewardship to man on earth.** Immediately, we can see that God has deliberately set limits to His authority and bestowed incredible authority to mankind. God created man to take dominion over the Creation, but it's not an unlimited license to participate in all activities. Scripture shows God like a Father, training and disciplining His sons toward responsible governance. This is all well and good—this "God in heaven" in a training relationship with "man on earth"—and perhaps many would agree that this is an accurate characterization of the big picture; but how does this apply to two Israels?

The first clue lies in a promise given to Abraham by the Almighty:

> ➤ **(Gen 22:17** NIV**)** *I will surely bless you and make your descendants as numerous as the <u>stars in the sky</u> and as <u>the sand on the seashore</u>.*

Notice those two phrases—the stars and the sand. They represent the heavenly and the earthly. Now, we could not infer from this alone that two groups are in view here. But further study will show this to be a perfect metaphor for the two Israels—a heavenly Israel and an earthly Israel.

What is the evidence for a heavenly Israel? Judaism has parallel concepts, but the Christian Apostolic writers of the New Testament clarified these concepts immensely. First, let's take note of one fact: Although Abraham was promised the Land of Canaan, neither he, Isaac, Jacob, or any of the sons of Jacob ever built a permanent dwelling in the Land. They dwelt in tents as foreigners in the Promised Land. There is no clear Biblical explanation for this. One could say that the time hadn't come yet, but the New Testament writers pick up on this curious fact:

> ➤ **(Hebrews 11:9)** *By faith he dwelt in the land of promise as in a foreign country, dwelling in tents with Isaac and Jacob, the heirs with him of the same promise.*

> *(Hebrews 11:13) These all died in faith, not having received the promises, but having seen them afar off were assured of them, embraced them and confessed that they were strangers and pilgrims on the earth.*

> *(Hebrews 11:10) For he waited for the city which has foundations, whose builder and maker is God.*

> *(Hebrews 11:16) But now they desire a better, that is, a heavenly country. Therefore God is not ashamed to be called their God, for He has prepared a city for them.*

> *(2 Corinthians 5:1) For we know that if our earthly house, this tent, is destroyed, we have a building from God, a house not made with hands, eternal in the heavens.*

> *(Philippians 3:20) For our citizenship is in heaven, from which we also eagerly wait for the Savior, the Lord Jesus Christ.*

It is unmistakably clear that Abraham had a dual promise—one directed toward eventual fulfillment on earth, but an even superior promise of citizenship in a heavenly country, and residence in the city of God, a city not made with hands. The Old Testament does not dwell on this heavenly aspect of the promise, giving almost exclusive attention to the earthly fulfillment, eventually known as **the Royal House of David.** Let's expand this idea of heavenly promises with more Scripture:

> *(John 1:12) But as many as received Him, to them He gave the right to become children of God, to those who believe in His Name:*

> *(Rom 8:23 NIV) Not only so, but we ourselves, who have the firstfruits of the Spirit, groan inwardly as we wait eagerly for our adoption as sons, the redemption of our bodies.*

These Scriptures reveal the "star" dimension of the promise to Abraham. It is no accident that Christianity has focused on issues of the heart, emphasizing the spiritual and heavenly dimensions. **To put it succinctly, Christianity, through Messiah Jesus, offers the right to participate in the heavenly calling of Abraham.** They have the right to literally be adopted into the family of God, to fulfill the original intent of God as recorded in Genesis 1, for men to become the "image of God" and to "rule" the universe. This is what Christianity boasts, and they should. This is the "good news." Men can be formed into the likeness of God; they can be sons of God, agents channeling divine energy to the world. By faith, this ministry and all its benefits are available to all men. Stated briefly, mankind's prophetic history is moving from an "earthly men" towards a "heavenly men" relationship.

Israel – One Becomes Two

We can see the conceptual basis for two Israels. But as the curtain went up 2000 years ago, we see Judaism and a Levitical economy functioning as the only Israel the world knew. So, it is out of this vestige of the Royal House of David that a new, heavenly Israel is brought forth. This song sounds familiar to one in our distant past when Eve was taken out of Adam. Apparently, Adam originally embodied both male and female attributes, until those attributes were divided into two distinct bodies. Then God commissions them for the high calling: *Therefore a man shall leave his father and mother and be joined to his wife, and they shall **become one flesh*** (Genesis 2:24). It's interesting that Christianity refers to itself as the "bride" of Christ, who is the last Adam. Separated from God by sin, through Christ we are invited back into the family of God. Then God commissions us for the high calling: *The two shall become one flesh. This is a great mystery, **but I speak concerning Christ and the Church*** (Ephesians 5:31-32).

Israel appears to have been designed likewise, and followed a similar pattern. The Nation of Israel, from its inception, embodied both heavenly and earthly Israels up until the coming of Messiah Jesus. Jesus came preaching the "Kingdom of Heaven" to a people that were anticipating the full restoration of the "Royal House of David." It would seem that, had Israel accepted Jesus, they would have remained invested with both dimensions of Israel. Jesus essentially made this offer: "I am the king of both Israels, if you accept my heavenly ministry, I am prepared to reestablish the Royal House of David now." The New Testament amply describes the outcome—*Israel stumbled over the "stumbling stone"* (Rom 9:32 NIV). In larger human terms, it was all for the best. *"Again I ask: Did they stumble so as to fall beyond recovery? Not at all! Rather, because of their transgression, salvation has come to the Gentiles" (Rom 11:11 NIV).*

The bride was paid for in blood and set apart for a new ministry. At the end of Jesus' ministry, He dealt with both Israels individually. In both cases He invoked Old Testament prophecy as the basis for His declaration. Dealing with the heavenly Israel, Jesus draws upon the "rejected Joseph" as imagery. Like Joseph's brothers rejected him, Judaism, as builders, rejected the capstone (Jesus). *Jesus said to them, "Have you never read in the Scriptures: 'The stone the builders rejected has become the capstone; the LORD has done this, and it is marvelous in our eyes'? 'Therefore I tell you that the **Kingdom of God** will be taken away from you and given to a people who will produce its fruit'" (Mat 21:42-43 NIV).*

The "Kingdom of God" will be "taken away" from the "builders" (Judaism) and opened to others. Messiah becomes the head (capstone) of a body of people who will produce the fruit of the Kingdom of God. As the verse implies, this is a permanent development. We should note that this "renewed Israel" in no way discriminates against individual Jews entering. Jews were the original founders; they are just as welcome as anyone, in fact, all things considered, they are still the "natural branches," and one would expect they would be more at home than pagans who have no instincts for Israel. Jesus said nothing about the end of Israel, or that this was some new religion that He was starting. The symbolic stones in Jesus' illustration were stones of a Temple. The New Testament furthered the role of the Temple by developing the concept of building the Spiritual Temple.

So what happens to the builders? Jesus clarifies their fate as well. *"O Jerusalem, Jerusalem, you who kill the prophets and stone those sent to you, how often I have longed to gather your children together, as a hen gathers her chicks under her wings, but you were not willing. Look, **your house is left to you desolate** (Mat 23:37-38 NIV).* A house left desolate! Jesus once again invokes Old Testament prophecy to show the prophetic expectation of His actions.

➢ *(Jer 22:5 NIV) But if you do not obey these commands, declares the LORD, I swear by myself that this palace will become a **ruin**.*

> ➤ (*Ezek 21:25-27* NIV) *"O profane and wicked prince of Israel, whose day has come, whose time of punishment has reached its climax, this is what the Sovereign* LORD *says: Take off the turban, remove the crown. It will not be as it was: The lowly will be exalted and the exalted will be brought low.* **A ruin! A ruin! I will make it a ruin!** *It will not be* **restored** *until He comes to whom it rightfully belongs; to him I will give it."*

This other Israel, the Royal House of David, would be brought low, ruined, made desolate—but not forever. This judgment was only for a season (2000 yrs), and so is not permanent. But Israel had reached a fork in the road, a path for both Israels. By Jesus' prophetic declaration, one was made two, but we should examine the practical reasons for the split.

Christianity—Brilliance & Blindness

From the very beginning, "Gentile" Christianity (non-Jewish Christianity) misconstrued the lesson to be learned from Judah's failure. Drawing from New Testament Jewish writings, Christianity began to accentuate the spiritual aspects of our relationship to God. It emphasized the internal or heart motivations of a "by grace through faith" based life. It connected deeply to the essence of Abraham's heavenly calling, and then catalogued its theology and articulated it to the world. Christianity devised a simple Gospel, however incomplete, and took on the burden of spreading this "light" of the God of Israel to the farthest corners of the world. Yes, Christianity did many things right, but regrettably, in its ignorance and immaturity, Christianity perceived the source of Judaism's failure to be it's legalistic system founded on the Mosaic Law. Christianity could not perceive of the need for all these complex rules and regulations, or a Temple and priesthood centered on archaic blood sacrifices. At best, this Law was a bitter lesson to show us why we need Jesus—and now that He's come, these old "Laws" need to be ruthlessly eliminated, lest they pollute our "newer," much superior system of grace and liberty.

What was wrong with Judaism was not the system of Mosaic Law, but human tendencies. Humans tend to remain within their safe comfort zone, rather than press on to a higher calling. Legalism, hard hearted-ness, and spiritual dullness are common to all humans and, therefore, all religions.

But knowing of this "heavenly calling" that is offered "free" to imper-fect flesh understandably produced some undesirable results—one of them being arrogance. The Gospel message invites an ignorant pagan, who doesn't know the true God in any way, into the King's palace as a son. You can see where this may inspire some very deviant behavior. This is what happened when the original Jewish apostles sent the "good news" out into the world of the Gentiles. Instead of humble gratefulness, Gentile Christianity, now with its superior numbers and superior man-date, eventually set about to devise theology that gleaned all the Jewish treasures (promises to Israel) for themselves, while holding up Judaism as an object of contempt and ridicule. Yes, Judaism, as an institution, had legally failed to live up to the "high calling." They had, for a second time, eliminated their strange brother "Joseph" (in this case Jesus) from their family. Yes, Israel throughout history has stumbled under the heavy demands of her calling. In 70 AD, God once again sent Israel (Judaism) into exile, and a new "kid" (Christianity) eagerly picked up the banner of the high calling. Stirred by Judaism's failure, Christianity developed anti-Semitic doctrines that would eventually become cast in stone; in a sense they would become "Christian tradition." In many cases they developed proper activities, but for the wrong reasons. Christianity became Law-less, and has remained so for close to 2000 years. In spite of this, the preaching of their simple, incomplete Gospel by the Christian (even the Catholic) church was a blessing for the world, but we cannot continue to operate in such darkness. As "heavenly Israel" moves into its final min-istry, these mistakes will have to be corrected.

Israel vs. Israel

You can now understand how we came to our current state of affairs. And more importantly, you can now see the major components of God's plan to bless humanity and establish an eternal government based upon "His righteousness." Both aspects of Israel, spiritual and physical, heavenly and earthly, have been utilized to set the stage for the ending drama about to unfold. Truth, like a coin, always comes with two sides. Israel's lack of faith allowed them to see only what was in front of them. As the original recipient of the covenant of Abraham and the Torah, the embodiment of knowledge and truth, they became totally distracted by the **physical kingdom** that God instructed them to build. They institutionalized an "earth only" kingdom. By the time their Messiah came declaring the "Kingdom of Heaven," Judaism had become spiritually deaf. In the hardness of their hearts, Jewish leadership had long since forgotten the heavenly calling of Abraham.

We can see the nature of Judaism and Christianity and how each expresses one aspect of the dual call of Abraham. We can now see the need, yes need, for two Israels. Judaism developed the earthly kingdom; while Christianity, dismissive of the Royal House of David, looked for the deeper meaning, the heart of Israel, and developed ideas compatible with the heavenly kingdom. Who's right and who's wrong? If we look at the big picture, we will see that in a very real sense, they both are! They both are based in truth; however as institutions, they have not, or will not, make room for ideas they don't understand. It's as if they are both "looking in a mirror, darkly." The higher truth seems so obvious; but the prophetic reality is such that both institutions will remain blind to it. Unless...

Working Together

Assuming that we can see two Israels as a single truth designed by God, the next questions are: Why and how do they interact with each other? A clear model on how these two Israels function harmoniously is still missing.

Once again, we can find the source of our answer back in the beginning. Before Abraham's covenant, even before the promise of an heir, we have a very brief account of Abraham's encounter with Melchizedek. Very little is said here, but we get a critical insight into the relationship of our two Israels. Melchizedek ministers blessings as from God, and Abraham gives offerings to Melchizedek as unto God. Through other Scriptures, we pick up more information. In the Psalms: *The LORD has sworn and will not change his mind: "You are a priest forever, in the order of Melchizedek" (Psalm 110:4 NIV).* Here we see that Melchizedek was not just a single priest, but an "order of priests." Messiah himself is a priest of this order of Melchizedek. Years later, when the Law is finally given on Sinai, we see a new priestly order established, the "order of Levitical priests." This is the priesthood of Jewish history, the priesthood of earth, the priesthood of the Royal House of David. In the New Testament, the Apostle Peter reveals more truth concerning our priesthood picture:

> ➤ *(1 Pet 2:4, 9-11 NIV) As you come to Him, the living Stone ... you also, like living stones, are **being built into a spiritual house to be a holy priesthood**, offering spiritual sacrifices acceptable to God through Jesus Christ. ... But you are a chosen people, a **royal priesthood**, a holy nation, a people belonging to God, that you may declare the praises of Him who called you out of darkness into His wonderful light. Once you were not a people, but now you are the people of God; once you had not received mercy, but now you have received mercy. Dear friends, I urge you, as **aliens and strangers in the world**.*

This fits perfectly into our "heavenly Israel" picture, as opposed to the Levitical priesthood, which has only earthy jurisdiction. It's not a stretch to see that God has designed a special priesthood for each Israel, each with its own responsibilities, functions, and jurisdiction. Speaking of the Messiah, the book of Hebrews says: *"If He were on **earth**, He would **not** be a **priest**, for there are already men who offer the gifts prescribed by the Law"* (Heb 8:4 NIV). Here's more evidence of the jurisdictional nature of both Israels and both priesthoods. They each have an important role in the functioning of the whole.

To help clarify the function of our two Israels, we associate a priestly order with each one. The Melchizedek order (royal priesthood) is central to the heavenly priesthood, and the Levitical priesthood is central to the earthly priesthood (Royal House of David).

What did God have in mind when he promised Abraham a city made without hands? Even the Levitical priests typified this spiritual call. They were not given a portion of the Land, God was there portion. The patterns are clear that there is a set-apart calling that does not directly include elements of this material creation. Its highest reward is relational, an identity tied to God himself, the very ministry of God. How can we say this without going science-fiction? God has made a place in His family and He is in the process of bestowing God-likeness on a remnant of humanity who will forgo the immediate pleasures of this beautiful "earth," and yet bless the people who don't.

The End-of-the-Age will see these two Israels manifested in two priesthoods, both being refined and activated. The Melchizedek priesthood, especially, has a divine responsibility to rule with Messiah and will begin that rulership before Messiah returns to earth. Levitical Israel will become the head of the nations and has earthly jurisdiction. Melchizedek Israel will speak for and manifest the rule of God over the earth. How these two Israels will interact will become clear over time, but it is through both priesthoods that the earth will enjoy the "stars" and the "sand" blessing of Abraham.

Conclusion

Thus far, we have only scratched the surface. Space does not permit further discourse at this time. The LORD Almighty willing, we will greatly expand on these ideas in the future. Perhaps the most practical reason to know Israel is that it helps us know ourselves. We will know who we are, "the seeds of Abraham" and heirs according to the promise. And we will know who we will be, the "sons of God." Understanding our identity just might make it a little easier to *keep on pressing on* toward the upward call in Y'shua the Messiah. Brothers and sisters, press on till we all come to the unity of the faith and of the knowledge of the Son of God, to a perfect man, to the measure of the stature of the fullness of Christ. And even greater works than He will we do.

Blessed be the Holy One of Israel.

Appendix D: Prophetic Themes Chart

Note: Read the Prologue (Page 14)
for the significance of the following chart.

For a larger printable version of this chart,
visit TheHeartOfDavid.com.

Prophetic Themes found throughout the Book | Prophetic Outcome for you as the Reader

These themes appear in each of these chapters: (columns) 1, 2, 3, 4, 5, 6, 7, 8, 9, 10, 11, 12, E

Blueprints & Patterns → Read the Blueprints and Patterns

Blueprints & Patterns	Read the Blueprints and Patterns
The Journey & Destination Captivity-Wilderness-Promised Land	Discover where you are on your spiritual journey.
Scriptural Blueprints & Prophetic Patterns	Able to recognize patterns & read the blueprints.
We have the keys, authority, & responsibility to solve the mysteries of the Kingdom of Heaven.	Identify the mysteries & discover your abilities to solve them.
Good stewardship: Reap where you have not sown! Precept upon precept, line upon line.	Accept the responsibility to take what has been given, build upon it, and then pass it along.
Man's blunders advance God's plan for His Kingdom.	God's plan will advance in spite of man's failures.
The double-edged sword & two sides of the same coin.	Learn to unify Biblical truths that appear to be contradictions.
The Wilderness is a place of supernatural provision.	Your wilderness experience will cause full dependence on God.

The Gospel of the Kingdom (TGOTK) → Become a Laborer for (TGOTK)

The Gospel of the Kingdom (TGOTK)	Become a Laborer for (TGOTK)
The Gospel of the Kingdom & the Kingdom of Heaven, The Govt. & Economy of Heaven	A working understanding of the Kingdom of Heaven and the Government of God.
The Gospel of the Kingdom vs. The Gospel of Salvation. Make the message clear!	Be able to identify and define the Gospel of the Kingdom. (Make the message clear!)
The Gospel of the Kingdom preached to all the world.	Able to preach the Gospel of the Kingdom.

The Forerunner → Become a Forerunner

The Forerunner	Become a Forerunner
The Wilderness Prophet	Recognize the Wilderness Prophet and his message. Distinguish him from false prophets.
The Remnant vs. The Masses Many are Called, Few are Chosen.	Know your role. Are you a forerunner?
The good report & the bad report & the two types of Spies.	Conclude which type of "spy" you are. Which report will you give? Or whose report will you believe?
Passing the mantle: Preparing the next generation & the double-portion outpouring of the Holy Spirit.	The authority will be passed. You must be prepared. A full dose of the Holy Spirit is coming.
The uncircumcised heart: A transplant (circumcision) is needed. Seek the Heart of David!	You should want to seek a circumcised heart. (Heart Restoration)

Prophetic Themes Found throughout the Book

These themes appear in each of these chapters:

Perfection — Know your upward Call in Christ Jesus

Prophetic Theme (Perfection)	1	2	3	4	5	6	7	8	9	10	11	12	E	Prophetic Outcome for you as the Reader
There is a high calling after salvation. This calling is the Gospel of the Kingdom (the Called vs. the Chosen).														Know the difference between the Gospel of the Kingdom and the Gospel of the Salvation.
The Prayer of David - It is the Believer's equivalent of the Sinner's Prayer. (Faith unto Perfection)														Move on to the high calling.
Sinlessness / Perfection (The fullness, stature and image of Messiah) & Perfect Ministry														Believe that attaining perfection is possible.
Manifestation of the Sons of God														All creation is waiting for you to embrace your full inheritance. There's a difference between obtaining this title & manifesting this position.
The Spiritual Temple (God's Institution)														It is the role of the Body of Christ to build the Spiritual Temple
Unity of the Faith														We are one faith serving one God. We WILL come to unity. Denominationalism is a root cause of disunity.
The Restoration of all Things (Elijah must come first).														There must be restoration before the second coming of the Lord.
Corporate and Individual Restoration														Coming to unity of the faith and perfection is not simply an individual accomplishment. It is a corporate achievement.

Torah: God's Laws & Instruction — The Torah is Holy and Just and Good

Prophetic Theme (Torah)	1	2	3	4	5	6	7	8	9	10	11	12	E	Prophetic Outcome for you as the Reader
Torah is for Christians today (Faith-Based Obedience). God's commandments are not too difficult/ burdensome.														You should develop a favorable opinion of Torah, and desire to keep the Feasts and weekly Sabbaths
Righteousness of faith and Righteousness of the Law. (Faith-based obedience vs. Your own righteous)														You should be able to distinguish faith-based obedience from legalism!
Holiness														Realize that all good things are not holy. Only God defines holiness.
The Feasts of the LORD														The Feasts are a joy and have deep prophetic significance.

| The number of major prophetic themes that appear in each chapter is: | 9 | 16 | 17 | 18 | 18 | 19 | 15 | 12 | 18 | 24 | 20 | 16 | 12 | 13 | Make the Message Clear! |

Printed in the United States
54550LVS00004BC/88-510